SAGE was founded in 1965 by Sara Miller McCune to support the dissemination of usable knowledge by publishing innovative and high-quality research and teaching content. Today, we publish more than 750 journals, including those of more than 300 learned societies, more than 800 new books per year, and a growing range of library products including archives, data, case studies, reports, conference highlights, and video. SAGE remains majority-owned by our founder, and after Sara's lifetime will become owned by a charitable trust that secures our continued independence.

Los Angeles | London | Washington DC | New Delhi | Singapore | Boston

Thank you for choosing a SAGE product! If you have any comment, observation or feedback, I would like to personally hear from you. Please write to me at <u>contactceo@sagepub.in</u>

—Vivek Mehra, Managing Director and CEO,
SAGE Publications India Pvt Ltd, New Delhi

Bulk Sales

SAGE India offers special discounts for purchase of books in bulk. We also make available special imprints and excerpts from our books on demand.

For orders and enquiries, write to us at

Marketing Department
SAGE Publications India Pvt Ltd
B1/I-1, Mohan Cooperative Industrial Area
Mathura Road, Post Bag 7
New Delhi 110044, India
E-mail us at <u>marketing@sagepub.in</u>

Get to know more about SAGE, be invited to SAGE events, get on our mailing list. Write today to <u>marketing@sagepub.in</u>

This book is also available as an e-book.

Governance, Conflict and Development in South Asia

Series Note

GOVERNANCE, CONFLICT AND CIVIC ACTION

Series Editors: David N. Gellner, Krishna Hachhethu, Siri Hettige,
Joanna Pfaff-Czarnecka, Gérard Toffin

Volume 1: *Local Democracy in South Asia: Microprocesses of Democratization in Nepal and its Neighbours*, eds David N. Gellner and Krishna Hachhethu

Volume 2: *Ethnic Activism and Civil Society in South Asia*, ed. David N. Gellner

Volume 3: *Varieties of Activist Experience: Civil Society in South Asia*, ed. David N. Gellner

Volume 4: *The Politics of Belonging in the Himalayas: Local Attachments and Boundary Dynamics*, eds Joanna Pfaff-Czarnecka and Gérard Toffin

Volume 5: *Facing Globalization in the Belonging and the Politics of the Self*, eds Gérard Toffin and Joanna Pfaff-Czarnecka

Governance, Conflict and Development in South Asia: Perspectives from India, Nepal and Sri Lanka

GOVERNANCE, CONFLICT AND CIVIC ACTION: VOLUME 6

Edited by

Siri Hettige
Eva Gerharz

The (Micro) Politics of Democrastisation:
European–South Asian Exchanges on
Governance, Conflict and Civic Action

 www.sagepublications.com
Los Angeles • London • New Delhi • Singapore • Washington DC • Boston

First published in 2015 by

SAGE Publications India Pvt Ltd
B1/I-1 Mohan Cooperative Industrial Area
Mathura Road, New Delhi 110 044, India
www.sagepub.in

SAGE Publications Inc
2455 Teller Road
Thousand Oaks, California 91320, USA

SAGE Publications Ltd
1 Oliver's Yard, 55 City Road
London EC1Y 1SP, United Kingdom

SAGE Publications Asia-Pacific Pte Ltd
3 Church Street
#10-04 Samsung Hub
Singapore 049483

Published by Vivek Mehra for SAGE Publications India Pvt Ltd, Phototypeset in 10/13pt Minion Pro by RECTO Graphics, Delhi and printed at Chaman Enterprises, New Delhi.

Library of Congress Cataloging-in-Publication Data Available

ISBN: 978-93-515-0100-8 (HB)

The SAGE Team: N. Unni Nair, Alekha Chandra Jena, Apeksha Sharma, Baibhav Bansal and Vinitha Nair

Contents

List of Abbreviations   vii
Preface   ix

Chapter 1
Introduction: Governance, Development and Conflict in South Asia   1
Siri Hettige and Eva Gerharz

PART I: THEORETICAL PERSPECTIVES ON DEVELOPMENT AND GOVERNANCE

Chapter 2
'Participation' and 'Empowerment' in the Development Discourse:
   Rethinking Key Concepts   23
Ravinder Kaur and Vinod K. Jairath

Chapter 3
The Idea of Development as Governance: India in the First
   Decade of Independence   44
Dilip M. Menon

PART II: EXPERIENCING DEVELOPMENT AND CONFLICT AT NATIONAL LEVEL

Chapter 4
Governance and Development in Post-independence Sri Lanka   69
Siri Hettige

Chapter 5
Rituals of Democracy and Development in Nepal   99
David N. Gellner

PART III: GOVERNANCE, CONFLICT AND DEVELOPMENT: EXPERIENCE AT THE GRASSROOTS

Chapter 6
Negotiating a Dual Governance System during
the Conflict in Nepal   131
Natalie Hicks

Chapter 7
Empowerment of Excluded Groups: Local Democracy and
Social Change in Rural Odisha, Eastern India   157
B.B. Mohanty

Chapter 8
Between Order and Chaos: Jaffna's Local Images of
Governance during Conflict   186
Eva Gerharz

PART IV: IDEAS AND INTERESTS IN GOVERNANCE AND DEVELOPMENT IN CONFLICT-RIDDEN SOCIETIES

Chapter 9
Economic Growth to Conflict Mitigation: Changing Aid
Strategies of Nepal's Donors   217
Laxman Acharya

Chapter 10
Good Governance and Development in a Shrinking Local
Policy Space: GATS and Service Sector Reforms   240
Dileepa Witharana

Glossary   273
About the Editors and Contributors   277
Index   281

List of Abbreviations

ADB	Asian Development Bank
ANM	assistant nurse midwife (programme)
BASE	Backward Society Education
BJD	Biju Janata Dal Party (India)
BJP	Bharatiya Janata Party (India)
CBO	Community-Based Organization
CEB	Ceylon Electricity Board
CPA	Comprehensive Peace Agreement
CPM	Communist Party of India (Marxist)
CPI	Communist Party of India
DDC	District Development Committee or District Development Chairperson
DSB	Dispute Settlement Body
ESAF	Enhanced Structural Adjustment Facilities
FAO	Food and Agriculture Organization
FAP	foreign aid policy
FECOFUN	Federation of Community Forestry Users Nepal (a national organization of Forest User Groups)
FFP	Friends for Peace
GATS	General Agreement on Trade in Services
GATT	General Agreement on Tariff and Trade
GNP	Gross National Product
HSZ	High Security Zones
IDP	internally displaced person
IFC	International Finance Corporation
ILO	International Labour Organization
INGO	International Non-Governmental Organizations
IPTA	Indian Peoples Theatre Association
JRY	Jawahar Rojgar Yojana scheme
JVP	Janatha Vimukthi Peramuna
KPAC	Kerala People's Arts Club
LDC	Least Developed Countries

LOTIS	Liberalisation of Trade in Services
LSSP	Lanka Sama Samaja Party
LTTE	Liberation Tigers of Tamil Eelam
MFN	Most Favoured Nation
MIGA	Multilateral Investment Guarantee Agency
MIT	Medical Institute of Tamils
MKSS	Mazdoor Kisan Shakti Sangathna
MLA	Member of the Legislative Assembly
MOF	Ministry of Finance in Nepal
MP	Member of Parliament
NDS	National Development Service
NGO	Non-Governmental Organization
OECD	Organisation for Economic Co-operation and Development
OPEC	Organization of Petroleum Exporting Countries
PAR	Participatory Action Research
PLA	People's Liberation Army
PRA	Participatory Rural Appraisal
PRGF	International Monetary Fund's Poverty Reduction Growth Facilities
RRA	Rapid Rural Appraisal
SAARC	South Asian Association for Regional Cooperation
SAP	WB's Structural Adjustment Programme
SLFP	Sri Lanka Freedom Party
SLMM	Sri Lankan Monitoring Mission
SPA	Seven Party Alliance
THO	Tamils Health Organization
TRO	Tamil Rehabilitation Organization
UML	Unified Marxist-Leninist
UN	United Nations
UNCTD	United Nations Conference on Trade and Development
UNDP	United Nations Development Programme
UNP	United National Party
USAID	United States Agency for International Development
USCSI	US Coalition of Services Industries
VDC	Village Development Committee
WB	World Bank
WTO	World Trade Organization
WUNC	worthiness, unity, numbers and commitment

Preface

This publication is the last in the series on Governance, Conflict and Civil Action in South Asia. It presents the outcome of the conference on Governance and Development in South Asia held in Kandy, Sri Lanka, several years ago. With its focus on the ways in which development, conflict and governance intersect, it captures dominant characteristics of political and social processes in almost all parts of South Asia. Development is a goal that the governments of South Asian countries pursue without exception, albeit the ideals and visions depend on the particular circumstances not just at national, but also at local levels. Moreover, there is a great deal of diversity in the region with regard to governance. While the popular aspiration among citizens in each of the countries is to see their countries being governed by democratically elected leaders keeping secular democratic values, standards of governance fall far short of expectations in much of South Asia. Individual, social and political rights, which are often taken for granted in mature democracies, are at times violated at the heads of powerful and privileged individuals and groups. Effective checks and balances on those who wield power and authority, be they individuals or institutions, need to be improved.

The achievement of political independence in South Asian countries following several centuries of Western colonial subjugation was followed by the enthronement of privileged, naïve political elites, often committed to secular, liberal values. The democratization of politics that followed the introduction of universal suffrage led to the political mobilization of the underprivileged strata enabling some members of these strata to rise up to the positions of power through the electoral process. As it turned out, many of these upwardly mobile politicians of a humble origin have tended to translate their positions of power and influence to positions of wealth and privilege. While the process of democratization has empowered hitherto underprivileged and marginalized groups in a society leading to the increased political representation of such groups and many significant social reforms, emergent patron–client politics, abuse of power and corruption have tended to hinder the principles of good governance such as transparency, accountability and the rule of law. The democratization of politics has not always led to good governance in South Asia. Although several countries have seen revolutionary uprisings and strong civil society activities, the scope for mobilizing the masses as citizens with equal rights and privileges has been limited. Instead, primordial divisions based on caste, ethnicity, religion and language have been reproduced within the political process. In some contexts, this has led to serious intrastate conflicts, which more often than not have become extremely violent, resulting in the death and displacement of large numbers of people in affected communities. The conflicts have also been costly in terms of the destruction of social and economic infrastructure and lost economic opportunities for both the affected communities and the country at large. The ensuing economic hardships and increasing social and political instability have encouraged many citizens to migrate, particularly the most educated and skilled sections of the labour force. As is well known, such brain drain has not only been a major hindrance to development, but has also significantly contributed to institutional decay in diverse spheres such as politics, public administration, law enforcement, education and public services.

So, governance, development and conflict in most South Asian countries are highly interdependent. What happens in one area, therefore, is more than likely to have significant implications on other areas. The key challenge for South Asian countries is to harmonize development goals with those of good governance and peace. The experience in almost all South Asian countries has amply demonstrated that this has not been easy due to many endogenous and exogenous circumstances.

The book is an outcome of the project 'Micro-Politics of Democratization in South Asia' funded by the European Commission under the EU-Asia-Link programme (2004–07). The project facilitated collaborative research, writing and publications on the overall theme involving junior and senior academics from a number of countries, namely, Germany, Nepal, the UK and Sri Lanka. Several conferences and workshops were organized in Nepal, the UK and Sri Lanka by the project partners: (a) Institute of World Society Studies, Bielefeld University, Germany, (b) the Centre for Nepal and Asian Studies (CNAS), Tribhuvan University, Kathmandu, Nepal, (c) the Social Policy Analysis and Research Centre (SPARC),

University of Colombo, Sri Lanka and (d) the Institute of Social and Cultural Anthropology (ISCA), University of Oxford, UK. This is the last volume in this series of publications.

This book would not have seen the light of day if not for the commitment, support and encouragement extended to us by a number of individuals, in particular, Joanna Pfaff-Czarnecka and David Gellner. While the publication was delayed considerably due to circumstances beyond our control, both Joanna and David continued to support and encourage us throughout this period. We acknowledge their role with great appreciation. Dharshi Thoradeniya who was attached to the SPARC, University of Colombo, from 2006 to 2009 in her capacity as an Administrative Coordinator played a significant part in organizing the conference on *Governance and Development in South Asia* in 2006 and later in the coordination of the editorial process leading to the present publication. We appreciate her valuable contribution towards this publication. We also record with appreciation the secretarial and administrative support extended to us by S.V.P. Sepalika and Thilini Withanachchi, both attached to SPARC, University of Colombo. We thank Daniela Urbansky, Katrin Renschler, Arne Oster and Anna Frings, who have provided valuable support in preparing the manuscript. Cassie Barton, David Phelps and Lisa Vissel have been of enormous help in editing the last versions of the chapters. Last but not least, we acknowledge the cooperation extended to us by the authors. We record with appreciation the patience and understanding they displayed over the last several years, in addition to making their significant contribution to this volume.

Siri Hettige
Eva Gerharz

Chapter 1

Introduction

Governance, Development and Conflict in South Asia

SIRI HETTIGE AND EVA GERHARZ

The themes of governance, development and conflict have figured prominently not only in the recent social science literature on South Asia (cf. Jalal, 1955; Vignaraja, 1989; Gupta, 1966; Raja, 1996; Shasma, 1999; Zaidi, 1999 and Mitra, 2006) but also in the wider public discourse, as is evident from frequent media coverage on such issues in the region and elsewhere. However, these phenomena are not always treated as closely intertwined, though there have been several attempts to explore some of their interconnections.[1] Viewed from both empirical and theoretical perspectives, particularly from a comparative historical viewpoint, it is quite clear that none of these topics can be discussed in isolation from the other two. This book is an attempt to examine governance, development and conflict from both a conceptual and an empirical perspective, and pays attention to particular configurations of governance and development that have shaped the recent history of South Asian states. The case studies collected here clearly point to the fact that governance, development and conflict are phenomena that have interacted with one another in very complex ways, depending on the nature of the particular endogenous and exogenous circumstances in different countries. India, South Asia's largest and most diverse country, has displayed greater resilience in terms of economic performance, democratic rule and socio-political stability,

[1] For several wide-ranging analyses, see Collier et al. (2003), Cramer (2002), Geneva Declaration (2010), Kaplan (2008), Meiden (2006), Murdoch (2004), OECD (2010) and Ostby (2008).

but other countries in the same region, such as Bangladesh, Sri Lanka and Nepal, have been adversely affected by internal conflicts leading to diverse negative outcomes. A persisting challenge for these countries is how to achieve economic development, nurture good governance and overcome social and political conflict (The World Bank, 1997, 2011). It is also important to recognize the fact that South Asian countries have not evolved in isolation of each other but have continued to be influenced by historical, socio-cultural, political and economic forces often operating across geographical and national boundaries (Shourie, 2010). Although this theme is not explicitly addressed in the present volume, it is of persisting relevance for development, governance and conflict in each of the countries in the region.

Development is a goal that all South Asian countries have pursued almost without exception, in spite of the diversity in the ideals and visions that have guided or inspired their respective political regimes over time. The region is also characterized by a high degree of diversity with respect to the nature and quality of governance, though the wider population in general seems to aspire for good governance based on secular democratic values. Yet, human rights, including social and political rights, are violated frequently by powerful and privileged actors in society. Effective checks and balances on those who wield power and authority are either absent or ineffective and the public demand for the restoration of such checks and balances is often resisted by vested interests.

Although this volume cannot adequately account for the enormous diversity within the South Asian region in terms of the experiences of different countries with respect to governance, development and conflict, it nevertheless brings together a number of in-depth analyses of the ways in which governance, development and conflicts have evolved over time. These interrelations are the product of colonial legacy, changing discourses of development and participation, institutionalization of democratic practices and the modes of accommodation of diverse population groups, in particular ethnic and other minorities, within the state. Firstly, this book explores the various ways in which particular modes of governance have emerged after colonialism and the challenges these countries face in achieving development and socio-political stability. Secondly, it uncovers the ways in which shortcomings in the political arrangements that lead to the exclusion of minorities and other marginalized groups often contribute to conflicts at national as well as at local level. Thirdly, it shows how diverse political cultures, that is, democratic and authoritarian, have influenced successes and failures of development as well as how (external) interventions and policy reforms in the name of development have led to unforeseen consequences. In the following, this introduction provides an overview of the possibilities and challenges for development and peace in the South Asian region.

CHALLENGES TO GOVERNANCE AFTER COLONIALISM

The achievement of political independence in South Asian countries after several centuries of Western colonial subjugation was followed by the enthronement of privileged, native political elites, often committed to secular, liberal and democratic values. But the democratization of politics that followed the introduction of universal suffrage in many countries in the region also led to the political mobilization of the underprivileged strata, enabling some members of these strata to reach high positions of power through the electoral process. As it turned out later, many of these upwardly mobile politicians of a humble background tended to convert their positions of power and influence into positions of wealth and privilege. While the process of democratization has empowered hitherto underprivileged and marginalized groups in society, leading to an increase in their political representation and several significant social reforms, emergent patron–client politics, abuse of power and corruption have tended to hinder the principles of good governance such as equity, transparency, accountability and the rule of law.

Those South Asian countries that constituted an important part of the British Empire inherited certain social and political institutions and practices as a result of the colonial legacy including representative government, formally organized public administration, judicial systems and political parties. However, such institutions did not get firmly established everywhere due to the continuing significance of traditional elites and emerging authoritarian tendencies. Consequently, when South Asian countries came under pressure to liberalize their economies and loosen up the grip of the state over economic resources, many countries in the region did not have a firm liberal political foundation that could withstand the pressures of rapid socio-economic transformation. So when the state gave way to the market, existing political and administrative institutions became even weaker and more fragile. This can be clearly observed in countries such as Sri Lanka and Bangladesh. The state has by and large failed to adequately regulate the market, which has led to failures or serious distortions. For instance, the rapid expansion of private health and educational services following economic liberalization in Sri Lanka has resulted in great inequities within the two sectors but the state has done little to arrest the trend. The growing interconnections between the ruling elites on one hand and the emerging business leaders on the other often prevented the adoption of public policies that would address some of the emerging issues such as income disparities and corruption. Growing social disparities, particularly between rural and urban areas, contributed to social and political unrest, at times feeding into violent conflict. Such developments have not helped to improve governance standards, as is clearly evident in the case of Bangladesh (Kabeer, 2003; Sobhan, 2004).

The state has been weakened due to both internal or external pressures. Internal pressures have often emanated from anti-systemic insurgencies such as separatist movements or radical resistance movements that necessitate substantive responses both at national and local levels, as Hicks' and Gerharz's ethnographies on local governance arrangements in Nepal and Sri Lanka, respectively, show. Many of these movements have been the result of the failure of the state itself. External debts, overdependence on worker remittances and falling terms of trade can put unprecedented pressure on weak, dependent states (see the chapters by Witharana and Laxman). On the other hand, a large country like India has a much greater capacity to withstand external pressures than small states such as Sri Lanka and Nepal. At the same time, it can be observed that a socially unregulated market may turn into a corrupting influence on political elites as well as others such as law enforcement agencies, public officials and the society at large. This, in effect, has a destabilizing impact on the political process itself. Market-led development is, thus, not always consistent with the imperatives of good governance (this argument is developed in Hettige's chapter with particular reference to Sri Lanka). Corruption, violation of rules and regulations, and the abuse of economic and political power by vested interests constitute major socio-political issues. The need to protect vulnerable groups, such as the poorer segments of society, minorities and migrant workers, continues to be a major challenge for almost all South Asian states.

Even casual observers of South Asian politics often sense that not all is well with the way in which the countries are organized as political communities. For instance, political instability, tension and conflict characterize the political landscape in much of South Asia. Such conditions have, on the one hand, contributed to a high level of violence between ethnic groups and communities, and the displacement and exodus of large sections of the population. On the other hand, the same conditions have also hampered social and economic advancement, as violent conflict and underdevelopment have tended to reinforce each other. Poverty and the marginalization of large sections of the population exacerbated by political conflict and violence have fuelled social and political unrest further.

Western colonialism in South Asia did not necessarily have a levelling effect on South Asian societies. In fact, some of the pre-existing divisions became even sharper during the colonial period. As Wolfert (1982) and many others (for example, Spencer, 1990) have pointed out, the roots of much of contemporary confrontations in South Asia can be traced back to the colonial period. This pattern has persisted or has been reinforced further following political independence. In this regard, it is necessary to note that the increasing population pressure on material resources, divisive politics and new politically expedient public policies have made a significant contribution to social and political conflicts. The latter in turn have hampered economic development and social stability, leading to increasing out-migration of people, in particular highly skilled professionals, with serious adverse consequences in most countries.

Persisting underdevelopment and socio-political instability have increasingly encouraged people to leave their own countries in search of greener pastures in the developed West. This has greatly contributed to a depletion of the skilled human resources that are necessary for building modern institutions in such diverse fields as education, science and technology, industry, politics or public services. The resultant weakening of the institutional fabric has hampered political, social and economic development in most South Asian societies. For instance, the lack of highly skilled human resources is a major hindrance to export-oriented industrialization. Migration policies in much of the developed world that favour skilled migration from the periphery have not helped to ease the situation in this regard in many countries. However, we also witness a strong trend towards brain gain to India, though this is not the case in the rest of South Asia. The reverse flow in India is a reflection of the expansion of private sector firms, in particular those dealing with technology-intensive products and services.

South Asia, like many other parts of the post-colonial world, witnessed an anti-colonial, nationalist backlash towards the end of colonial rule. While this eventually contributed to de-colonization, the initial unity among nationalist forces was later undermined by various divisions in the society based on ethnic and other loyalties. These divisions, in turn, have come to dominate more recent local and national politics in South Asia. Various attempts to contain pressures emanating from different social and cultural forces have led to public policy shifts in diverse fields, with significant social, economic and political implications. For instance, the state-led central planning approach to development in several South Asian countries was largely the result of the growing influence of socialist parties there. Many egalitarian social reforms in such areas as land ownership and education were inspired by leftist movements as well as by changing development thinking (see Mohanty's and Kaur and Jairath's chapters).

EXCLUSION OF MINORITIES AND CONFLICT

The democratization of politics has not always led to good governance in South Asia. Although several countries have seen revolutionary uprisings and strong civil society movements, the scope for mobilizing the masses as citizens with equal rights and privileges has been limited. Instead, primordial divisions based on caste, ethnicity, religion and language have been reproduced and eventually deepened through popular, democratic political processes (for Sri Lanka see Tambiah, 1986). In some contexts, this has led to serious intrastate conflicts that often have become extremely violent, resulting in the death and displacement of large numbers of people in affected areas, as the case of Sri Lanka's conflict amply illustrates. The conflicts have also been costly in terms of the destruction of social and economic infrastructure and lost economic opportunities for both the affected communities and the country at large. The ensuing economic hardships and increasing social and political instability have encouraged many citizens to migrate, particularly the most educated and skilled sections of the labour force. This kind of migration induced by violent conflict has led to the formation of diasporas, whose transnational activities have had ambivalent effects. Such brain drain phenomena have not only been a major hindrance to development, but also significantly contributed to institutional decay in diverse spheres such as politics, public administration, law enforcement, education and public services [for Sri Lanka, see Gerharz (2014)]. Moreover, the weakening of public institutions has undermined good governance in a number of countries.

Although ethnic and religious diversity has posed a serious challenge to social and political stability in South Asia in general, it is astonishing that a vast country like India characterized by great diversity has nurtured strong democratic institutions that have been able to accommodate diversity to some extent. It almost looks as if the size and the diversity have been a source of resilience of her democratic institutions than a serious threat to them. In most of the other South Asian countries, however, ethnic and religious diversity has been regarded as an obstacle to national integration, which has eventually led to a violent conflict. Most of these countries have been less successful in following similar trajectories in the process of political and economic development as it has been the case in India over the last 50–60 years. Even in countries where democratic institutions were initially established, they have later come under pressure or have been undermined by military or violent non-state forces. Sri Lanka, for example, which has experienced one of the bloodiest civil wars in the post-colonial history of Asia, is today ruled by an increasingly illiberal regime whose legitimacy largely depends upon the legacy of having defeated the Tamil insurgency. Bangladesh's democracy has been repeatedly under threat and is challenged by stiff competition between two opposing political parties, each one struggling to come to power by any means. Nepal's post-conflict situation is dominated by power struggles and infinite difficulties in finding common ground with regard to a viable power-sharing arrangement. And even India experiences a variety of challenges concerning public security, with the Northeast continuously under emergency rule.

In spite of persisting and widespread poverty and other issues of social and political development, India stands out as the dominant player in the regional economy and is a leader on the world stage. The country's early and continuing public investments in science and technology, strengthening of public institutions and continuation of a broadly democratic framework of governance, undoubtedly helped India to benefit from economic reforms and global integration (Gujral, 1979; Stein and Subramaniyam, 1996). Though there have sporadically been outbreaks of political violence and ethno-religious riots in several regions of the country, these have hardly undermined the social and political stability of the country as a whole. In contrast, political violence and social instability have been the order of the day in countries such as Nepal, Pakistan, Sri Lanka and to some extent also in Bangladesh. A large share of public funds has been diverted into defence expenditure, leading to a significant curtailment of social investments that have a long gestation period before benefits can be reaped. Persisting social and political instability has discouraged long-term private investment in vital sectors of the economy such as modern industries. Persisting underdevelopment, widespread poverty and regional disparities have contributed to social and political conflict that in turn has reinforced authoritarian tendencies and elevated the national security apparatus to a preeminent position in national politics. These developments tend to adversely affect basic freedoms and the functioning of civil society organizations.

GOVERNANCE AND THE DEVELOPMENTALIST STATE

Although much of South Asia was part of the British colonial empire and transformed into politically independent states almost simultaneously after the Second World War,[2] not all South Asian states have followed identical trajectories during the post-colonial period. As Ludden (1992; 2005) has pointed out, India and Sri Lanka acquired an increasingly developmentalist character. Their close ideological affinity to the socialist bloc led by the Soviet Union influenced their leaders to adopt policies that made them fit more clearly into this state model and the idea of central planning figured prominently in the context of domestic development thinking at the time.

Independent Pakistan comprised spatially separated western and eastern territories as a result of the partition. Bangladesh was born after an

---

[2] An exception is Bangladesh, which belonged to Pakistan after 1947 and became an independent state only in 1971 after a bloody liberation war.

independence struggle against West Pakistan in the early 1970s (Alauddin and Hasan, 1999). Both countries have been under military rule from time to time, and this undoubtedly has weakened their democratic institutions and traditions. Nepal and Bhutan remained two independent monarchical states with their own historical experiences and encounters with the outside world (Karan and Ishii, 1996; Ministry of Commerce, 2000). The fact that they did not come under Western colonial domination has been highly significant. However, India as their giant southern neighbour, as well as China to the north and east, has influenced both these states to a great extent. Development issues have been addressed by these governments in the region in different ways, and each case needs to be viewed individually. However, the emergence of violent conflict in some countries is related to both, the politics of development and the ways of governance. With a special focus on Nepal, Sri Lanka and India, this book targets the nexus between governance, development and conflict from both conceptual as well as empirical perspectives. An important prerequisite for understanding the ways development has become prominent as a discourse and as practice requires a careful analysis of the history of the nation-state and the culture of governance that have evolved after colonialism (see Kaur and Jairath's as well as Gellner's contributions).

Judged by international standards, almost all countries in South Asia are relatively poor,[3] though social and material disparities have deepened in recent decades. Access to basic social and physical infrastructure facilities, such as health, education, housing, transport, water and electricity, is by no means assured everywhere. It is widely assumed today that the state alone cannot get these countries out of their present state of underdevelopment; civil society (Gellner, 2009; 2010) and the market are expected to play an increasingly significant part in the development process. Economic liberalization does not necessarily accompany greater political freedoms as increasing market pressures generate popular protests that, in turn,

---

[3] Per capita income has increased in all countries in recent years, though significant variations are also evident. For instance, according to IMF data for 2010, per capita income in the region varied from 1,250 US dollars in Nepal to 5,600 US dollars for Bhutan. The relevant figures for Bangladesh, India, Pakistan, the Maldives and Sri Lanka are 1,600, 3,339, 2,789, 5,483 and 5,108 US dollars, respectively. These incomes are relatively low in comparison to many East Asian countries, such as South Korea, Japan and Malaysia.

encourage governments to adopt anti-democratic measures to contain or suppress them. In others, governments role back economic reforms partly to avoid confrontations with agitated population groups. Yet, the advocates of market reforms continue to point to the failure of social-ist states to achieve a higher level of development, human freedom and choice, and seek to explain it in terms of the suppression of the market forces and individual initiative. Especially with regard to India and Sri Lanka, it has been argued that protectionism and excessive state control over the economy constituted critical factors holding back development in the recent past.

In spite of various measures taken by post-colonial regimes in South Asia, the countries in the region have not been able to break away from underdevelopment and widespread poverty due to various circumstances. Many critics, both from within and outside, began to blame state domina-tion over the economy as the critical factor. When the international finan-cial institutions came forward to recommend drastic economic reforms to allow market forces to operate freely, South Asian countries did not see alternatives. Subsequent implementation of economic reforms resulted in a significant transformation of their economies leading to their closer integration with the world economy. Yet, how and to what degree each country is integrated with the global economy differs widely and depends on both the structure of their respective economies as well as the level of development of their social, economic and political institutions.

What is evident from the discussion so far is that governance, develop-ment and conflict are not discrete phenomena but are interconnected in complex ways. The experience of most South Asian countries over the last few decades clearly attests to this fact. While social and political stability facilitates good governance and development, social and political conflicts weaken liberal democratic form of government and impede the process of economic development. At the same time, illiberal tendencies and economic stagnation feed into social and political conflict, and in spite of liberal economic reforms and increasing integration with the global system of production and exchange relations, most South Asian countries have not been able to achieve either social and political stability or a high level of economic development in comparison to East and South East Asian countries such as China, South Korea, Malaysia and Singapore. While this volume makes no attempt to engage in a comparative analysis, its different chapters here directly and indirectly address the South Asian dilemma from a number of different social science perspectives.

STRUCTURE OF THE BOOK

One of the key challenges for South Asian countries is to harmonize development goals with those of good governance and peace. Experiences in almost all South Asian countries have amply demonstrated that this has not been easy, owing to many endogenous and exogenous circumstances. This book addresses these issues paying attention to critical discourses on participation and modernity in relation to development and governance. It further addresses the ways in which governance and development evolved as paradigms, with ensuing effects on the nation-building process. Several case studies probe deeper into the processes of governance and development at the local level and in relation to external influences.

This introduction is followed by a section on development and governance from a conceptual perspective, largely pertaining to post-colonial India. The first contribution by Ravinder Kaur and Vinod K. Jairath draws on contemporary debates and looks at the shifting notions of 'participation' and 'empowerment' in development practice. Beyond critically evaluating the approaches applied over time—from early concepts of 'community development' to more recent priorities on 'participatory governance' and 'citizenship participation'—they unravel the complex mechanisms of participatory inclusion and exclusion. According to the authors, this aspect is revealed most obviously in the accentuation of citizenship not only as a legal framework, but also in terms of the relationship between state and citizen. In order to enliven this relationship, they argue that it is necessary to overcome ill-/narrowly defined concepts of distinct 'localities' and homogeneous 'communities', which de facto tend to impede processes of citizen participation.

In the third chapter, Dilip M. Menon reviews the 'making of' modernity in post-colonial India. Illustrated by examples covering the spheres from fine arts to science and technology, he figuratively dissects the representation of the modern in the newly emerging nation state. He pays particular attention to the (re)arrangement of the relationship between the state and its people, manoeuvring between traditional/earlier concepts of the people as masses that had to be disciplined and mobilized, and post-colonial ideas of a particular version of modernity—still in waiting and buttressed by a quest for authenticity. Moreover, he argues that governance has to be conceived not merely as *for* the people, but also in fact as undertaken *by* the people. Strategies of development have to bring people back in as active participants and partners, instead of making them passive recipients of the benefits of the state's distributive and managerial activities.

The second section of the book deals with experiences of development and conflict at a national level. It brings together two chapters that develop a historical perspective on the ways in which nation-building projects were shaped by development policies and discourses. Siri Hettige's contribution unpacks the nexus between development and (good) governance in relation to the conflict in Sri Lanka. Efforts made by the Sri Lankan state to change the colonially inherited structure of the economy soon led to a domination of the state (particularly in the social sector), while the private sector, in turn, became marginalized. At the same time, the state-led development model nourished ever higher and more unrealistic expectations which were not fulfilled amidst the economic, political and social crises since the 1970s. The radical shift towards an open economic policy that followed, rendering large numbers of the population unemployed, set the stage for (increasingly violent) anti-state resistance. Market liberalization created new opportunities for private consumption; but the poor regulation of the new economy also encouraged a political culture of corruption and abuse of power, particularly in the urban centres. The rural population, in contrast, remained largely marginalized, without adequate sustainable income opportunities. At the same time, major shifts occurred on the political level. Through the introduction of an executive presidential system of government, power became increasingly concentrated in the hands of the executive president—which gave rise to considerable protest by the political opposition. The heavily unbalanced constellations of powers have triggered a range of problems in other domains of governance, most notably in the sectors of civil society, the judiciary, the organization of political parties, state bureaucracy (including increasing abuse of power by public officials and political leaders) and political interference with freedom of expression in the media landscape. Rising horizontal and vertical inequalities reinforced existing tensions and contributed to the intensification of the (ethnically driven) conflict in

Sri Lanka. The conflict came to an end in 2009 with the military defeat of the separatist Liberation Tigers of Tamil Eelam (LTTE); but the issues of governance and conflict have become more serious since the war owing to an increasing concentration of power at the centre.

In Chapter 5, David Gellner deals with the performance of democracy and development in Nepal. Reconstructing the vicissitudinous last decades, he works out the close links between (inter)nationally applied approaches to development and the national conceptions of democracy. He particularly emphasizes the ideas and ideals of modernity and related representations in the spheres of governance and development during the then Hindu kingdom (high-caste Parbatiya culture as a modernized national identity). Following the course of events, including the 12 years of multiparty government and the Maoist insurgency, he points out the way the Maoists in their struggle for the support of the Nepali people have actually reverted to the same vocabulary and strategies (performance of meetings, rallies, forms of protest such as bandh, marches and burning effigies) as their opponents. Far from condemning the modalities of development and the steps towards democracy as imitations or even fake, the author recognizes the value of and the need for what he calls performance to negotiate included notions of modernity and to enact new ways of thinking.

The third section is devoted to an analysis of how governance, conflict and development intersect at the local level. The three chapters in this section bring out the way in which governance is negotiated in people's everyday lives—with case studies on Sri Lanka and Nepal dealing with the ambivalences emerging from dual governance in conflict-ridden localities and that on India scrutinizing the reproduction of social inequalities in the context of local governance. Case studies based on empirical material from India, Nepal and Sri Lanka reveal how citizens negotiate the slippery terrain of local governance in everyday life. On the basis of field research in Nepal conducted in 2005–06, Natalie Hicks reveals the complexity of the interaction between rural community members and the international and political elite in the capital, Kathmandu. She points to the factors that led to the competing systems of government during the conflict and argues that the Maoists utilized the existing ignorance on the part of capital-centred politics of political and social realities in rural Nepal to establish village people's governments as an alternative to the inefficient governmental administration so as to address grievances in the rural areas. The Maoist ideology gained rural support for a new vision for the future Nepal (articulated in the 40-Point demand), because—in comparison with the rather self-interested Kathmandu-centred governance system—it promised to deal with the interests of the villagers. Clashes between Maoists and villagers emerged when promises were clearly undermined: not only in terms of the extraction of taxes, but also in terms of education. Indoctrination stood in stark contrast with the self-declared aim of universal education for all. Hicks analyses negotiations over the dual governance system in everyday life in rural areas by contrasting three exemplary cases: negotiations over education in Dhankuta district, agricultural services in Morang district and the fight against crime in Jhapa district. Her findings reveal that the villagers were not simply trapped between opposing military and political forces, but actively developed elaborated strategies (agency) to navigate through the dual governance systems, for example, so as even within the dire situation of conflict to benefit from public services and security from both sides.

B.B. Mohanty's contribution investigates the unequal distribution of power across gender, caste, class and political party affiliation during the early days of the system of *panchayati raj* (rule by local councils). Particularly in rural areas, women, as well as scheduled castes and tribes, were excluded from local decision-making processes. Whereas formal inclusion of these groups through the 73rd Constitutional Amendment in 1993 has been accomplished, the question emerges as to how far this has been actually implemented. By taking the example of the Indian state of Odisha, Mohanty argues that post-Independence planning turns a blind eye towards prevailing inequalities. Rather, it buttresses existing structures, replacing the notion of caste by class. The political overrepresentation of the higher castes is scarcely challenged, owing to the absence of collective action on the part of the disadvantaged castes. At best there is only moderate inclusion of women into politics, and many of them being of rural and low-caste origin suffer from multiple deprivations. A comparative study of three panchayats in Kendrapara district reveals ambiguous tendencies: though the institutional inclusion is formally implemented, the hitherto excluded groups remain discriminated against. Female representatives are merely included as proxies for their male relatives, and members of the lower and scheduled castes have been co-opted by the privileged groups.[4] Nevertheless, while established structures of dependence (for example, landlord–tenant) and mutually accepted notions of respect, prestige and authority impede an effective inclusion, this pro forma participation has created at least a certain level of awareness of local governance among the otherwise almost totally neglected segments of the population. In the light of the prevailing situation and the data available at present, however, it is doubtful whether the steps taken have reduced persistent inequalities at a local level.

Chapter 8 deals with the images of governance in the context of the Sri Lankan conflict. In her contribution, Eva Gerharz focuses on the Tamil-dominated Jaffna peninsula, which was particularly characterized by a state of dual governance involving the LTTE and the government forces. By means of the concept of locality (understood in terms of local space, with aggregated interactions, providing scope for identity constructions), she explores local relations between the society and the state, closely connected with the local images of governance in Jaffna. The peninsula had come under LTTE control from the mid-1980s onwards and remained without much government influence until military forces recaptured the territory in 1995. Until the end of the war in 2009, Jaffna was under two systems of governance. Officially, the military and civil administration represented the central state, whereas the LTTE acted as a shadow government, influencing decisions and creeping into the civic realm by alternative means of 'governance'. This situation was critically observed by the local population, which was caught between the two forces. The LTTE was often seen as more efficient and legitimate and more capable of ensuring law and order and providing human security. The LTTE, thus, stood in stark contrast to the government forces, which were regarded as a foreign occupation. However, the LTTE rule, with its authoritarian tendencies, was not a problem-free enterprise, but shaped by an ambivalent relationship between the LTTE and civilians in Jaffna. Whether international involvement with the aim of restructuring the system of governance would have stabilized this situation remains unanswered, as the Sri Lankan military

---

[4] The empirical findings presented by Mohanty are not uncontested. On the basis of her fieldwork on Uttar Pradesh and Himachal Pradesh, Strulik (2008) comes to a different conclusion and highlights the agency of female politicians.

defeated the LTTE and continues to maintain control, with a high level of militarization.

The last section of the book deals with ideas and (foreign) interests in governance and development in conflict-ridden societies. In Chapter 9, Acharya Laxman considers the relationship between the Nepalese government and modalities of foreign aid. Proceeding from the increasing inflows of financial aid within the past decades, he critically evaluates the trends of spending these allocations and finds fault with the insufficient system of aid management and administration. While the donors long pursued the objective of bridging existing financial gaps in order to mobilize internal resources, the author finds today's Nepal more dependent on aid than ever before. And in similar fashion to the country's experience with economic development, he considers the donors' idea of stabilizing the political situation through aid as an essentially failed venture too, as the Maoist insurgency most vividly shows. In view of the deteriorating political and social situation, Laxman demonstrates how the global shifts in development paradigms during times of conflict were wide off the mark with regard to the country's actual needs. Notwithstanding, he finds cause for optimism, particularly with regard to recent developments: the commonly shared aim to promote social inclusion and good governance fits better with the socio-economic realities of the conflict-affected population. In the backdrop of the current state of affairs—here the author highlights the necessity to understand Nepal as a country still in a state of conflict rather than following the international community's tendencies to already open the repertoire of post-conflict reconstruction—it remains to be seen whether and how these strategies will be successfully implemented.

By taking the example of the General Agreement on Trade in Services and Service Sector Reforms in Sri Lanka, Dileepa Witharana investigates good governance and development in a shrinking local policy space. He argues that contradictory tendencies characterize the current world order: on the one hand, concepts of good governance and sustainable development are widely discussed and are often integral part of strategies and policies promoted by representatives of the government, civil society and the private sector. On the other hand, these intentions are hardly reflected in the actual situation of the population at the local level, which is rather characterized by the want of opportunities for participation in the processes of decision-making. 'Local policy space', conceptualized as 'the freedom of choice to adopt and implement development policies that respect the principles of sovereignty of states and self-determination of the people through autonomous and semi-autonomous forums at different levels', and the options for decision-making therein are curtailed by international trade and financial institutions, and multilateral agreements. Taking the example of electricity and water reforms in Sri Lanka, he shows how declining policy space increasingly concerns local levels of authority, because competitive free trade and the privatization of services are seen as a threat to both the national economy and the assurance of public services. A major issue is the neglect of the voices of small- and medium-scale traders and producers and their representatives as a fundamental violation of any ideas of good governance. He argues that the theoretical understanding of good governance and sustainable development is sophisticated and sufficiently elaborated, but extremely difficult to enforce in practice, in a dependent, developing-country context. Deteriorating economic, social and environmental conditions lead to popular unrest; but the capacity and the willingness of the state to address issues of inequality, injustice and exclusion are undermined by external economic pressures and poor governance at home.

As is clear from the various chapters included in this volume, persisting issues of governance, development and conflict characterize the socio-economic and political landscape of South Asia. In this regard, we have observed significant variations in the region and across the countries. India, in spite of persisting political controversies and conflicts and great inequalities, both socially and regionally, has recorded high rates of sustained economic growth, leading to steadily increasing per capita income, rapid expansion of its middle class and the strengthening of public institutions, including civil society organizations, the media and the judiciary. The resilience and the vibrancy of the democratic system of governance there, despite its imperfections, seem to provide the basis for sustained economic development. A strong civil society movement with its diverse manifestations and an independent media not only keep the political establishment in check to a considerable extent, but also help articulate social issues and mobilize large sections of the population around them, persuading political leaders to respond in a democratic fashion, through new legislation, state policies and programmatic interventions like the Mahatma Gandhi Rural Employment Guarantee Scheme (Joshi, 2010).

Poor economic performance, political instability and weak democratic institutions are characteristics of much of the rest of South Asia. Sri Lanka had some of the important pre-conditions for sustained, economic, political and social development at the time of independence. Yet the lack of unity among diverse ethnic communities contributed to increasing political instability, conflict and divisive policies. The culmination of these developments was the three-decade-long brutal ethnic war that came to an end in 2009. The end of the war created a window of opportunity to address long-standing issues that led to the conflict and take advantage of economic opportunities available for the country. Yet the lack of political will and institutional weaknesses have prevented serious attempts at national reconciliation. The country, thus, faces an uncertain future, in spite of the end of the war.

The challenges faced by other South Asian countries in achieving sustained economic development, good governance and socio-political stability are equally or even more daunting. On the other hand, it is difficult to imagine how these countries could ensure peace and a decent standard of living for their citizens without achieving a higher level of economic development, equitable distribution of the fruits of development, democratic and accountable government and harmonious coexistence of the diverse segments of the population. While there is perhaps no universally valid formula that can be followed in order to create a contended and relatively more harmonious society, a single-minded pursuit of economic growth without balancing it with social and political considerations such as equity, social justice, civil and political rights and transparent and accountable governance is unlikely to lead to sustainable development and social and political stability.

REFERENCES

Alauddin, M. and S. Hasan. 1999. *Development, Governance and Environment in South Asia: A Focus on Bangladesh*. London: Macmillan Press Ltd.
Collier, P. et al. 2003. *Breaking the Conflict Trap: Civil War and Development Policy*. Washington, D.C.: The World Bank.
Cramer, C. 2002. 'Homo Economicus Goes to War: Methodological Individualism, Rational Choice and the Political Economy of War'. *World Development*, 30(11): 1845–64.

Gellner, D. (ed.). 2009. *Ethnic Activism and Civil Society in South Asia*. New Delhi: SAGE Publications.

Gellner, D. 2010. *Varieties of Activist Experience: Civil Society in South Asia*. New Delhi: SAGE Publications.

Geneva Declaration. 2010. *More Violence, Less Development: Examining the Relationship between Armed Violence and MDG Achievement*, Geneva.

Gerharz, E. 2014. *The Politics of Reconstruction and Development in Sri Lanka. Transnational Commitments to Social Change*. London: Routledge.

Gujral, M.L. 1979. *Economic Failures of Nehru and Indira Gandhi*. Ghaziabad: Vikas Publishing House.

Gupta, B.S. 1966. *India: Problems of Governance*. New Delhi: Konark Publications.

Jalal, A. 1955. *Democracy and Authoritarianism in South Asia; A Comparative Historical Perspective*. Cambridge: Cambridge University Press.

Joshi, A. 2010. 'Do Rights Work? : Law, Activism and the Employment Guarantee Scheme'. *World Development*, 38(4): 620–30.

Kabeer, N. 2003. 'Growing Citizenship from Grassroots: Nijerkori and social mobilization in Bangladesh'. *Bangladesh Development Studies*, 29(3&4): 1–20.

Kaplan, S.D. 2008. *Fixing Fragile States; A New Paradigm for Development*. Westport, CT: Praeger Security International.

Karan, P.P. and H. Ishii. 1996. *Nepal: A Himalayan Kingdom in Transition*. Tokyo: UN University Press.

Ludden, D. 1992. 'India's Development Regime', in N. Dirks (ed.), *Colonialism and Culture*. Ann Arbor, MI: University of Michigan Press. pp. 247–87.

———. 2005. 'Development Regimes in South Asia: History and Governance Conundrum'. *Economic and Political Weekly*, 40(370): 4042–51.

Meiden, M. 2006. 'China's Africa Policy: Business Now, Politics Later'. *Asian Perspective* 30(4): 69–93.

Ministry of Commerce. 2000. *Perspectives for Nepalese Economy*. Kathmandu: Ministry of Commerce.

Mitra, S.K. 2006. *The Puzzle of India's Governance: Culture, Conduct and Comparative Theory*. New York: Routledge.

Murdoch, J.C. 2004. 'Civil Wars and Economic Growth: Spatial Dispersion'. *American Journal of Political Science*, 48(1): 138–55.

OECD. 2010. *Do No Harm: International Support for State-building*. Paris: OECD.

Ostby, G. 2008. 'Inequalities, the Political Environment and Civil Conflict: Evidence from 55 Developing Countries', in Frances Stewart (ed.), *Horizontal Inequalities and Conflict: Understanding Group Violence in Multi-ethnic Societies*. Basingstoke: Palgrave Macmillan.

Raja, G.T.C. 1996. *Democracy, Security and Development in India*. New York: St. Martin's Press.

Shasma, S.D. 1999. *Development and Democracy in India*. Boulder, CO: Lynne Reiner.

Shourie, A. 2010. 'India and Its Neighbours', in T.T. Young (ed.), *Challenges of Economic Growth, Inequality and Conflict in South Asia*. New Jersey: World Scientific: 1–22.

Sobhan, 2004. 'Structural Dimension of Mal-governance in Bangladesh'. *Economic and Political Weekly*, 39(36): 4041–148.

Spencer, J. (ed.). 1990. *Sri Lanka: History and Roots of Conflict*. New York: Routledge.

Stein, B. and S. Subramaniyam. 1996. *Institutions and Economic Change in South Asia*. Delhi: Oxford University Press.

Strulik, S. 2008. 'Engendering Local Democracy Research: Panchayati Raj and Changing Gender Relations in India', in D.N. Gellner and K. Hachhethu (eds), *Local Democracy in South Asia. Microprocesses of Democratization in Nepal and its Neighbours*. New Delhi: SAGE Publications, pp. 350–79.

Tambiah, S.J. 1986. *Sri Lanka. Ethnic Fratricide and the Dismantling of Democracy*. Chicago/London: Chicago University Press.

The World Bank. 1997. *World Development Report 1997: The State in a Challenging World*. Oxford: Oxford University Press.

The World Bank. 2011. *Conflict, Security and Development*. Washington, D.C.: The World Bank.

Vignaraja, P. 1989. 'The Challenges', in P. Vignaraja and A. Hussain (ed.), *The Challenge in South Asia: Development, Democracy and Regional Cooperation*. New Delhi: SAGE Publications.

Wolfert, S. 1982. *Roots of Confrontation in South Asia*. Oxford: Oxford University Press.

Zaidi, A. 1999. *The New Development Paradigm: Papers on Institutions, NGOs, Gender and Local Government*. Oxford: Oxford University Press.

PART I
THEORETICAL PERSPECTIVES ON
DEVELOPMENT AND GOVERNANCE

Chapter 2

'Participation' and 'Empowerment' in the Development Discourse

Rethinking Key Concepts

RAVINDER KAUR AND VINOD K. JAIRATH

To involve the "patients" in their own care was the instrumental task which the participatory concept has been assigned by development.

—Rahnema, 1997: 165

Over the past thirty years participation has become one of the shibboleths of contemporary development theory and practice, often linked to claims of 'empowerment' and "transformation".

—Hickey and Mohan, 2005: 238

INTRODUCTION

'Development' has always been seen as a contested idea, with a multiplicity of meanings and understandings. It is not surprising, therefore, that the concepts, particularly those which are common to different development discourses, carry contested meanings in ideological battles and practices of development. Scholars and practitioners/activists are engaged in defining, redefining and relocating prominent concepts such as social capital, participation, empowerment and community. In the process, one finds attempts to appropriate and sanitize any radical connotations of such terms used in development discourses. Therefore, it is necessary to understand the historical trajectory, assumptions, methodological devices used and the political implications in practice for each of these concepts. In this chapter, our primary focus is on 'participation' and some of its related concepts. We hope that our evaluation will help in understanding the nature of contestation in the larger issues of governance and development. The idea of participation has existed in the field of development for several decades now, but it has carried different meanings depending on historical context. Hickey and Mohan (2004b: 6–8) have summarized the variety of terminology, with different connotations, popular during different decades. The terms used are: 'Community development' (colonial: 1940s–50s), 'Community development' (post-colonial: 1960s–70s), 'Political participation' (1960s), 'Emancipatory participation' and 'Liberation theology' (1960s–70s), 'Alternative development' (1970s–90s), 'Populist participation in development' (1980s–present), 'Social capital' (1990s–present) and 'Participatory governance and citizenship participation' (late 1990s–present). This does not represent any evolutionary scheme. But different types of participation can be categorized in terms of two analytically distinct approaches: efficiency-based participation and agency-based participation (see Puri, 2004). While the former is seen as instrumental and utilitarian (see, for example, the social capital approach), the latter may be termed a 'social capability' approach, emphasizing empowerment, equity and voice. The first type of participation is associated with the objective of achieving specific development goals, while the second type is seen as a value in itself. However, these analytical types of participation are in fact intertwined, and they impinge upon each other in practice.

One of the early 'social capability' approaches emerged in the 1960s–70s (under the banners of 'Emancipatory participation' or 'Liberation theology'). Freire (1970) popularized the 'radical' and transformative understanding of 'participation' (although he did not use the term) in his work *Pedagogy of the Oppressed* (see Rowlands, 1996). He wished to transform the 'culture of silence' of the dispossessed into critical awareness/consciousness through 'dialogical' encounters. He saw the potential of education as a subversive force that could transform the mute dispossessed into 'free subjects', who would participate actively and creatively in the transformation of their own conditions by changing the structure of their society. For Freire, '... their perception of themselves as oppressed is impaired by their submersion in the reality of oppression' (Rowlands, 1996: 45). Through dialogic encounters, 'each individual wins back the right to say his or her own word' (Shaull, 2006: 33). These issues were also important to activist-scholars such as Franz Fanon and Erich Fromm during the 1960s–70s. For example, Erich Fromm in *The Heart of Man* sees the invisible process of oppression and submission thus:

> One way is to submit to and identify with a person or group having power. By this symbolic participation in another person's life, [men have] the illusion of acting, when in reality [they] only submit to and become a part of those who act. (Fromm, 1964: 31)

It was this condition of oppression and submission that needed to be changed through capability-building and empowering 'participation'; the object was to generate a critical consciousness capable of understanding the structure of oppression, so that the structure which created these conditions could be radically transformed.

But during the 1980s–90s, 'participation' was transformed into a set of techniques whose rhetoric emphasized the 'bottom-up' approach, meant to be inclusive and democratic, emphasizing self-help at the local level. This approach had several components—introduction of new methods of community engagement such as 'Participatory Action Research' (PAR) and widespread acceptance of the role of grassroots development organizations (or 'non-governmental organizations', NGOs) as agents of social change. These ideas went well with the neoliberal prescription of 'retreat of the state', preceded by the marketing of 'failure of the welfare state'. However, in recent years, there have been serious attempts at rethinking the concepts and techniques of participation and empowerment. But, first of all, we will examine in the next section how the idea of 'participation' emerged and evolved.

THE EMERGENCE OF THE CONCEPT AND STRATEGY OF PARTICIPATION IN DEVELOPMENT

After the Second World War, the 'discovery' of mass poverty in the third world gave Western nations, especially the US, a new role in the third world (Escobar, 1994). Accordingly, the removal of poverty became a major objective of development strategies, which, in the McNamara era, carried both political and economic salience in the context of the

Cold War. Development interventions during the two decades following the Second World War were, thus, a peculiar mix of wisdom drawn from modernization theory and ideas of socialist planning. The logic of planning gave a large role to the knowledge of the 'expert', who would draw up plans to transform the condition of 'underdevelopment' seen to characterize much of the third world. In most developing countries, a mix of national and international experts took up the task of 'doing development', the objective of which was mainly to improve standards of living in the third world through transfer of technologies and skill development in agriculture, irrigation, health, sanitation and education. As discussed later, the assumptions of backwardness in third world economic actors underlay many such interventions.

Despite the efforts of international and local experts, the 1960s–70s turned out to be a period of disillusionment with this development strategy, as poverty remained stubbornly resistant. In a book titled *Pyramids of Sacrifice*, Berger (1974) called development a myth, arguing that nowhere was it delivering the promised goods. However, his questioning of the entire Western-centred development paradigm received little support at the time, and the failure of development projects and poverty alleviation programmes was attributed to the non-participatory nature of approaches to development. The theorist at the forefront of the formulation of this critique was Robert Chambers, who from the 1980s onwards shaped the empirical strategy of participatory development. His critique pointed out that top-down approaches excluded subjects from the process of development and disregarded the validity of local knowledge, and its importance to the development process. He and other proponents of participatory development argued that those initiating development interventions (planners, administrators and development experts) had a poor understanding of the needs, priorities and circumstances of those they were trying to 'develop' and whose poverty they were trying to alleviate (Chambers, 1983, 1997; Jodha, 1988). The development expert (scientist and social scientist) had a cursory interaction with the field, through short visits made at a time convenient to him or her. Chambers (1983, 1997) discusses how the academic and the expert often arrived in the field after harvest time, and so witnessed prosperity and not poverty. Monsoons, which are a difficult time for villagers (especially the poor) in terms of food availability, were always avoided by 'development experts'. Thus, failure was attributed not to any structural reasons caused by inequality of access to resources or unequal power, but to a lack of sufficient expertise, knowledge and participation. Chambers (1983, 1997) argues that the exclusion of local knowledge from development policies and strategies was based on the assumption that the Third World farmer or the 'tribal' was illiterate, poor and backward; and that he or she needed to be introduced to new methods and technologies to manage agriculture, improve yields and bring change in related spheres. The knowledge of the natives was discounted by earlier planners as being 'unscientific superstition', to be replaced by rational and scientific methods. The peasant was routinely condemned as being 'risk averse', disinclined to adopt newer and better methods of production.[1]

Ethno-science approaches developed by anthropologists such as Conklin (1967) and Tyler (1969) had previously highlighted the 'rational' nature of 'farmers' science' and of systems of indigenous knowledge. These approaches provided theoretical justification for paying attention to local knowledge and including local people in development interventions. There was also recognition of the need to apply a contextual understanding of farmers' practices and understand the constraints—low incomes, low assets and lack of access to community resources—within which poor people had to organize their lives.

To redress the methodological lacunae in earlier approaches, Chambers (1983) recommended PAR (which took its inspiration from Freire and Gramsci) as a way of engaging communities in the process of their own development. The PAR approach, incorporating a more democratic outlook and attempting to break down the hierarchy between the villager and the expert, was attempted by the Bangladesh Rural Advancement Committee, in which the rural poor participated in mapping the resources and power structure of their own villages. Simultaneously, the techniques of Participatory Rural Appraisal (PRA) and Rapid Rural Appraisal (RRA) allowed experts and planners a better basis for planning development projects. As an example of RRA, Chambers (1995) pointed to the work

---

[1] This was very clear when the technology of the Green Revolution was introduced in India. Poor or marginal farmers, who could not adopt the technology as it required purchasing seeds, fertilizer and pesticides, and ensuring irrigation, were termed 'risk averse' and backward.

of Wolf Ladejinsky, who toured Bihar and Punjab to study the impact of the Green Revolution and came up with several useful insights. Over a period of time, these methodologies were refined and turned into 'techniques' to study rural people and came to be widely adopted by the development community all over the world. However, Chambers himself recognized the limitations of such techniques: they were ultimately introduced by outsiders and could do little about altering local power structures (Chambers, 1995). Whether the adoption of these methodologies achieved any real 'participation' in the development process remains a moot point. Additionally, such practices isolated themselves from other forms of social and political action—that is, they were depoliticized. It is in this context that recent interrogations of participation have raised fundamental questions regarding the 'political ambiguities of participation' (Cornwall, 2004: 78).

More recent studies (Kothari, 2001) have also argued that despite development professionals' attempts to privilege local knowledge, a subtle Eurocentrism continues to shape the interventions carried out by non-local development workers and experts. Kothari (2001) argues that there is a danger of PRA turning into a set of 'ritual practices'. These ritual practices lead to local knowledge 'produced' by outsiders which is cleaned up through mapping and codification and which ends up marginalizing the spaces for challenging the status quo. She argues that local knowledge is not something given but is arrived at through a process of negotiation between different actors—it has a constructed nature and outside experts often tend to reify 'local' knowledge, interpreting practices engendered by necessity as 'cultural variables' (Kothari, 2001). However, as Mosse points out, in PRA, local knowledge is a 'collaboratively produced normative construct' (2005: 95) highlighting that agency of local people is a part of the construction.

ADDRESSING INCLUSION—EMPOWERMENT THROUGH PARTICIPATION

Research had also shown that poor and marginalized groups, such as marginal farmers and lower castes on the one hand, and women on the other, have been excluded from the development process albeit in different ways.[2] Due to entrenched unequal local power structures, they were unable to give voice to their concerns and interests. State resources for development were equally subject to elite capture. Participation required drawing excluded groups into the ambit of development decision-making and allowing them access to resources. Two strategies for operationalizing participation emerged: state-initiated processes of democratic governance and decentralization, and the involvement of grassroots organizations (that is, NGOs).

Thus, in the Indian context, the process of decentralization was initiated by the 73rd Amendment to the Indian Constitution. It delegated powers to village-level bodies and provided for inclusion through the reservation of seats in all governance structures for the marginalized sections of society, such as the lower castes and women. This mandatory representation of hitherto excluded groups was a step towards legal participation and the empowerment that comes with it. Much has been written on the impact of this 'formal' inclusion and participation of earlier disempowered groups (see Jayal et al., 2006). It is outside the scope of this chapter to evaluate its impact and examine the lacunae in the state's efforts at formal inclusion. Inclusion unfolds both at the empirical and conceptual levels; at the conceptual level, the debates focus on the possibilities of radical citizenship, and we take this up for examination later in the chapter.

At the empirical level, adoption of participatory methods by organs of the state works through an incentive structure for participation. This can be seen clearly in many government programmes, such as those for family planning or the more recent programmes to create self-help groups. Local workers are rewarded in terms of the number of self-help groups they help to set up, the amount of bank loans they manage to disburse and other similar targets.[3] As Rahnema (1997) states, 'this is "forced participation"

---

[2] In fact, ultimately, the strategy adopted for spreading the Green Revolution was 'betting on the strong', that is, rich farmers who could afford all the inputs required to make the new seeds a success (see Shiva, 1991). Similarly, studies have shown that women were often ignored by development practitioners (see Kabeer, 1994; Agarwal, 2001 on women's exclusion from formally participatory institutions in India and Nepal).

[3] Participation in recent 'micro-credit' schemes has turned lethal, with some borrowers who were indebted to multiple creditors taking their own lives (see Sharma, 2006).

and is limited to projects and programmes that have been visualized at the level of Central and State governments or by donor agencies'. Participation in the formulation of plans and priorities by local groups remains minimal, if it exists at all. Programmes often collapse once the incentive structure is withdrawn and rarely lead to the building of the social capital. Mosse shows how 'participation' itself ended up being made into a commodity and marketed, for its success to be recognized. He shows how the processes and needs of donors and their partners required that measurable outcomes be visible while involving participatory processes at the ground level. Deconstructing the project he worked on in India, he states:

> The project system was simply not capable of transferring power to communities or dealing with the uncertainty that would result from allowing Bhil farmers to develop their own ways of doing things, making their own decisions, taking risks and making mistakes. But, when interpreted through the assumptions of the project model, the impressive landscape of well laid out soil and water conservation bunds, improved varieties, newly planted woodlots, deepened wells and operating pumpsets, could nonetheless be read as demonstrating the success of the donor goals of people's participation and farmer-managed development and self-reliance. *Both participation and its denial in practice were necessary to the management of reputation and the marketing of success* (italics added). (Mosse, 2003: 24)

A parallel movement to the strengthening of democratic decentralization has been the involvement of NGOs in development work (Fisher, 1997; Kamat, 2004). Both the retreat of the state from the social sectors and the perceived failure of the state made the development community look towards other actors who could initiate change in poor and backward areas. This created space for the entry of NGOs, the main civil society actors, who could help in building social capital without challenging the existing structure of the society in any serious manner. The 1980s, thus, saw a new turn in participatory ideology, with a large-scale entry of civil society organizations (developmental NGOs) into the development arena. As funding for development and poverty alleviation continued to increase, these non-state actors increased their presence with support from governments and international donor agencies. There was a tacit perception among organizations such as the World Bank that NGOs would succeed where the state had failed.

There is currently a wide variety of NGOs in India engaged in development, each with different ideologies and levels of expertise and commitment. Many NGOs were already active in the field, as part of voluntary movements initiated during the period of the Indian nationalist movement; some were embedded in local areas and were involved in including people in the development process through processes of conscientization, organization and capacity-building. It was rationalized that, being a part of the civil society, NGO actors would be able to understand the genuine needs and problems of people and achieve their involvement in development. It was also expected that they would perform the role of mediators between the state and society, and help local people in accessing the bureaucracy.

However, as discussed below, the majority of the NGOs were co-opted by the development machine and tended to lose their pro-poor bias and their ability to devise innovative strategies for intervention and inclusion. Apart from a few, they remained closely linked to the mainstream development agenda as defined by the international and national development community (see Kamat, 2004; Pearce, 2004). Few among them presented alternative visions of development or subverted existing power structures in any way. As professional organizations, they participated in development efforts oriented around projects in various areas such as agriculture, afforestation, watershed management, health and education. Post the 1980s, NGOs came to be regarded as representatives of people's will. But as Kamat (2004) points out, the analysis of NGOs as the representatives of civil society and of the interests of the poor has remained somewhat atheoretical, ignoring the articulation of NGOs with the market economy. The proliferation of various types of NGOs—grassroots, advocacy, business and industry associations and public interest NGOs—has lead to a pluralization of the public space with many of these NGOs representing key private interests. She says, 'The notion of a "common partnership" constitutes a central discursive device through which the multiple and disparate entities of civil society are integrated into a unified whole in which each representational body has different, albeit complementary responsibilities' (Kamat, 2004: 166). What this supposedly common partnership of NGOs, as civil society at the global level, does in actuality is to privatize the public sphere. The non-discriminatory attitude of multilateral organizations, which have increasingly begun to rely on NGOs as representatives of public interest, marginalizes pro-poor and anti-capitalist agendas of grassroots or advocacy NGOs.

PROFESSIONALIZATION OF 'CHANGE AGENTS'

The 'post-development school', represented by scholars such as Escobar, Sachs and Rahnema, has been highly critical of various attempts to alter the paradigm of development. For instance, Rahnema (1997) is very critical of outsider intervention by 'change agents' (grassroots activists) whose supposed role is to bring out a positive outcome for poor and marginalized people. Change agents work at the grassroots level through advocacy, organizing and informing, in order to make collective action possible. In a Freirian sense, they attempt a dialogical method to change local people's own understanding of their situation to enable them to define their own agendas and access state resources for development. Rahnema, however, believes that such genuine actors (animators) are few (Rahnema, 1997). Movements in India such as the Chipko (an ecology and livelihoods movement in the lower Himalayas) and Swadhyaya (a movement for village renewal in Maharashtra) were successful due to charismatic change agents. The vast majority of individuals in NGOs are, however, merely translators for already conceived and existing development projects, seeking to bring greater efficiency to the project. Hence, both NGOs and change agents are quickly co-opted by donors. Their strategies, meant to be empowering for local people, are routinized and incorporated into the implementation of the same kinds of plans and projects. Grassroots workers who begin with a 'vision' often end up institutionalizing their efforts, thereby losing the potential for genuine or radical change. Based on the work of several scholars, Kamat (2004: 167) argues that new challenges have forced community-based NGOs into a process of professionalization at the organizational level and depoliticization at the grassroots level. According to her, these studies show that the shift has been to a managerial and functional approach to social change and a move away from education and empowerment programmes that involve structural analysis of power and inequality (Kamat, 2004: 168). NGOs are useful to donors if they water down their political character and focus more on an efficiency-based approach.

However, the view of critics such as Rahnema may be overly pessimistic; for, if justified, the serendipitous effects of interventions by the state and by NGOs may sometimes move in the direction of a radical agenda.[4] Their initial efforts may sow the seeds of new thinking or new ways of acting, which can corrode existing structures to some extent. In this context, it is possible to argue that a genuine space for participation could be created by interventions such as reserving seats for women, Dalits (former 'untouchable' castes in India) and the so-called tribals in local development bodies. The initial ineffectiveness of such interventions may eventually be overcome through an enhancement of capabilities, developed through involvement in practices of participation such as meetings, visits for training, learning to do accounts and interacting with higher level administrators and decision-makers.[5] This, as we have seen in various states of India, can be a step towards empowerment. Over time, as participants become aware of and begin to demand their rights, it is hoped that they might make a difference to the development agenda.[6]

Critiquing the appropriation of the concept of participation, Rahnema (1997) refers to 'manipulated, or teleguided, forms of participation' and distinguishes them from 'spontaneous ones'. The teleguided form of participation, he says, has become merely a 'politically attractive slogan' and 'a good fund-raising device'. One of Rahnema's most important concerns is that 'participation has come to be "disembedded" from the socio-cultural roots which had always kept it alive' (Rahnema, 1997: 160). While valorizing 'vernacular' cultures and society, Rahnema is critical of all forms

---

[4] The Right to Information Act in India was brought to fruition by the efforts of a rural-based NGO, MKSS (Mazdoor Kisan Shakti Sangathna).

[5] There is evidence from Rajasthan and several other states that women who initially became panchayat members through reservation have won back seats in later rounds on the basis of the good work they were able to do in their communities. In the first round, they may have been 'proxy sarpanches', with work being handled by their husbands, but in the following rounds, they acted in their own capacity. See also Kabeer (2005) on women's participation in self-help groups.

[6] This is evident in the recent National Rural Employment Guarantee Programme in India. In Madhya Pradesh, an NGO (Jagrut Adivasi Dalit Sangathan) has been at the forefront of helping programme implementation and is leading people to become empowered and demand their rights. The hope is that the outcomes will be improved rural development and a more equal social structure. See Khera (2008).

of participation that involve outside intervention, including the 'Freirian methods of dialogical action and conscientization'. He sees certain types of social movements (for example, the Gandhian, the Chipko, the Lokayan and the Swadhyaya) as 'genuine grassroots movements', which necessarily include a spiritual dimension and are aided by some 'very sensitive "animators", able to listen to their own people, to the world at large and to the roots of their common culture' (Rahnema, 1997: 170).

Many scholars have agreed with most of Rahnema's criticisms of populist notions and practices of participation but do not share his love for tradition and the vernacular and his rejection of any form of the modernity project. Several participatory and empowering movements such as democratic decentralization in Kerala, participatory budgeting in Brazil, the 'REFLECT' approach to literacy generation, the Right to Information movement in Rajasthan, etc. (see Hickey and Mohan, 2004c) are seen as signs of hope in a world where anti-globalization movements gained strength towards the end of the twentieth century, with strong participation by some NGOs at various levels.

HAS PARTICIPATION WORKED?

Following this 'new orthodoxy' in conceptualizing participation, a gamut of other concepts and terms such as social capital, empowerment and decentralization were widely adopted by the development community. However, experience on the part of various development actors (donor organizations, NGOs, government agencies) with participatory methods and interventions has not led to dramatic success in the development context. As with many other such ideas, two things happen—the concept is appropriated in a particular way by those promoting development and it is also appropriated or functions in particular ways in the local context. As pointed out before, in the process of transfer and adoption, radical connotations are often sanitized. As Rowlands (1996: 91) says, 'There is, however, a worrying temptation to use them (concepts such as "participation", "capacity-building", "sustainability" or "institutional development") in a way that takes the troublesome notions of power, and the distribution of power, out of the picture. For in spite of their appeal, these terms can easily become one more way to ignore or hide the realities of power, inequality and oppression. Yet it is precisely those realities which shape the lives of poor and marginalized people, and the communities in which they live'. In the sections below, we discuss more recent critiques of participation which, from a deconstruction perspective, seek to lay bare the barriers to empowerment.

CONTEMPORARY CRITIQUES OF PARTICIPATION

In recent literature, populist participation—efficiency- and agency-based—has been subjected to serious scrutiny. While the earlier critiques of participation focused on the limitations of method or the workings of the practitioner, the recent critiques provide a conceptual and ideological examination of the theory, method and practice of participatory development. The responses can be divided into two types: pessimist and optimist. Both tend to agree broadly in their critiques of populist/official participation, but they disagree on alternative possibilities. As Hickey and Mohan (2004b) put it,

> [T]he past decade witnessed a growing backlash against the ways in which participation managed to "tyrannize" development debates without sufficient evidence that participatory approaches were living up to the promise of empowerment and transformative development for marginal peoples. (Hickey and Mohan, 2004b: 3)

This was vividly captured in a book entitled *Participation: The New Tyranny?* (Cooke and Kothari, 2001), which focused explicitly on 'participation' in the form of PRA. Few contributors to the *Tyranny* collection envisaged a positive future for participatory development.

The post-development perspective, represented by, among others, Majid Rahnema is not merely critical of participation but finds even the idea of development itself tyrannical. However, a mood of optimism, based on critical evaluation of populist participation, is seen in the response to the *Tyranny* volume in the form of the collection put together by Hickey and Mohan (2004a), *Participation: From Tyranny to Transformation?*, which explores new spaces and places, political alliances and social movements wherein a potential for emancipatory transformation exists. As an alternative approach, Mohan and Hickey theorize 'a radical approach to participation based around citizenship while rooting our normative premise in a critical modernist epistemology' (Hickey and Mohan, 2004a: 59). Whereas the 'radical' is defined as being socialist and transformative, the notion of citizenship is also radicalized as a set of 'practices' (juridical, political, economic or cultural) as opposed to an abstract legal definition concerning the formal status of citizens.

Interrogating 'Community'

A serious criticism of the participatory approach has been that it functions with an understanding of the community as 'homogenous' and, thus, fails to deal with various diversities and power equations inherent within 'the community'. Puri (2004) problematizes the idea of community as an 'uncontested whole' with systemic biases against the underprivileged sections of society. Such assumptions are passed on to the local facilitators or built into government programmes. PRA techniques are biased towards seeing the 'communities' as consensual and harmonious while concealing 'powerful interests at the intracommunity level' (Mohan and Stokke, 2000: 253). The lack of attention to heterogeneity and hierarchy in communities has very frequently been responsible for the failure of many 'participatory' development projects. This is because development is often aimed at villages or blocks seen as geographical entities and not as entities which are essentially systems of dense social relations. Local facilitators, who are aware of the complexities of communities, may ignore this factor until a development project flounders on caste, religious community or class fault lines.[7] Equally, local facilitators who are part of the government machinery and also members of local communities may act to orient processes and projects towards their own class, caste, community or towards the local elite. Building consensus over development priorities

---

[7] One example is a social forestry project with which one of the authors was involved. Afforestation was being carried out on village common lands. The location to be afforested had been agreed to by the village representative body. However, the plants which were put in were constantly found uprooted. It was later found that in this multireligious village, the land put under afforestation was actually a burial ground for the local Muslims, who had not agreed to the afforestation plan but whose voice had been suppressed by the dominant Hindu community.

in complex communities is challenging and time consuming; it is fruitful only with long-term investment in capacity-building and sensitization, and demonstrated success of programmes.

'Participation', with a depoliticized notion of 'community', may also lead to what Agarwal (2001) has called 'participatory exclusion'. To understand how spaces and strategies of participation can determine outcomes, Cornwall (2004) makes a distinction between popular spaces and invited spaces:

> Distinguished from 'popular spaces', those arenas in which people join together, often with others like them, in collective action, self-help initiatives or everyday sociality, 'invited spaces' bring together, almost by definition, a very heterogeneous set of actors among whom there might be significant differences in status. (Cornwall, 2004: 76)

Participation in such 'invited spaces' in governance and development bodies such as panchayats and natural resource management committees may lead, according to Puri (2004), to a 'multiplication of authority and power' in the hands of the dominant group. While a *gram sabha* (village assembly) may bring together all adult members of the village, the complex decisions regarding development priorities or their funding end up being taken by the smaller group of upper caste and landed individuals who may dominate panchayat bodies even when they do not hold formal membership.

Interrogating 'Locality'

Similarly, privileging the idea of the local, especially in practice, distances the role of the state and non-state actors from the complexities of 'participation', especially in a globalized world. Hickey and Mohan point to 'the overly localist approach of many participatory approaches to the exclusion of broader, more structural patterns of injustice' (Hickey and Mohan, 2004b: 9; see also Mohan and Stokke, 2000). In fact, the privileging of the local contributes towards the depoliticization of the development process and makes power and the politics of difference invisible. Many successful and empowering participatory movements have demonstrated the need to link up with institutions at different levels and forge contextual alliances, based on commonalities. The problem can be addressed through the concept of 'linking' social capital (sometimes also known as the 'enabling environment'), and its understanding is crucial for analysing differences and alliances in social and political movements, and their impact on empowerment, critical awareness and potential for structural transformation.

Understanding Power

Similarly, although 'participation' and 'participatory development' have become part of the accepted jargon and strategy of development practice, questions of power and possibilities of inclusion and voice have not been taken up seriously.

It is instructive to look at the question of 'power' in the critiques of 'participation'. Kothari (2001), in the *Tyranny* volume, and Cornwall (2004), in the later *Tyranny to Transformation* volume, both approach the problem of power from the writings of Foucault. However, Kothari produces a more pessimistic reading of Foucault whereas Cornwall finds optimistic possibilities of transformation in Foucault's approach to power.

For Kothari, following Foucault, 'power is everywhere' and it is 'found in the creation of norms and social and cultural practices at all levels' (Kothari, 2001: 141). In the process of deconstructing 'people's knowledge' or 'local knowledge', so essential in the 'new orthodoxy' of participation, Kothari states that knowledge is constituted through 'an accumulation of social norms, rituals and practices that, far from being constructed in isolation from power relations, is embedded in them (or against them)' (Kothari, 2001: 141). Thus, participatory techniques as methods of knowledge accumulation reproduce power-relations at the micro-level through the use of these approaches (see also Mosse, 1995). In fact, 'the very act of inclusion, of being drawn in as a participant, can symbolize an exercise of power and control over an individual' (Kothari, 2001: 142). Such forms, suggested by various scholars, of 'adverse incorporation' or 'insidious modes of inclusionary control' prevent people from challenging the existing inequalities and power structure in society, thereby manufacturing consent and conformity, and, hence, control through inclusion.

However, Kothari (2001: 142) does suggest the possibility of subversion by some non-conforming participants who may then be excluded from participatory processes. Such exclusion can, under certain conditions, set the individuals or groups free from the need to conform. It can embolden and empower them to challenge existing structures of domination and control. In that sense, for Kothari, exclusion may even be a necessary condition for empowerment.

On the other hand, Cornwall (2004) represents the emerging view of optimism, hope and a sensing of the possibilities of subversion of entrenched power structures and genuine transformation through participation at certain sites which may not always be the excluded ones. 'By illuminating the dynamics of power, voice and agency, *thinking spatially* can help towards building strategies for more genuinely transformative social action' (Cornwall, 2004: 75; emphasis added). Cornwall points to the distinction made by other scholars between 'popular spaces' or 'sites of radical possibility' that are 'chosen, fashioned and claimed by those at the margins' and 'invited spaces [...] into which those who are considered marginal are invited' (2004: 78). Like Kothari above, Cornwall also sees the constraints of power when she states that, 'Spaces in which citizens are invited to participate, as well as those that they create for themselves, are never neutral. Infused with the existing relations of power, interactions within them may come to reproduce rather than challenge hierarchies and inequalities' (Cornwall, 2004: 81). However, she is much more optimistic about the possibilities of transformation. 'For "government" is no monolith and the project of "governmentality" is an ever partial, contingent and contested enterprise: a constantly moving dance of domination and resistance' (Cornwall, 2004: 81). Transformative participation requires active citizen engagement in both 'popular' as well as 'invited' spaces. But this game has no rules which can be standardized and taught in training sessions as a set of techniques.

There are many stories of success in South Asia and elsewhere in the world. As Gaventa states,

[T]he emerging evidence suggests that, at least in some conditions, [interventions] can lead to positive pro-poor and pro-democracy outcomes. But they do not always lead to such outcomes. A further set of questions must be asked about the conditions under which such outcomes might occur. (Gaventa, 2004: 33)

Referring to the 'successful' Kerala experiment, Heller (2001) has pointed to the presence of the following: (a) a strong central state capacity, (b) a well-developed civil society and (c) an organized political force with strong social movement characteristics. This last factor, the mobilization of people in wider movements, seems to be vital in encouraging people to participate in the development process.

Referring to the 'closed', 'invited' and 'claimed/created' spaces in any society, Gaventa emphasizes that, 'these spaces exist in dynamic relationship to one another and are constantly opening and closing through struggles for legitimacy and resistance, co-optation and transformation' (Gaventa, 2004: 35). These different possibilities of co-optation, resistance and transformation can be seen in the complex dynamics of emerging political alliances, possibilities and constraints in 'local democracy' in the wake of the 73rd Constitutional Amendment in India.

CONCLUSION

Critiques of 'official' instrumental notions of participation in recent literature have led to a shift in focus from efficiency-based participation to capability-based participation. The emphasis has, therefore, shifted from participation in management of local development projects to the wider issue of empowerment and inclusion of hitherto excluded sections of society. This aspect is captured in the modification or redefinition of the concept of citizenship.

> On the one hand, citizenship has traditionally been cast in liberal terms, as individual legal equality accompanied by a set of rights and responsibilities and bestowed by a state on its citizens. Newer approaches aim to bridge the gap between citizen and state by recasting citizenship as *practised* rather than as given. (Gaventa, 2004: 29; emphasis added)

The over emphasis on the 'local' in mainstream understanding and practice of participation has also been challenged. 'Localism' makes larger structures of power and control (policies, bureaucracy, markets, international relations, etc.) invisible and, furthermore, it tends to prevent the possibility of vertical political alliances in various social movements such as those against the World Trade Organization, global seed companies, powerful soft-drink companies, privatization of water and displacement from large development projects such as dams. It is important to understand that the local is impinged upon by other state and non-state actors, institutions and policies, and similarly that the potential for participation locally can be influenced by wider forces.

Many participatory projects assume local communities to be homogeneous, uncontested wholes and fail to see, or ignore, the structural inequalities which impose long-term constraints on participation by marginal sections of the 'community'. In fact, actual practice of participation in such heterogeneous communities leads to 'participatory exclusion' and 'multiplication of power and control'. This remains one of the most serious challenges to the idea of participation.

However, recent years have also seen the emergence of various successful social movements amidst poor and marginalized communities throughout the world, which challenge the established power structures through actions in 'popular' and 'invited' spaces. This has given rise to a new optimism about the possibility of transformation through inclusionary participation or subversion after exclusion.

Despite this hope and optimism, it must be recognized that ideological battles continue at the levels of discourse and practice, and newer forms of engagement and contestation are devised every day. The nature of resistance, co-optation and transformation through participation and responsive and accountable governance will be determined by the dynamics of the balance of power.

REFERENCES

Agarwal, B. 2001. 'Participatory Exclusions, Community Forestry, and Gender: An Analysis for South Asia and a Conceptual Framework'. *World Development*, 29(10): 1623–48.

Berger, P. 1974. *Pyramids of Sacrifice: Political Ethics and Social Change*. New York: Basic Books.

Chambers, R. 1983. *Rural Development: Putting the Last First*. Essex: Longman Scientific & Technical.

———. 1995. *Poverty and Livelihoods: Whose Reality Counts?* Copenhagen: Institute of Development Studies Sussex, UNDP.

———. 1997. *Whose Reality Counts? Putting the First Last*. London: IT Publications.

Conklin, Harold C. 1967. 'An Ethnoecological Approach to Shifting Agriculture'. *Transactions of the New York Academy of Sciences*, 17: 133–42.

Cooke, B. and U. Kothari (eds). 2001. *Participation: The New Tyranny*. London: Zed Books.

Cornwall, A. 2004. 'Spaces for Transformation? Reflections on Issues of Power and Difference in Participation in Development', in S. Hickey and G. Mohan (eds), *Participation: From Tyranny to Transformation?* London/New York: Zed Books, pp.: 75–91.

Fisher, William F. 1997. 'Doing Good? The Politics and Antipolitics of NGO Practices'. *Annual Review of Anthropology*, 26: 439–64.

Freire, P. 1970 [1968]. *Pedagogy of the Oppressed*. New York: Continuum.

Fromm, E. 1964. *The Heart of Man*. New York: Harper and Row.

Escobar, A. 1994. *Encountering Development: The Making and Unmaking of the Third World*. New York: Princeton University Press.

Gaventa, J. 2004. 'Towards Participatory Governance: Assessing the Transformative Possibilities', in S. Hickey and G. Mohan (eds), *Participation: From Tyranny to Transformation?* London/New York: Zed Books, pp. 25–41.

Heller, P. 2001. 'Moving the State: The Politics of Democratic Decentralization in Kerala, South Africa and Porto Alegre'. *Politics and Society*, 29(1): 131–63.

Hickey, S. and G. Mohan (eds). 2004a. *Participation: From Tyranny to Transformation?* London/New York: Zed Books.

———. 2004b. 'Towards Participation as Transformation: Critical Themes and Challenges', in S. Hickey and G. Mohan (eds), *Participation: From Tyranny to Transformation?* London/New York: Zed Books, pp. 3–24.

———. 2004c. 'Relocating Participation Within a Radical Politics of Development: Insights from Political Action and Practice', in S. Hickey and G. Mohan (eds), *Participation: From Tyranny to Transformation?* London/New York: Zed Books, pp. 159–74.

———. 2005. 'Relocating Participation within a Radical Politics of Development'. *Development and Change*, 36(2): 237–62.

Jayal, N.G., A. Prakash and P. Sharma (eds). 2006. *Local Governance in India: Decentralization and Beyond*. New Delhi: Oxford University Press.

Jodha, N.S. 1988. 'Poverty Debate in India: A Minority View'. *Economic and Political Weekly*, Special Number (November): 2421–27.

Kabeer, N. 1994. *Reversed Realities: Gender Hierarchies in Development Thought*. Brooklyn/London: Verso Books.

———. 2005. 'Is Microfinance a "Magic Bullet" for Women's Empowerment?'. *Economic and Political Weekly*, 40(44&45): 4709–18.

Kamat, S. 2004. 'The Privatization of Public Interest: Theorizing NGO Discourse in a Neoliberal Era'. *Review of International Political Economy*, 11 (February): 155–76.

Khera, R. 2008. 'Employment Guarantee Act'. *Economic and Political Weekly*, 30 (August): 8–10.

Kothari, U. 2001. 'Power, Knowledge and Social Control in Participatory Development', in B. Cooke and U. Kothari (eds), *Participation: The New Tyranny*. London: Zed Books, pp. 159–74.

Mohan, G. 2001. 'Beyond Participation: Strategies for Deeper Empowerment', in B. Cooke and U. Kothari (eds), *Participation: The New Tyranny*. London: Zed Books.

———. 2000. 'Participatory Development and Empowerment: The Dangers of Localism'. *Third World Quarterly*, 21(2): 247–68.

Mohan, G. and S. Hickey. 2004. 'Relocating Participation Within a Radical Politics of Development: Critical Modernism and Citizenship', in S. Hickey and G. Mohan (eds), *Participation: From Tyranny to Transformation?* London/ New York: Zed Books, pp. 59–74.

Mohan, G. and Stokke, K. 2000. 'Participatory Development and Empowerment: The Dangers of Localism', *Third World Quarterly*, 21(2): 247–68.

Mosse, D. 1995. *Social Analysis in Participatory Rural Development* (PLA Notes No. 24), IIED, October, pp. 27–33.

———. 2003 'The Making and Marketing of Participatory Development', in C. Quarles van Ufford and A. K. Giri (eds), *A Moral Critique of Development: In Search of Global Responsibilities*. London, Routledge, pp. 43–75.

———. 2005. *Cultivating Development: An Ethnography of Aid Policy and Practice*. London: Pluto Press.

Puri, E. 2004. 'Understanding Participation: Theoretical Foundations and Practical Implications'. *Economic and Political Weekly*, 39(24) 2511–17.

Rahnema, M. 1997. 'Participation', in W. Sachs (ed.), *The Development Dictionary*. New Delhi: Orient Longman.

Pearce, Jenny. 2004. 'Development, NGOs and Civil Society: The Debate and its Future', in Jenny Pearce (ed.), *Development, NGOs and Civil Society*. Great Britain: Oxfam.

Rowlands, J. 1996. 'Empowerment examined', in Mary B. Anderson, *Development and Social Diversity*. Oxford: Oxfam.

Sharma, S. 2006. 'Death by Microcredit'. *Times of India* (September 26).

Shaull, R. 2006. 'Preface (to Freire, P. [1970])', *Pedagogy of the Oppressed*. New York: Continuum.

Shiva, V. 1991. *The Violence of the Green Revolution*. Penang: Third World Network.

Tyler, S.A. (ed.). 1969. *Cognitive Anthropology*. New York: Holt, Rinehart and Winston.

Chapter 3

The Idea of Development as Governance

India in the First Decade of Independence

DILIP M. MENON

An age becomes an age, all else beside
When sensuous poets in their pride invent
Emblems for the souls consent.

—Archibald MacLeish, The Metaphor

As India embarked on its post-colonial journey in the 1950s, development and modernization were the watchwords of the political class. Public rhetoric was characterized by an obsession with questions of political economy that inevitably came to provide the frame for the project of governance—the mission of 'achieving our country', to borrow a phrase from the American philosopher Richard Rorty (1999). There was not much of a public debate on the form and substance of post-colonial governance. While the political transition may have been marred by the violence of Partition, the institutional transition was presumed to have been smooth, with India getting the cream of the Civil Services. The question remained unasked as to how independent India would be governed by its elected representatives within the inherited colonial apparatus of law, bureaucracy and policing. Independence was seen as the prerequisite for the belated transition to modernity: a leap into an industrial society that required an acceleration of historical stages of development.

This chapter argues that the staging of an idea of the modern was central to the post-colonial enterprise. The deployment of art, film and theatre sat alongside the state's rhetoric of development, which anthropomorphized dams, scientific establishments and nuclear reactors as the heroes of the post-colonial nation. The 'telos' was unambiguous and implied a happy ending: a modern, developed and democratic nation. Each of these categories was presented both as cause and effect, both as existing and yet to be achieved. The actors in this national drama were heroic: Nehru, a cast of thousands of politicians who had come through the fire of colonial repression through the collective discipline of Satyagraha, and the scientific and other 'experts' who would be the makers of modernity in India (see Mitchell, 2002). The audience, a grateful nation of Indians united in their diversity, would watch the show being staged for them by the chosen.

Some hissing and booing was allowed from the sidelines. The Shankar's Weekly—a satirical weekly with cartoons, founded in 1949 and published from Delhi—lampooned the Congress government, Nehru and the national leadership through its distinctive cartoons and broad humour, continuing a tradition honed under colonial rule. O.V. Vijayan, novelist, political satirist and cartoonist, wrote later of Shankar's cartoons that, pictorially, they shunned the British notion of refinement; they were crowded with figures, many of them idle bystanders—the atmosphere was that of a fair (Vijayan, 2002). However, this was old-fashioned proscenium theatre, not agitprop; the audience was not allowed to take over the stage. It was about spectating, not participating. The people of India, who were perceived either as unmodern or yet-to-be modern, were scripted in only as a sentimental metaphor ('the people of India') or as spectre ('the anti-national'). Governance was not for the people, by the people or of the people; it was about ruling the people.

The 1950s increasingly appear as a decade of closure—in questions of politics as much as aesthetics. Further, it is these two themes—the visualizing of modernity as state-led development and a closure of the idea of popular participation in governance—that this essay deals with, albeit in a provisional and tentative formulation. This closure was reflected in three arenas. First, in the process of state-led development. This came to be determined by the parameters of a passive revolution, which involved—among other things—the short-circuiting of radical land reform (Herring, 1983). Second, in a notion of modernity that envisaged a landscape of a techno-future studded with dams, nuclear establishments and steel mills to which the citizen would be a mere witness, if anything at all. It would be the political elite and the expert that would oversee this transition and the people of India were to be the beneficiaries of this oversight: an oversight that precluded their actual participation. Third, the very idea of the 'people' was rendered as a romantic abstraction, with their way of life frozen in an idea of a timeless romantic popular culture that evacuated any historical process. No better expression of this can be found than in the Gandhian phrase—'India lives in its villages'—that acquired a new life amidst the bustle of change and progress. As India forged ahead, there was to be a space within which, paradoxically, an authentic India survived, where civilization would always trump the idea of modernity.

In the political arena, intimations of an emphasis on disciplining the people over mobilizing them were evident, reflecting continuity with Gandhian nationalist practice. The reaction of the nationalist leadership, particularly Nehru, to the Royal Indian Navy Mutiny of 1946 had already shown the Congress as a government in waiting, impatient of popular unruliness (Pandey, 1988; Guha, 1998). The horrors of Partition in 1947–48 were followed by a war of diplomacy between the independent nations of India and Pakistan over the repatriation of women abducted during the Partition riots, where the body of women was a proxy for territory (Das, 1997; Butalia, 2000; Pandey, 1998, 2001). The Constituent Assembly, and subsequently the first Parliament, became theatres of masculinity as Indian men debated the future of Indian womanhood. The long shadow of this debate about rights and masculinity that haunted the formation of the nation became evident when the Constitution was finally adopted in 1950, and the distinguished artist Nandalal Bose and his students from Santiniketan were asked to provide illustrations for each chapter. Significantly, the chapter on Fundamental Rights was headed by an illustration showing Rama returning triumphant from Lanka with his wife Sita, having defeated Ravana and redeemed both dharma and his masculinity.

THE POETICS OF PASSIVE REVOLUTION

When thinking about questions of aesthetic representation, it is important to remember that they cannot be separated from the discourse on the reconstruction of independent India along the axes of modernity, development and equity. Both aesthetics and development had to reckon with the persistence of 'tradition' and 'people' for whom modernity was to be staged, since the nationalist movement had never envisaged a revolution of the Indian masses. Two framing arguments could be borne in mind: the Gramscian idea of 'passive revolution' and an emerging national consensus across ideologies (Gramsci, 1973). Gramsci glosses passive revolution as a historical situation in which the old feudal classes are demoted from their dominant position to a 'governing' one, but are not eliminated. No attempt is made by the emergent state to liquidate them as an organic whole; instead of a class they become a 'caste' with specific cultural and psychological characteristics, but no longer with predominant economic functions. On the question of development, Chakravarty (1987) has observed that the central problem was one of reconciling accumulation with legitimation. This necessitated the evolution of the ways of avoiding the unnecessary rigours of an industrial transition as well as attempting to resolve a conflict through change—but not a radical change. Thus far and no further, the post-colonial project of the Indian state concerned itself with the means by which the condition of modernity could be brought about. Paradoxically, at the same time, it was visualized as an already existing, indigenized and naturalized state of being. Development was seen through the metaphor of sculpting out a figure that was embedded in a notion of a national economy that had been covered over by the detritus of colonial policies of economic retardation. This is of a piece with Nehru's epiphanic *Discovery of India* as something already existing since the dawn of time, which obscured the construction of this very entity in the throes of the nationalist movement.

Nationalist political activity had largely left pre-capitalist sites, structures, and classes intact, even in the process of mass mobilization (the Gandhian notion of trusteeship, as much as colonial traditions of political compromise with landed elites, was responsible for this). Moreover, as in most ex-colonies, passive revolution became the characteristic mode of transition. The establishment of a nation state was the priority, and a process of reform from above would follow this. The institutional structures of 'rational' authority set up by colonial rule—of law or of administration—were neither broken up nor were they transformed. Chatterjee (1998) has argued that the new framework of rule was not a representative mechanism operated by individual agents; rather, it incorporated entire structures of pre-capitalist community. In the political field this was manifested in the idea of vote banks. In the economic field, the notion of community development presumed already existing and harmonious communities (Chatterjee, 1998). This timorousness on the part of the state towards a fundamental alteration of the hierarchies of community led to a certain degree of suspicion in popular perceptions towards its rhetoric. While the post-colonial state claimed to lead from the front, it seemed clear, at times, who was pushing it.

There was also a broad consensus emerging on issues relating to industrialization and the village. Nehru, the left and Gandhi are conventionally seen as exemplifying distinct positions on a scale running from outright and rampant industrialization at one end to a valorization of the village on the other. By the 1950s, arguably, the vocabularies had become quite indistinguishable and the differences were more rhetorical than substantive. Nehru's *Discovery of India* concluded with a critique of modern industrial society that could have been penned by Gandhi. He wrote of 'excessive individualism', the prevalence of 'competitive and acquisitive characteristics' and the avid enthronement of wealth above everything else (Nehru, 1946). Gandhi plumped for an ethical socialism premised on the immoral character of capitalist economic institutions. He denounced both private property and production for profit as fundamental causes of exploitation. When he writes in *India of My Dreams* (1947) that, 'land and all property is his who will work for it' or in *Towards Non-violent Socialism* (1951) that the capitalist was committing theft when appropriating 'surplus value' as profit, he sounds no different from the Kerala communist theoretician K. Damodaran, writing his 10 popular Malayalam primers on Marxism in the 1950s. Marxism and Socialism in India were heavily influenced as much by the experience of Gandhism as they were by participation in the Nehruvian dream of modernity and development. To rephrase the American philosopher, Rorty (1999), perhaps for us Indians it is important not to let Marxism influence too much the story we tell about our own left. We need to reflect seriously on what this consensus and confluence of ideas mean: the consequences of running Gandhi, Nehru and the left together, as it were.

WRITING THE HISTORY OF THE MODERN

The political orientation of the Indian intelligentsia was significantly affected by the Gandhian refashioning, even reinvention, of the past and tradition so that it exemplified both the evidence of 'ancient moral glory' and a certain romanticization of the idea of the people. This was reflected, too, in constructions within the historical profession of the 'Golden Age' in India's history, which could be mined for already existing traditions of republican government, rational bureaucracies and realpolitik (Altekar, 1955; Sastri, 1955; Mookerji, 1957). There was no contemporary elaboration of an uncompromisingly radical modernity that spoke of freeing incipient citizens from the shackles of the past; towards the idea of the contemporary there was only a profound ambivalence. An active engagement with the idea of a past was treated with suspicion; the past had ostensibly been superseded by the very act of gaining freedom. The conception of the people as a historical force for change, an idea that may be seen as central to any notion of good governance, came to be recast by seeing them as the repositories of a timeless wisdom. In art, this ambivalence towards tradition expressed itself in more complex ways.

In a series of insightful essays, Gita Kapur has argued that the idea of modernism is not as yet fixed in its meaning and has no stable and canonical position in India. To be progressive (or modern) is sometimes understood by artists as involving a deployment of tradition in order to alter its meanings and at other times as subverting the very idea of tradition itself. The modern, therefore, acquires an emblematic, or as she puts it, a 'heraldic' value; newness has to enter the world invoking the name of the modern. There is a further entailment. The idea of 'modernism' arises in the decolonized world at the chronological conjuncture of the achievement of nationhood and the consequent aspiration to modernity. This conjuncture necessarily means that the desire for modernism is at the same time embroiled in the demand for the revealing of an authentic national self (located in the idea of a singular Indian 'tradition'). The process of 'modernization' becomes both desired and abhorred as the national self, or the idea of the citizen, oscillates between the contradictory pulls of what Kapur calls 'the modern' and 'the authentic'. The dominant rhetoric of the state and the newly emergent nationalist elite conflates modernization (the process), modernity (the desired state of being) and modernism (the aesthetic form of the modern). This may be seen as a characteristic of developing post-colonial societies, adding a further dimension to the 'heraldic' modern. As Kapur astutely puts it, it was a euphemistic modernism, never sure of itself and implicated in the desire of the nation state to kick start modernity, that finally emerged and which kept in tow notions of a people's culture, or folk/tribal art as a legitimating genealogy (Kapur, 1990, 1991, 1996, 2000a). What indeed were the consequences for cultural practice or politics of this sentimentalizing of the people as a sign of authenticity? We shall return to this question again when looking at both film and political theatre.

The invocation of the idea of the modern necessarily involves imagining a national culture that shall break free of the distortions of a colonial modernity. It requires a sense of history, as well as a sense of past, present and future imagined along a continuum, each in dialogue with and bearing an organic relation to the other. However, the compromise of the passive revolution rendered both the past and the future into ambivalent, even suspect, categories. To imagine too radical a future raised the spectre of social upheaval on a large scale. Srinivas' (1952) idea of Sanskritization, which has dominated the thinking on India (perhaps even the subcontinent) since the 1960s and remains the *doxa* of most Indian sociological speculation, addressed itself specifically to this idea of harmonious social transformation and the task of nation-building. The concept addressed centrally the question of authenticity: Would India's unique civilizational values be undermined by too rapid a change, the kind of change implicit in the modernization theories that were regnant then and which emanated from the West? For the progressive intellectual of the 1950s whose thinking was shaped by that peculiar mixture of nationalism and socialism, the past lay too close at hand, coiled around the present. The deadweight of the past was manifested in structures and attitudes, as well as in the all-embracing metaphor of feudalism that was the counterpoint to the modernity that the Indian state and political processes sought to establish. Visualizations of modernity—the imagining of national culture—reflected this central tension. The present, rendered as the contemporary, worked with an idea of the past that stretched into 'the dark backward and abysm of time' and was imbued with the aura of ancientness. On the other hand, the past was also a spectre that needed to be, and could be, exorcized through the incantation of the modern. The future became a mere proleptic gesture disconnected from the immediate social and historical space. The contemporary, thus, lay between an under-theorized past rendered as embodying civilization and a hyper-modern, beyond-history future. The idea of development helped to suture the rupture; it broke away from the past and represented both the work of, as well as the work towards, realizing the future.

THE FETISH OF SCIENCE AND NATIONAL INSTITUTIONS

The dominant visualization of the developed future was determined by the fetish of science and technology. While Nehru's famous 'scientific temper' was harder to inculcate in a country oscillating between reverence for the past and genuflection to the idea of a future, what came easier was the representation of science through artefacts. Abraham (1998) calls it a socialist realist style of monumentality—represented through the photographs and publicity material of the Directorate of Audio-Visual Publicity and the Films Division documentaries. Dams, such as the Bhakra Nangal, the Durgapur Steel Mills (built with British collaboration), the hyper-modern city of Chandigarh where grids ordered human irrationality and, above all, the gleaming domes of the Bhabha Atomic Research Centre indicated an oxymoronic already-present yet-distant future (Kalia, 1990, 2004; Scott, 1999). These visual representations were accompanied by the fetishized litany of numbers—of tons of steel, miles of road—and invocations to the ineffable power of the atom. The very size and awesomeness of these monuments seemed to locate them in a disconnected future inhabited not by the ordinary Indian, but by categories such as the engineer and the expert. It was a landscape 'sans' the human, a hyper-modern geography of catwalks, girders and gleaming shapes. The eighteenth-century colonial picturesque of the Daniells had created a sense of the sublime and of awe through a depiction of India's landscape and ancient monuments dwarfing the loincloth-clad native. This was a high modern picturesque in which the factory and reactor loomed over the Indian people. Albeit from the 1960s, Mitter Bedi's photographs—classic black and white projections of a future—are a case in point. They feature the smokestacks of the Dhuwaran power station, the coolant towers of the National Organic Chemicals Industries Ltd (NOCIL) plant—a landscape of the future without people (Hoskote, 2000). One can put alongside the classic documentary *The Story of Steel* directed by Harisadhan Dasgupta in 1956, with music by Ravi Shankar and scripted by Satyajit Ray. Here again, it was the product (the emblem of India's striving to be a modern industrial nation) rather than labour that was visually glorified.

Let us get back to ideas of art and culture, and the grid of development discourse within which they functioned. The 1950s process of institution-building—the National Museum (established in 1948) and the National Gallery of Modern Art (1954), both in New Delhi, and the Film and Television Institute, Pune (1959)—was possibly an attempt to modernize through a centralized mandate. It has been suggested that centralized action by the nation state was a way of disentangling the modern from earlier nationalist polemic (which had to speak in the name of tradition). There are several consequences that follow, the least being the idea of a state that stands outside and above while shaping what is within. Kapur (1991) observes that Indian modernism developed without an avant-garde. State patronage for the arts absolved progressive elements of adopting confrontational initiatives.

To return to our argument about the disconnectedness of past, present and future in India's visualization of modernity, let us look at the museum and the idea of the past. Nehru was convinced of the power of the museum's ability to visually represent the past for the people of an illiterate country. The citizens would discover their India through sight alone even as Nehru had done through reading and reflection in the uncertain comfort of colonial jails. In 1948, an exhibition of sculpture and miniature paintings that was held in the halls of the Government House, Delhi, presaged the formation of the National Museum. What was clearly excluded was any reference to the modern, even though modern Indian paintings had been included when the exhibition had travelled to England earlier. As an aside here, it is significant that when the National Gallery of Modern Art opened in Delhi, the core representative collection comprised of the paintings of Amrita Sher Gil—the part Hungarian painter who had honed her images in Paris. The National Museum, Guha-Thakurta (1997, 2004) has argued, objectified and memorialized the past in sharp dissociation from the present—the 'masterpieces' of Indian art were very clearly associated with achievements in early Indian sculpture. Moreover, the collection embodied Nehru's delightfully vague characterization of what was central to Indian civilization—'that worthwhile something', as he put it. The pastness of Indian art came to be expressed in that reified, static opposition between Western realism and Indian idealism—the spiritual, transcendental, civilizational spirit. If E.B. Havell and A.K. Coomaraswamy had looked back to early Buddhist art to escape from the anxiety of Greek influence, now an all-embracing notion of what was Hindu was jerry-built as the master tradition of Indian art, engulfing Buddhist genres in the idea of a great Indian synthesis (Guha-Thakurta, 1997).

The past came to be rendered as distinct from the present, and indeed excised from it. It was also given a religious, civilizational colour. There was another problem—one of silencing. If the hyper-modern future lay under the sign of the factory and the reactor, with the people absent or at an awed distance, the reified past was similarly rendered as an object of wonder. Its organic connection with the people was severed. Nowhere is this more evident than in the ironic story of the 'museumization' of the Didarganj Yakshi from eastern India (Guha-Thakurta, 2004). The Yakshi was the object of intermittent popular worship and dispensed her aura under a makeshift shrine. Once identified as an object of art, and an icon of India's civilizational depth, she was plucked away and planted in Patna museum, the first station of the cross in a journey that was to end in the National Museum, Delhi. Over the next few decades, icons were to be recovered from 'inappropriate' uses and locations and 'rescued' from popular village worship. The past was excised from the present and also from the people, who were characterized as the inappropriate guardians of value. Moreover, in the spectacle that was to be India's art heritage, the 'modern' was to be conspicuously absent. This reluctance—even refusal—to incorporate the idea of the people as a historical entity, moving towards an idea of the modern, was to be the failure in the imagining of a national culture. Modernity was to be enacted for a static body of the people: they were to be the audience rather than actors in the drama of the post-colonial nation.

The idea and rhetoric of development under the stewardship of the state came to stand in for the deeper and more democratic project of envisaging governance. The whole project of nationalist mobilization had been premised on the disciplined figure of the Satyagrahi, who stood in a disciplinary relation to the masses and had not thought through the idea of a collective political enterprise. The transition from subjecthood to citizenship that the post-colonial constitution envisaged (with the detailed enumeration of rights and liberties) should have entailed the involvement of the people in governance. The post-colonial state with its predilection for the commanding heights and its fear of mass involvement was loath to experiment with the participation of the citizen in defining the project of the state and administration. This had to wait till the 73rd Constitutional Amendment of 1993, which finally took the idea of *panchayati raj*, or devolution of power to the villages, seriously.

THE ROMANTICIZATION OF THE PEOPLE

In Gandhi's *The India of My Dreams* (1947), the romanticization of the people and their rendering as abstractions received its classic enunciation.

> [T]he moment you talk to [the Indian peasants] and they begin to speak [...] wisdom drops from their lips [...]. Take away the encrustations, remove his chronic poverty and his illiteracy and you have the finest specimen of what a cultured, cultivated free citizen should be. (Gandhi, 1947)

The association of popular forms only with the 'common people' was a stark expression of elite dissociation from a culture in which they had earlier participated.

The search for the authentic in the visualization of national culture was an attempt also to straddle the debate on tradition versus modernity. In the case of Satyajit Ray, representation in the realist genre became a way out of the dilemma (Kapur, 2000b). A painstaking attention to the lucent representation of the grain of peasant life is only one end of Ray's conviction regarding the inexorable autonomy that modernity grants to the individual. When the American critic Stanley Kauffmann, speaking of Ray, drew a parallel with Joyce's Stephen Dedalus forging in the 'smithy of his soul the uncreated conscience of his race', he was not far wrong. Ray's *Pather Panchali* trilogy was in a significant sense the *Portrait of the Artist as a Young Nation* that linked modernization with individual autonomy. The anecdote goes that when Ray ran out of money while shooting *Pather Panchali* he approached Dr B.C. Roy, the then Chief Minister of West Bengal. Some money was allotted out of the road-building programme of the Public Works Department, both because of the English title *The Song of the Road* as well as its realist documentary appearance. The twinning of the ideas of modernization and modernity are also evident in the fact that the train sequence in *Pather Panchali* was the first to be shot, although it appears late in the film. Apu and Durga, running across a field, encounter a train for the first time in one of the most poignant moments in the film. This encounter with the modern is a watershed followed by a series of deaths, including that of Apu's beloved sister Durga, that inexorably propel his departure from the village towards a sovereign identity. The final shot of *Apur Sansar* (Satyajit Ray, 1959), with Apu's son perched on his shoulder, looks beyond to an unsentimental modernity. Ray was different, indeed unique, in his commitment to modernity, stemming both from his cosmopolitan *Brahmo* background as well as his location within an international film aesthetic. Reconstruction of folk tradition, middle-class urban life and intellectual existential angst could be kept separate and distinct: the rural fairy-tale world of *Gupi Gyne Bagha Byne* and the urban alienation of *Pratidwandi*—which is set in the time of post-colonial disillusionment with the ability of the state to deliver development, let alone employment—have little in common.

The Hindi film industry was another entity, what Salman Rushdie called 'a love song to India's mongrel self'. While there were attempts at authentic neorealism, as in films like *Do Beegha Zamin* and *Dharti Ke Lal* (the latter with its authentic footage incorporating peasant union marches), we must be clear as to the nature of this realism. The call for realism arose from the need to project images of India as she should be rather than as she was (hence, the controversy over the starkness of *Pather Panchali*). Ideas of realism came to be conflated both with a social conscience and with a desire for modernity, which would retain the special, idealistic nature of an Indian essence. The same issues that characterized the debate on development, as of heritage, surface here. Material affluence and the very idea of money came to be tainted, as was the idea of excessive accumulation: the irascible hero was always pitted against industrialists, moneylenders and the feudal rich or the smuggler. Poverty was to be embraced but in a sentimental formulation: it was the act of becoming poor, not the state of being poor, which attracted the filmic imagination. Whether in Raj Kapoor's *Shri 420* (1955), *Jagte Raho* (1956) or Guru Dutt's *Pyaasa* (1957), poverty came to be detached from the poor and was conflated with the civilizational idea of renunciation (the taking up of a life of poverty, as it were). This was a closure of any further debate on the question of the conjoined fates of poverty and modernity (Chakravarty, 1993).

Even in the overtly 'social film' of the 1950s the people are abstractions (Vasudevan, 1993, 1995, 2010). Urban streets, shot as metaphors of India's diversity, teem with newspaper vendors, hawkers, construction workers, pimps and layabouts, but the people are only the backdrops against which the moral vicissitudes of the hero are played out. For instance, in a famous precursor to the social films of the 1950s, *Neecha Nagar* (1946), directed by Chetan Anand, went on to win the Grand Prix at Cannes. It is the story, allegorical in conception, of a town where the industrialist and the rich occupy Ooncha Nagar while Neecha Nagar holds honest, working folk. The conflict is staged as the hindrances in the love between Balraj from Neecha Nagar and the daughter of the industrialist. There is an epidemic caused by leakage of dirty water. Balraj leads the protest; the industrialist dies, the lovers are united and presumably the hero will now run the industry with a social conscience (Chakravarty, 1993). The representation of the people is romantic—the happy, singing poor who provide an honest diversion from the protagonist's travails. The rendering of social hierarchies and the possibility of transformation in the form of love requited stemmed from the passive revolution that India had undergone. It was an effective solution rather than a political one that was offered; akin to the Gandhian formula of a change of heart, whether from the upper caste or the capitalist.

Recent film criticism has suggested that the Hindi film is best apprehended as melodrama with its stereotypical, morally bipolar characters and the narration itself being driven through the awareness of a single character (Prasad, 1994; Vasudevan, 2010). Within the genre of melodrama the class structure remains resolutely feudal: the distinction between the hero and the other characters are as between King and peasants. The film critic Madhava Prasad has argued that within Narodnik rhetoric of 'the people' what ensues is an aristocratic self-legitimation—where the hero/noble is in an organic relationship with his subjects. He becomes their metaphor and subsumes them. In a typically modern manoeuvre, it is an egalitarian feudalism, all are presumably equal, but the hero is nearly always well born. Love opens up the possibility of crossing over, of opening up a space, but within a peculiarly modern rendering in which the only difference can be one of class. Intercaste, interreligious or even taboo love such as that of desiring widows is inconceivable. In a modernity premised on a passive revolution and driven by it, the pre-modern lurks beneath the rhetoric of the modern, as that which dare not speak its name. After all, as I have argued, the very idea of development had little to do with social change or transformation; becoming modern was to be achieved through a modernization that would be stage-managed by the state from its commanding heights.

There are two other issues to be considered here. Films such as Raj Kapoor's *Aawara* (1951), Chetan Anand's *Taxi Driver* (1954) and Guru Dutt's *Aar Paar* (1954) present the street—the space of the people—as the space also of a possibility of the dissolution of the hero's social identity. Within that space, however, the hope of social renewal or redemption is never closed off—but only as far as the hero is concerned (Vasudevan, 1993). Becoming one of the people, and one among them, remains a liminal activity. Moreover, the narratives of films remained rooted in the present and reflected a troubled engagement with the past—either literally a personal secret or trauma, or figurative peasant selves of the modern hero. The future remains outside the space of the narrative and is deferred to a non-existent space outside the film. This may not be surprising, and indeed to be expected within a mainstream cinema concerned with representation rather than Utopias.

RADICAL THEATRE AND ITS COMPROMISES IN SOUTHERN INDIA

In the final part of this essay, we turn to the southern state of Kerala and the visualization of a modern, radical culture in the plays of Thoppil Bhasi (1924–92), who became synonymous with the cultural productions of the Kerala People's Arts Club (KPAC), the cultural wing of the Communist Party in Kerala. Bhasi's plays were avowedly about social transformation and reflected an attempt to create a new radical cultural practice founded on the lives and actions of 'the people'. Bhasi's turn to the theatre also reflected his faith in immediacy, which he felt could not be translated onto the screen. The KPAC was founded in 1950 in Ernakulam by a group of committed student activists at the Law College. In 1951, they staged a play *Ente Makananu Sheri* (My Son is Right) that caused only a minor ripple. It was with Bhasi's *Ningal Enne Kammyunistu Aaki* (You Made Me a Communist) of 1952 that KPAC became a force to reckon with both regionally as well as nationally, through its association with the IPTA (Indian Peoples Theatre Association) based in Bengal. The 1950s saw six major productions starting with *Ningal Enne*; *Surveykallu* (Survey Stone) in 1954, *Visakunna Karinkali* (The Hungry Scab) in 1955, *Mudiyanaya Puthran* (The Prodigal Son) in 1956, *Muladhanam* (Capital) in 1958 and *Puthiya Maanam Puthiya Bhumi* (New Sky, New Earth) in 1959 all followed in quick succession. Bhasi, who himself had been accused in a conspiracy case and had spent four years between 1948 and 1952 both in jail and in hiding, wove his own experiences into the plays. The plays appeared with dedications to the heroes and heroines among the common people who had given him refuge.

Before we look at the plays themselves, a brief excursus into the history of communist politics in Kerala becomes necessary. In northern Kerala (Malabar), the formation of peasant unions from the 1930s had led to a whole-scale questioning of feudal modes of landholding as much as those of imposed caste behaviour. A live culture of reading rooms, processions and performances of plays—particularly K. Damodaran's *Rent Arrears* (1938) and *Draught of Blood* (1939)—had led to the crystallization of an incipient, alternative proletarian aesthetic. In southern Kerala, comprising the princely states of Cochin and Travancore, the struggle had been directed more against the intransigent monarchy than against the colonial state. The communist movement here had to contend primarily with the politics of caste and community associations more than the feudal landholding system as in Malabar. With the People's War Line of 1942, the Communist Party of India (CPI) aligned itself with the British war effort; the attack on the Soviet Union by Germany had transformed the war into an anti-fascist campaign. While this put the brakes on radicalism and precipitated the moves towards an agrarian consensus, the post-independence period saw the outbreak of radical activity yet again. Alongside the Tebhaga agitation in Bengal and the insurrection in Telangana, the Malayali region witnessed the first working-class revolt in India in 1946 at Punnapra Vayalar and militant agrarian radicalism in Malabar. The calling off of the Calcutta thesis of 1948, which envisaged rural revolution, was brought about as much by state repression as by revolutionary fatigue (Menon, 1994).

The decade of the 1950s was to be different. If the earlier decade had been one of militant popular activity, where the masses were perceived with approbation as agents making their own history, the discourse by the state on popular movements now assumed different overtones. The 1950s began with the acceptance by the Communist Party of the people's participation in the electoral process: the move towards 'parliamentary cretinism' as Damodaran (1984) put it in Marxist argot. Debates had begun and were reaching a head around the issue of the linguistic reorganization of states. On 1 November 1956, the Malayalam speaking areas of the southwest coast were brought together as the state of Kerala. And in 1957, the first communist ministry to be elected to power anywhere in the world assumed office in Kerala. These three conjunctures of parliamentary communism, linguistic statehood and the communist ministry were also to transform communist cultural expression towards a more conservative practice, centred on the state rather than the people.

One of the most important expressions of a growing closure had been E.M.S. Nambudiripad's book of 1948, *Keralam Malayalikalude Mathrubhumi* (Kerala, the Motherland of the Malayalis). This was primarily concerned with the linguistic and cultural region of Kerala and sought to find the unities underlying differences and inequalities. One of Nambudiripad's fundamental concerns was to posit an intellectual challenge to the Dravidian position that the Brahmins, who were foreign to the Dravida space, had historically wrought inequality in South India. The issue of caste hierarchy had come up within the party in 1944 when the senior Tiyya labour organizer C.H. Kanaran had been removed from the district committee. There had been accusations of casteism and a lot of soul searching in the party, almost precipitating the resignation of Krishna Pillai, one of the founders of the movement itself. Nambudiripad in his text looked forward to linguistic statehood and put forward two simple and telling propositions: first, caste had been a rational form of economic organization in its day, allowing for the creation of a class responsible for cultural production, that is, the Nambudiri Brahmins, and second, it was Brahmin cultural production, that is, a high culture, which could form the organic basis of the new state. This moment of manoeuvre was not unique. In Tamil Nadu, the Dravidian movement put the lid on the caste question and the challenge from untouchable groups by an exaltation of the glorious Tamil culture and the personification of the Tamil language as mother. Linguistic statehood, I would argue, represented the closure of the caste question and lower-caste radicalism much more than Gandhi's intervention in the 1930s (Ramaswamy, 1997; Menon, 1998).

When Bhasi put pen to paper, these transformations were already in place. One way of exploring the context of his writing is to compare his plays with the plays put up by IPTA in the early 1940s, particularly Bijon Bhattacharya's *Nabanna* (1944), dealing with the Bengal famine. They were largely performed by peasant and working-class squads much as K. Damodaran's plays of the 1930s had been. It was a localized people's art merging folk traditions with the exigencies of a contemporary politics (Bharucha, 1983). The concern was less with an aesthetic form of the play and more with the political present and its transformation. While Bhasi's plays too are concerned with the transformation of the present—the evolution of the protagonists is always towards a political ideal and an association with everyman (within limits which we shall discuss later)—there is an anxiety regarding form. 'You Made Me a Communist' appeared with a preface by the theoretician of the CPI, C. Unniraja, remarking on how Bhasi had freed Malayalam drama from the song and dance tradition of Tamil theatre. His second play, *Surveykallu*, carried a glowing introduction by Joseph Mundassery, a powerful Marxist literary critic of his time, signifying that Bhasi had enlivened a moribund tradition. Alongside these were brief notes recording Bhasi's own indebtedness to the lives and words of ordinary people made heroic by circumstances. These opening pages reflect the contrary pulls on Bhasi's own aesthetic—Were the plays to be well wrought and conforming to the canon or were they a form of political practice?

NEW HORIZONS AND A NEW EARTH

I have argued that the 1950s represented a moment of closure after the opening up and culmination of the national movement in the 'tryst with destiny'. If during the national movement the masses had been held in thrall by the disciplined *Satyagrahi*, the post-colonial discourse of development offered the engineer and the scientist as the objects of devotion. If earlier the people were to be disciplined and mobilized, now they were to be the mute witnesses to the drama of development being staged for them. I shall take up three themes within Bhasi's plays to show how even a radical regional cultural practice came to share in the discourse of modernization envisaged by the post-colonial state.

The first theme is Bhasi's construction of the idea of the people, particularly the untouchable Cherumas and Pulayas. In 'You Made Me a Communist', the Cheruman Karamban is shown as part of the moral community of the Nair household. He is characteristically obedient and hesitant about involving himself in political activity. The one moment in the play when he shakes off his trepidation and timidity is when Gopalan, the upper-caste Nair peasant union organizer (and Karamban's patron), is beaten up. Karamban and the other Cherumans impulsively reach for their implements and sticks and wish to seek revenge for their master. They have to be disciplined and reminded of political norms. Karamban's character—obedient, impulsive and emotional—undergoes little transformation during the play. He remains someone who will witness the political activity of the upper-caste protagonists who lead him into controlled political participation. In 'The Prodigal Son', the Pulayan Chathan is a stereotype: largely ineffectual, impulsive, emotional and given to believe in black magic. His one desire is to get his daughter Chellamma married to a lecherous politician, the former member of the Legislative Assembly, Sastri. Chathan constantly reiterates dependence as a matter of honour: Pulayas work for the master's house rather than a wage. Again in 'The Hungry Scab', Kittu is a tubercular opium addict given to long-winded anecdotes and constant harking back to a dismal past when he lost his wife and child. These are static, ethnographic sketches of an idea of the people—the vestiges of a past in the present, which the central characters have to leave behind. There is no redemption, progress or transformation for them.

At the same time we have to look at another dramatic device. One of the reasons behind the phenomenon called the KPAC were the songs written by O.N.V. Kurup and Vayalar Rama Varma. While a number of them were exhortatory political songs speaking of a redemptive future, the majority were based on folk tunes and rhythms and represented a veritable invention of a tradition of *Naadan Pattu* or folk songs. Here again, we see a romantic recovery of the folk with female characters such as Chellamma the Pulayi and Thankamma the coir factory worker of 'Hungry Scab', who breaks into song as a matter of habit expressing a range of moods. While upper-caste women such as Sumam in 'You Made Me a Communist',

Vasanthi in 'The Survey Stone' and Radha in 'The Prodigal Son' sing because they have been trained in music, the lower-class/caste women sing in the spirit of the indomitably happy poor. The plays are suffused by nostalgia for a rural idyll of the happy peasant. The problem here is that of carrying the peasant into modernity, while retaining the structures of deference as well as a culture structured around the lost routines of work in the fields. There is a sentimental rendition of labour as the site for production of folk culture, rather than as demeaning or backbreaking.

While these are in a sense political plays, they are structured around love fulfilled, thwarted or betrayed. Why is the question of politics rendered as one of affect? Social stasis, decay and inequality are captured and represented in the impossibility of love within a space as yet to become modern. In 'You Made Me a Communist', the love of Mala, the untouchable Cherumi, for Gopalan, the Nair political organizer, is thwarted by the barriers of caste. In one scene, Gopalan contemplates marrying Mala by giving up Sumam, the woman who loves him. At the end of the play, we are left with the assumption that he will indeed marry Sumam, though Gopalan has said nothing to revise his altered position. In 'Survey Stone', Kesavan and Vasanthi's love is destroyed by the incessant feudal litigation over land between their families. In 'Hungry Scab', Thankamma refuses to countenance Sankaran's love for her after he becomes a blackleg to feed his family. His refusal to aspire towards class-consciousness away from an attachment to family marks him as less than modern. In 'Capital', Ravi's family is scattered and his wife commits suicide, presumably because of the functioning of capital itself. The refrain is that when our *sarkar*, the government of the people, is established there shall be no incomplete families or indeed, unfulfilled loves. The structuring of the idea of political transformation around the idea of the possibility of love is a distinctly melodramatic mode that brings Bhasi's plays in line with popular cinema. This may indeed explain why former members of the KPAC then found their way into mainstream Malayalam cinema, draining the KPAC of its talent and force. Where the plays fall in line with the closure affected in popular cinema is evident in the loves that are *not* countenanced. In 'Prodigal Son', the protagonist Rajan Nair loves Chellamma the Pulaya woman, but his own martyrdom at the end prevents the consummation of a love that dare not speak its name. We have the figures of Sankaran the Hindu and Thankamma the Christian in 'Hungry Scab', and Gopalan and Mala in 'You Made Me a Communist', who do not realize their love. The world of the upper-caste Nairs is what Bhasi is most comfortable with, and there are brilliant portrayals of crumbling households, litigious families, shady land deals and a critique of Nair nostalgia. Paramu Pillai, the small landlord of 'You Made Me a Communist' and one of Bhasi's most memorable characters, moves from being mired in the past to holding up the red flag in the last scene. As anchors of the plays, the Nairs undergo transformation towards a universal consciousness, while the others remain trapped within their stereotypical renditions. The future remains vague and located in a space outside the text: the metaphor of the red flag has to serve instead. The plays, in keeping with the national imagination, work with the notion of a hypostatized past, a present in flux witnessed by a passive 'people' and a future indeterminate and unimagined. Whether it is Paramu Pillai finding redemption from his feudal past through holding the red flag, or Sankaran the scab, finding expiation in a planting of the red flag, it has become merely a politics of gesture.

Bhasi's plays reflect at the regional level the contradictions within the cultural practice of the 1950s. His plays are remarkable in terms of the trajectory that they chart away from a radical politics of peasant mobilization (albeit controlled) to a participation in the national rhetoric of development to which the people shall be witness. If his first play dealt with the progressive radicalization of a small landlord towards an acceptance of 'communism', the play with which he ended the 1950s, 'New Sky, New Earth', is a paean to the development project, and the peasant organizer has been displaced by the engineer as hero. Ironically, the play itself is dedicated to the first 'martyr' (*raktasakshi*) in the cause of progress: the British engineer Alexander Minchin, who contracted malaria while building the Pechipara dam. Sukumaran, the engineer protagonist of the play who is in charge of building a dam, constantly refers not only to the litany of numbers characteristic of development (kilowatts of power, acres to be irrigated and so on) but also to his sense of duty towards the nation and its people. In this play, Bhasi moves beyond regional concerns to participate in the task of building the nation. The people of the village for whom the dam is being built are represented as unquestioning, obedient, docile and emotional, and Sukumaran's relation to them is one of patient patronage (or of ineffable condescension!). In a revealing moment Sukumaran tells Ponnamma the village girl:

> My relation to all of you has got entangled in my emotions. My relation to my job too has become emotional. Was the relation of your father to his ox only that of a man towards an animal on which he had spent sixty or seventy rupees?

Even as the father learnt to love his ox, the engineer learnt to love the people for whom he constructed.

The closure of a radical political and social imagination went hand in hand with the process of nation-building. Peasants, who had been rallied around the red flag to reject hierarchy and build a new world, had now to be trained in citizenship, which meant that they had to hand over volition to the state and its experts. In the radical theatre of the KPAC we can see this rehearsal for citizenship going on as the communists, initially the opponents of what they called a 'false independence', came to share in the project of development and modernity. Along with the dam, the reactor, the museum and the Hindi film, radical theatre, too, helped create an audience for state engineered modernity and development through the production of emblems for the soul's consent. There were some dissenting strains in the 1950s to this hegemonic subsumption of the imagination: the most significant being B.R. Ambedkar's conversion to Buddhism along with more than 400,000 members of the Mahar caste in 1956. The architect of the Constitution, with its unremitting and intransigent insistence on equality, had lost faith in the politics of deferral that characterized the post-colonial state engagement with issues of social equality. The 1960s were to see more insistent and urgent demands on the state by a resurgent popular politics, particularly the growth of the Maoist movement and its insistence on agrarian revolution. The 1950s in that sense was a decade of hope as much as a lost decade; the waiting room for mutinies yet to come. The fundamental question of how the people were to be brought back in as citizens, participating in the building of a new society through incorporation in governance, remains an unresolved issue. In the struggle over land rights led by the Maoists, in the popular movements against the handing over of land to mining cartels in eastern India, in the protests against big dams and in the demands for resettlement, we see the problems raised by the delinking of the question of development and governance in post-colonial India. Development for the people has to be replaced by the idea of development by the people, where governance is seen as a participatory exercise rather than an exercise in management by the state and its experts.

REFERENCES

Abraham, I. 1998. *The Making of the Indian Atomic Bomb: Science, Secrecy, and the Post-colonial State.* London: Zed Press.

Altekar, A.S. 1955. *State and Government in Ancient India.* Varanasi: Motilal Banarsidass.

Bharucha, R. 1983. *Rehearsals of Revolution: The Political Theatre of Bengal.* Honolulu: University of Hawaii Press.

Butalia, U. 2000. *The Other Side of Silence: Voices from the Partition of India.* Durham, NC: Duke University Press.

Chakravarty, S. 1987. *Development Planning: The Indian Experience.* Oxford: Clarendon Press.

———. 1993. *National Identity in Indian Popular Cinema: 1947–1987.* Austin, TX: University of Texas Press.

Chatterjee, P. 1998. 'Development Planning and the Indian State', in T.J. Byres (ed.), *The State, Development Planning and Liberalization in India.* New Delhi: Oxford University Press, pp. 82–103.

Das, V. 1997. *Critical Events: Anthropological Perspectives on Contemporary India.* New Delhi: Oxford University Press.

———. 2006. *Life and Words: Violence and the Descent into the Ordinary.* Berkeley, CA: University of California Press.

Gandhi, M.K. 1947. *The India of My Dreams.* Ahmedabad: Navajivan Press.

———. 1951. *Towards Non-violent Socialism.* Ahmedabad: Navajivan Press.

Gramsci, A. 1973. *Selections from the Prison Notebooks.* London: Lawrence and Wishart.

Guha, R. 1998. *Dominance without Hegemony: History and Power in Colonial India.* New Delhi: Oxford University Press.

Guha-Thakurta, T. 1997. 'Marking Independence: The Ritual of a National Art Exhibition'. *Journal of Arts and Ideas*, 30–31: 89–114.

———. 2004. *Monuments. Objects, Histories: Institutions of Art in Colonial and Post-colonial India.* New Delhi: Permanent Black.

Herring, R.J. 1983. *Land to the Tiller: Political Economy of Agrarian Reform in South Asia.* New Haven: Yale University Press.

Hoskote, R. 2000. 'In Black and White'. *Hindu Magazine* (October 22).

Kalia, R. 1990. *Chandigarh: The Making of an Indian City.* New Delhi: Oxford University Press.

———. 2004. *Gandhinagar: Building National Identity in Post-colonial India.* New Delhi: Oxford University Press.

Kapur, G. (1990). 'Contemporary Cultural Practice: Some Polemical Categories'. *Social Scientist*, 18(203): 49–59.

———. (1991). 'Place of the Modern in Indian Cultural Practice'. *Economic and Political Weekly*, 26(49): 2803–06.

———. (1995/6). 'When was Modernism in Indian art?', *Journal of Arts and Ideas*, 27–28: 105–27.

———. 2000a. 'Sovereign Subject: Ray's Apu', in N. Chandhoke (ed.), *Mapping Histories: Essays Presented to Ravinder Kumar*. New Delhi: Tulika Press, pp. 291–319.

———. 2000b. *When was Modernism? Essays on Contemporary Cultural Practice in India*. New Delhi: Tulika Press.

Menon, D.M. 1994. *Caste Nationalism and Communism in South India: Malabar, 1900–1950*. Cambridge: Cambridge University Press.

———. 1998. 'Being a Brahmin the Marxist Way: EMS Nambudiripad and the Pasts of Kerala', in D. Ali (ed.), *Invoking the Past: The Uses of History in South Asia*. New Delhi: Oxford University Press, pp. 55–90.

Mitchell, T. 2002. *The Rule of Experts: Egypt, Technopolitics, Modernity*. Berkeley, CA: University of California Press.

Mookerji, R. 1957. *Hindu Civilisation*. Bombay: Bharatiya Vidya Bhavan.

Nehru, J. 1946. *The Discovery of India*. New York: Meridian.

Pandey, G. 1988. *The Indian Nation in 1942*. Calcutta: KP Bagchi.

———. 1998. *The Construction of Communalism in Colonial North India*. New Delhi: Oxford University Press.

———. 2001. *Remembering Partition: Violence, Nationalism and History in India*. Cambridge: Cambridge University Press.

Prasad, M. 1994. *Ideology of the Hindi Film: A Historical Reconstruction*. New Delhi: Oxford University Press.

Ramaswamy, S. 1997. *Passions of the Tongue: Language Devotion in Tamil India, 1891–1970*. Berkeley, CA: University of California Press.

Rorty, R. 1999. *Achieving Our Country: Leftist Thought in 20th Century America*. Cambridge, MA: Harvard University Press.

Sastri, K.A.N. 1955. *Colas*. Madras: University of Madras.

Scott, J. 1999. *Seeing Like a State: How Certain Schemes to Improve the Human Condition Have Failed*. New Haven: Yale University Press.

Srinivas, M.N. 1952. *Religion and Society Among the Coorgs of South India*. Oxford: Clarendon Press.

Vasudevan, R. 1993. 'Shifting Codes, Dissolving Identities: The Hindi Social Film of the 1950s as Popular Culture'. *Journal of Arts and Ideas*, 23–24: 51–84.

———. 1995. *Film Studies, the New Cultural History and the Experience of Modernity*. *Research in Progress Paper*, Second series, CV. New Delhi: Nehru Memorial Museum and Library.

———. 2010. *The Melodramatic Public: Film Form and Spectatorship in Indian Cinema*. New Delhi: Permanent Black.

Vijayan, O.V. 2002. *A Cartoonist Remembers*. New Delhi: Rupa and Co.

PART II
EXPERIENCING DEVELOPMENT AND CONFLICT AT NATIONAL LEVEL

Chapter 4

Governance and Development in Post-independence Sri Lanka

SIRI HETTIGE

INTRODUCTION

The relationship between governance and development has been a widely discussed issue over the last few decades.[1] This is understandable given the fact that sustainable development and good governance are considered by many to be prerequisites for achieving a higher standard of living and political stability. On the other hand, both good governance and development remain contentious issues, as there is no consensus on what they entail or how they should be achieved. In fact, these notions have changed over time, depending on the specific local conditions and the historical circumstances. However, in more recent years there has been greater convergence of ideas on a global level, giving rise to a widely shared understanding of governance and development. The collapse of the socialist system in the late 1980s and the spread of neoliberal development thinking across the world have prepared the ground for the emergence of the above convergence. Today, many academics and practitioners share the view that governance and development are closely intertwined and that one cannot be discussed without reference to the other (Overseas Development Institute, 2006). The main purpose of this chapter is to provide an overview of governance and development in post-independence Sri Lanka.

---

[1] For wide-ranging analyses from different disciplinary perspectives, see De Silva (1998), Abeyratne (2000), Ranugge (2000), Sarvananda (2005), Kelegama (1999), Lakshman (1977), Manor (1984) and Moore (1990).

Sri Lanka has been hailed in the development and governance literature as a country that has maintained a democratic political framework from the time of independence to the present without descending into a military or civilian dictatorship (Jayasuriya, 2010). It has also been praised as a country that has achieved a disproportionately high level of human development given the country's relatively low per capita income (UNDP, 2010). Both these assertions need to be reviewed in the light of more recent developments, particularly those that have occurred over the last three decades. We will return to this issue later in the chapter.

The post-war developments in the global political economy have been the subject of extensive discussion and analysis by many writers of diverse theoretical and ideological persuasions. The developed Western countries, including Japan, Australia and New Zealand, evolved into three distinct politico-economic systems, widely described as liberal democratic, corporatist and social democratic (cf. Esping-Anderson, 1990; Kollmayer, 2001). Meanwhile, the eastern European socialist bloc countries led by the then Soviet Union, as well as China, Cuba and Vietnam, remained virtually cut off from the developed Western countries. African, Asian and Latin American countries, most of which gained political independence from their European colonizers after the Second World War, embraced diverse politico-economic ideas in shaping their post-colonial economies and social systems (Hyden et al., 2004). Many of the native political elites of the newly independent states drew inspiration from the socialist bloc, at least partly due to their anti-colonial, anti-Western inclinations. Some regimes soon descended into military or civilian dictatorships.

Unlike the developed, industrialized countries, the ex-colonial developing countries could not be easily classified into any of the three politico-economic systems mentioned earlier. Their economies were decisively shaped by the colonial experience and remained mostly underdeveloped at the time of independence. Therefore, their main aspiration was to develop their economies and satisfy at least the basic needs of their growing populations. Most of these states faced serious challenges in transforming their economies due to various constraints, largely emanating from the structure of their own economies. Besides striving to bring about structural changes, they were also eager to find ways and means of satisfying the increasing demands of competing groups of citizens. Yet many countries did not have the resources needed to do so, and the persistent poverty and gross social inequalities led to social and political conflict.

The development trajectories of post-colonial states, from the time of their independence to the present, have varied widely due to diverse historical and contemporary circumstances. This is true even within a single region like South Asia. It is a vast and complex theme and no attempt is made here to engage in a discussion on it. More recent developments in the global economy, guided by neoliberal economic thinking and the forces of globalization, have not spared many countries across the world. Though economic inequalities across countries and regions continue to characterize the world, they no longer clearly correspond to old divisions alluded to earlier.

It is also noteworthy that the adoption of neoliberal reforms by individual countries has been voluntary to some extent, though the influence of global financial institutions such as the World Bank (WB) on weaker developing countries has not been insignificant. On the other hand, the lure of foreign capital and access to global markets has been too strong to resist for countries faced with acute difficulties regarding their balance of payment, lack of financial capital and technology, and serious domestic problems such as poverty and widespread unemployment.

However, not all post-colonial countries rushed to liberalize their economies and some continued to keep foreign competition away from their import substituting industries, at least until they were ready to face international competition. Meanwhile, those who opened their economies prematurely saw their local industries collapse due to stiff competition from cheaper or better quality imports.

It is significant that many post-colonial states, under the influence of their own anti-colonial social and political movements, sought to reduce the dependence of their economies on Western countries by adopting protectionist and nationalist policies. These policies did not always produce anticipated outcomes and the countries concerned soon faced serious difficulties such as growing trade deficits and unemployment.

It is in the context of the changing global political economy outlined above that Sri Lanka's economic and political developments after independence need to be discussed. In the remaining pages of this chapter, an attempt is made to do this. In doing so, attention is focused on the efforts made by post-independence regimes to change the structure of the economy that the country inherited from the British colonial rule, aptly described by contemporary analysts as a dual economy comprising a vibrant plantation sector and a vast, subsistence-oriented rural peasantry (Snodgrass, 1963).

GOVERNANCE AND DEVELOPMENT IN POST-INDEPENDENCE SRI LANKA

As mentioned earlier, development approaches and governance frameworks have varied widely over time and across countries. When different ideas about development emerge from theoretical discussions, political debates and actual practices, they often get translated into policies, programmes and projects.

Sri Lanka's post-independence development trajectory is often assumed to have evolved through several distinct stages. Firstly, the period from independence in 1948 to 1956 did not mark any radical departure from the already established liberal, developmentalist state model. While the state adopted a clearly welfare-oriented approach, private capital was allowed to operate in the economy unhindered. The increasing influence of the political left represented by socialist and Marxist parties and affiliated civil society organizations could not be ignored by the conservative political establishment and, thus, resulted in the adoption of redistributive policies, such as land reforms, and universal welfare services, such as free health and education.

The year 1956 marked a watershed in the development history of the country. The outcome of the 1956 general elections not only brought to power a coalition led by the left-of-centre Sri Lanka Freedom Party (SLFP), but also further increased the influence of the political left, led by the two main Marxist parties in the country, namely, the Lanka Sama Samaja Party and the Communist Party. The result of these changes became clearly evident over the next few years. The state became the dominant player in the economy, steadily marginalizing the private corporate sector. Social sectors became almost completely dominated by the state, leaving little room for private investments in areas such as health, education, public transport, housing and rural infrastructure. The state became the main provider of life chances, in particular for the lower strata of society.

The underprivileged people naturally looked to the state for their sustenance, making political power the main source of redress for a host of problems. A rapidly growing population with increasing expectations for a higher standard of living continued to exert pressure on the available resources, soon leading to an unhealthy imbalance between welfare expenditure and productive investment (Marga Institute, 1974). The widening gap between higher aspirations on the one hand and unrealistic expectations on the other led to tensions, frustrations and conflicts. By the early 1970s, the country was in the midst of a major crisis that had economic, political and social ramifications. While the political left continued to believe that the resolution of the crises required further socialist reforms, the advocates of liberal economic reforms put forward an entirely different perspective that emphasized the crucial role of private capital in leading the economy out of the prevailing crises. Economic, social and political crises that converged in the early to the mid-1970s to produce widespread popular resentment and frustration culminated in the defeat of the incumbent, left-of-centre regime at the 1977 general elections, bringing into power the United National Party (UNP), which was committed to liberal economic reforms.

The main feature of the period from 1956 to 1977 was the dominant interventionist role played by the state. State interventions were guided by a socialist ideology. Interventions guided by the dominant (official) political ideology at the time included radical land reforms, nationalization of private business assets and firms, establishment of state-owned enterprises, state control over imports and exports, wholesale and retail trade, provision of extensive subsidies to producers and consumers and political control over public administration. Even though successive governments had established many import substitution industries, the country's economy continued to be dominated by primary production, including export-oriented plantation production (see Table 4.1). The worsening terms of trade coupled with the first oil shock in the mid-1970s forced the government to restrict imports. Economic stagnation in a context of rapid population growth[2] resulted in high rates of unemployment and

---

[2] Sri Lanka's population in the 1946 Population Census was just over 6 million, but by 1971 the population had increased to over 12 million. This was largely due to the eradication of malaria, a major cause of mortality for many decades.

Table 4.1
Distribution of Employment by Sector in Sri Lanka

	1953		1963		1971	
	Number of employees	Per cent	Number of employees	Per cent	Number of employees	Per cent
Peasant agriculture	1,584,141	52.00	1,681,937	52.60	1,823,957	50.40
Plantation agriculture	856,110	28.60	784,872	24.70	927,263	20.00

Source: Department of Census & Statistics, The Population in Sri Lanka, 1974.

widespread poverty. However, the left-of-centre government advocated greater self-reliance, austerity and import substitution as remedies. In the run-up to the 1977 general elections, it became apparent that economic liberalism was gaining ground at the expense of the socialist central planning model that had hitherto dominated the country's political landscape.

The dominant role that the state played in the management of the economy and the regulation of the market did not threaten the multiparty system in the country. Political parties and media institutions facilitated public discussion on economic and political issues. Changes of government, although they did not lead to radical policy shifts, helped to maintain political pluralism. On the other hand, state domination over the economy and the increasing political control over public administration curtailed the autonomy of the business community and public officials. Egalitarian policies pursued by successive governments helped contain both class and regional disparities within reasonable limits, reinforcing the legitimacy of left-of-centre regimes.

A significant political landmark during the pre-liberalization period was the drafting of a republican constitution in 1972. The event marked the severance of the country's allegiance to the British throne. The island, hitherto referred to as Ceylon, was renamed Sri Lanka. The 1972 constitution did not respond to the grievances of the minority Tamils who had been agitating for regional autonomy for the north and east. Another sticking point in the constitution was the special place accorded to Buddhism. Moreover, the new constitution ensured the continuation of the centralized, parliamentary system of government, contrary to the long-held aspiration of the Tamil minority for a federal form of government[3] that would have given considerable political autonomy to the northeast region in which they were dominant (Rizvi, 2008).

As is well known, social welfare policies adopted by the post-independence regimes continued to produce positive social outcomes, indicated by high physical quality of life indices. Yet some of the same policies facilitated the emergence of large alienated youth constituencies, aided by a high rate of population growth after independence. Disadvantaged rural youth, educated in the vernacular, became increasingly restless due to actual and perceived injustices and increased unemployment. What was also significant was the clear division of the youth population along ethno-linguistic lines, as they became increasingly monolingual and were socialized within almost exclusive ethno-linguistic enclaves. In other words, the young population of the country was clearly differentiated vertically, on social class lines, and horizontally, on ethno-linguistic lines. As I have discussed elsewhere, these divisions provided the basis for violent youth politics in the country from the early 1970s onwards (Hettige, 2004).[4]

The state-led development model that continued to guide policy-making came under pressure due to the economic crisis in the mid-1970s. Its opponents carried out a successful campaign against it and it was replaced by the open economic policy of the post-1977 regime. This naturally marked a radical shift which was bound to be resisted by left-leaning political constituencies—in particular, socialist trade unions affiliated to leftist parties. The new regime changed the constitution and introduced an all-powerful executive presidential system. Political developments in the years that followed have been described by commentators as anti-democratic. Various forms of resistance to new developments were dealt with by the

---

[3] The formation of the Federal Party at the time of independence by a powerful section of the Tamil political leadership was a clear indication of their desire to establish a federal system of government in the country.

[4] Political independence in 1948 did not immediately bring any major policy shifts. English continued to be the official language, and it also remained the medium of instruction in secondary schools and the university. The policy environment changed radically following the election of a Sinhala nationalist regime in 1956. While Sinhala replaced English as the official language, Sinhala and Tamil became the media of instruction in both schools and universities. For a detailed discussion on the political and social implications of the policy changes, see Hettige (2011).

government deploying violent party cadres, in particular trade union activists affiliated to the ruling party. The large-scale dismissal of public sector workers who took part in a general strike in 1982 was a severe blow to the country's left-leaning trade union movement. The 1982 referendum on extending the life of the parliament by another term was marred by violence and gross irregularities, and was later considered even by some leading members of the ruling party as an undemocratic, unwise move.

On the other hand, the thinking on the part of the reformers appears to have been that a soft approach was not helpful in changing the pre-existing social and moral order. What was envisaged was a major ideological shift and a transformation of the status quo. Since the leaders wished to attract foreign capital, in addition to incentives such as tax holidays and infrastructure facilities, they wanted to create a workforce that would fit into a new industrial environment. The free trade zones that were established following economic liberalization did not allow their workers to form trade unions.

Addressing the problem of unemployment was undoubtedly a priority issue for the newly elected government. The government made public pronouncements about the availability of a large pool of educated, trainable youth that could be tapped by potential foreign investors. Yet the type of work created in the newly established free trade zones was not attractive to upwardly mobile, educated youth, who instead looked for white-collar jobs in the state sector. It appears that the unskilled and semi-skilled positions in the new economy were filled by almost redundant rural workers who were engaged either in agricultural labour or in rural industries that were adversely affected by the influx of cheap imports after economic liberalization.

Meanwhile, the educated yet non-English speaking rural youth remained largely unemployed, as they could not be absorbed into the shrinking state sector or the expanding private corporate sector that used English as the main business language. The recruits to white-collar jobs in the private sector mostly hailed from urban middle-class backgrounds. The *Janatha Vimukthi Peramuna* (JVP), who staged the first anti-state youth rebellion in 1971, continued to attract alienated rural youth in large numbers, and many observers felt that it was only a matter of time before the JVP launched a second rebellion. This came to pass in the late 1980s, this time partly as a reaction to the political reforms intended to

Table 4.2
Sri Lankan Youth by Preferred Employment Sector and Ethnicity
(in Percentages)

Which employment sector would you prefer to work in?	Ethnicity				
	Sinhala	Tamil	Moors	Other	Total
State sector	72.2	61.6	66.1	66.7	69.9
Private sector	18.0	16.1	17.4	0.0	17.6
Self-employment	9.1	20.4	15.6	33.3	11.6
Other	0.7	1.9	0.9	0.0	0.9
Total	100.0	100.0	100.0	100.0	100.0

Source: National Youth Survey, 2009, SPARC, University of Colombo, Sri Lanka.

defuse the anti-state uprising spearheaded by rebellious Tamil youth in the north and the east. Agitations by the alienated Tamil youth began in the mid-1970s and gradually evolved into a violent separatist struggle. These Tamil youths shared many grievances with their Sinhalese counterparts, but being members of a minority community, their relationship to the Sri Lankan state was different. I have discussed this issue elsewhere (Hettige, 2008).[5] It should be noted that youth aspirations were similar across ethnic divisions. As Table 4.2 shows, the vast majority of youth in the country, irrespective of their ethnic identity, aspired towards state sector employment (SPARC, 2010).

The post-1977 period is highly significant in the recent history of Sri Lanka. The developments with regard to governance and development during this period were far-reaching. While successive governments continued to press ahead with liberal economic reforms, leading to a massive social transformation, politics became increasingly violent due to agitations in both the south and the north. It is significant that neither did persistent political turmoil and violence derail economic reforms, nor

[5] Most of the educated youth, irrespective of their ethnic background, strived for upward social mobility through higher education and state sector employment. Free education enabled them to secure educational credentials but finding state sector employment was not easy, particularly after economic liberalization when there was a deliberate effort by successive governments to cut back on public sector employment.

did the change of regimes appreciably slow down the progress of such reforms. However, this does not mean that violent political conflicts since 1977 have not impeded economic development. In fact, the direct cost of the northeast war alone has been enormous (Strategic Foresight Group, 2004), in addition to many lost opportunities.

SOCIAL AND ECONOMIC CHANGES AFTER 1977

Economic liberalization brought about significant changes in the country's opportunity structures: free trade zones, the urban construction boom, expansion of the service economy and the urban informal sector attracted rural labour, creating wage pressure in the rural economy. Rising cost of production and food imports made rural farmers vulnerable as their profit margins dwindled. This naturally caused more rural people to look for alternative sources of livelihood, both in urban areas and abroad. The liberal economic environment also facilitated the exodus of labour to overseas labour markets, in particular the Middle East. As the available data shows, migration of Sri Lankan labour to the Middle East and elsewhere increased steadily after economic liberalization (see Table 4.3).

Table 4.3
Number of Departures for Foreign Employment:
Annual Departures 1976–2007

Year	Male		Female		Total
	Number	Percentage of total	Number	Percentage of total	
1976	524	99.05	5	0.95	529
1981	27,287	47.50	30,160	52.50	57,447
1986	10,618	67.16	5,191	32.84	15,809
1991	21,423	32.97	43,560	67.03	64,983
1996	43,112	26.53	119,404	73.47	162,516
2001	59,807	32.50	124,200	67.50	184,007
2006	90,605	44.45	113,236	55.55	203,841
2007	102,629	47.20	114,677	52.70	217,306

Source: Statistical Handbook on Migration (1999), Sri Lanka Bureau of Foreign Employment Annual Report, 2008. Central Bank of Sri Lanka.

The expanding import and export trade continued to create more and more opportunities for private consumption of goods and services. Increasing demand for consumer goods and privately provided services in sectors such as education, health and transport contributed to a rapid expansion of the urban-based service economy. The result was an increasing gap between rural and urban areas. While higher income groups tended to rely more on privately provided services, low-income groups continued to rely mostly on publicly provided services, the quality of which began to deteriorate as the elites gradually moved away from them. This situation naturally encouraged more and more people to look for new income opportunities so that they could also take part in modern consumption. Private and international schools, private hospitals, supermarkets, modern luxury housing complexes, expensive motor cars, etc., became part and parcel of a new urban consumerist lifestyle that persuaded many people to look for new income opportunities. Naturally, the new business elite based in Colombo took the lead, setting examples for the others to follow. While the professionally qualified groups such as lawyers, doctors, engineers and architects used their professional skills to earn money and adopt the new consumerist lifestyle, the political elites used their power and influence to engage in rent-seeking behaviour. Prominent public school teachers and principals left public service to establish private and international schools, in an attempt to attract the children of new rich parents in urban areas. The economic pressure and the lure of modern consumption persuaded others to look for both legitimate and illegitimate sources of income. These developments in turn prepared the material basis for the spread of corruption and abuse of power.

It is widely recognized today that corruption is a major social issue in Sri Lankan society. Many people who are in positions that allow them to engage in rent-seeking behaviour have continued to do so. Politicians at all levels, public officials, law enforcement officers and the military are all implicated. Corruption is already a major governance issue in the country. International agencies, the media and civil society organizations have highlighted the issue as a major factor impeding good governance and development.

Post-1977 developments in Sri Lanka point to a symbiotic relationship between governance and development. The transition from a highly regulated economy to one which was loosely managed also signalled a breakdown of the normative framework of society, where different actors became pragmatic and began to freely use the opportunities afforded by an open economy. In fact, many institutions were established outside of a clear regulatory framework. For instance, private and international schools were established without the involvement of any educational authorities; newly established private hospitals were not regulated by the health authorities; private bus services were allowed to flourish without transport authorities setting minimum standards; labour recruitment agencies sending workers abroad mushroomed in the country, and many of these were not regulated by the relevant state authorities; and so on.[6]

There was no explicit regulation of fees charged by professionals. Medical doctors employed in the public sector were allowed to engage in paid work in the private sector after normal working hours. This naturally enabled them to earn additional income but the same practice had an adverse effect on the quality of the publicly provided health services. The same seems to have been true for other professional groups. Government teachers began to offer private tuition, forcing most pupils to rely on private tuition in an increasingly competitive education system. Deteriorating public transport services compelled more and more people to find their own solutions, such as the purchase of cars, motorbikes and vans.

All of the above adaptations and adjustments exerted considerable economic pressure on the general population. People living in rural areas had few opportunities to engage in lucrative income-earning activities. Some of them began to migrate to urban areas or overseas countries for employment, but the majority of the rural population left behind remained poor. Rural–urban disparities became more pronounced. This situation compelled the government and international agencies to develop strategies to address widespread rural poverty. The first poverty alleviation programme after economic liberalization in Sri Lanka was launched in 1989. The government also implemented Integrated Rural Development Projects in many districts in the country in the 1980s, but these projects

---

[6] The emergent situation can be contrasted with the pre-liberalization period when state control over economic activities was all-pervasive. For instance, imports were strictly regulated and controlled. Most of the consumer goods were imported by state agencies and marketed through a network of state owned, cooperative retail outlets. Similarly, foreign exchange transactions were highly controlled and overseas travel was extremely restricted as a result.

did not have an appreciable impact on poverty in rural areas. It was estimated at the time that nearly 50 per cent of the population of the country fell below the poverty line and the poverty alleviation programme was intended to cover this population.

The adoption of liberal economic policies stimulated the private sector, resulting in expanded economic activities in many areas. These included the export-oriented garments sector, the construction industry, the urban service economy, informal economic activities focused on personal services, the retail trade and overseas employment. No doubt the persistence of political conflicts and uncertainty had a negative impact on the economy. On the other hand, poor governance also made a significant contribution to economic stagnation and its related problems. In the remaining pages of this chapter, an attempt is made to analyse why the governance situation in the country leaves much to be desired.

ISSUES OF GOVERNANCE IN POST-LIBERALIZATION SRI LANKA

The adoption of an open economic policy in 1977 facilitated closer and more intense economic ties with the outside world. Multilateral and bilateral donor agencies came forward to support the Sri Lankan government in implementing various development and infrastructure projects. The government also became increasingly dependent on donor funding to bridge the widening trade gap. However, the same policies produced popular resistance and resentment due to increasing poverty, a widening gap between the rich and the poor, increasing cost of living and deteriorating public services. The government's attempts to deal with popular resistance resulted in the suppression of civil liberties and the persecution of political opponents. In fact, elections at all levels became violent and disorderly from the early 1980s onwards.

An analysis of the quality of governance in the post-1977 period cannot be discussed without reference to the rapid socio-economic changes that followed economic liberalization.

As mentioned above, open economic policies brought disproportionate benefits to certain sections of the population. The business community, professional groups, civil society groups linked to international organizations, migrants, the new rich, ruling party politicians and their close associates, etc., all made considerable gains. They had access to a disproportionate share of the newly created wealth. The inflow of donor funding also created opportunities for a number of privileged groups such as professionals, intellectuals, senior public servants, development-oriented civil society leaders and politicians. The emerging new urban middle class became the reference group in terms of consumption and lifestyle. On the other hand, rural peasants, urban workers, artisans, disadvantaged rural youth, plantation workers, lower and middle level public sector employees, etc., who constituted the vast majority of the population, did not gain much by way of new or improved income opportunities (Hettige, 1995). Moreover, these groups came under greater economic pressure due to the increasing cost of goods and services such as food, health, education, transport and housing.

The political leaders who were responsible for introducing liberal economic policies after 1977 undoubtedly felt that such policies could pave the way for rapid economic growth, which would eventually eliminate poverty and bring prosperity to everybody. They often cited the case of Singapore. The fact that Singapore did not promote popular democracy and civil liberties, but instead relied on strict discipline and rule of law, would have persuaded the post-1977 regime to take high-handed measures to deal with industrial unrest and popular resistance. However, the influence of the Singaporean example appeared to end there. For instance, the zero-tolerance position on corruption and the technocratic orientation of the state that characterized Singapore's political system did not figure in Sri Lanka's case. In fact, leading political activists belonging to the ruling party engaged in political favouritism, politicization of state institutions and widespread rent-seeking; this did not create a level playing field for businesses to thrive, in spite of the privatization of non-performing state enterprises and the removal of barriers to foreign trade.

In 1978, steps were taken to move power away from parliament and into the hands of the president, through the introduction of an executive presidential system of government. Parliament continued to be the national legislature, but the president—being the Head of State and the Head of Government—had sweeping powers, including the power to dissolve parliament and call for fresh elections. In fact, the incumbent president publicly proclaimed that his powers were so pervasive that he could do anything except turn a man into a woman or vice versa! The concentration of unprecedented powers in the hands of the executive president was a deliberate move on the part of the incumbent government to forge ahead with liberal economic reforms even against strong opposition from the left-leaning political forces. The issue of concentration of power in the hands of the executive president and the semi-authoritarian nature of presidential rule came under severe criticism and gave rise to considerable agitations by the political opposition. So much so, that by 1994 there was virtual consensus across the political spectrum that the presidential system should be abolished or at least that certain presidential powers should be removed. The main opposition party, which called for the abolition of the system, did not show much enthusiasm to do so once elected to power. In fact, the executive presidency soon became a non-issue for ruling party leaders, irrespective of which party was in power. This does not mean that the political conflict between the president and the parliament could be ignored; this became quite obvious in 2001 when the President, Chandrika Kumaratunga, and the Prime Minister, Ranil Wickramasinghe, belonged to two rival parties, namely the SLFP and the UNP respectively. Today, the president can cripple an opposition government not to his or her liking—even if it is backed by a parliamentary majority—by making it virtually impossible for the prime minister elected by the parliament to function. The president, being the Head of State and Head of Government, can appoint the cabinet, change its ministers, keep any ministry for himself or herself, dissolve parliament after a lapse of one year and call for fresh elections. Even if the people vote a party into power in order to form a government of their choice, the president can act contrary to popular will.

Another important aspect of the presidential system is the authority given to the president to appoint people to important public institutions, including secretaries to the ministries. This became a major issue in the recent past, and the opposition parties managed to introduce the seventeenth Amendment to the Constitution in 2000 to remove some of the sweeping powers that the president enjoyed in this regard. However, the provisions specified in the amendment were never implemented. The president continues to enjoy the power to appoint heads and statuary boards of many state institutions, and this often leads to nepotism, cronyism and the politicization of public institutions. The trend was further reinforced in 2010 when a new amendment to the constitution repealed the seventeenth Amendment altogether.

The situation described above has persisted from 1978 to the present day. The enactment of the 1978 constitution that paved the way for the establishment of the executive presidential system prepared the ground for the prevailing institutional problems in the political domain. These problems have also spilled over into other domains. The result is a lack of clarity with respect to lines separating different domains, often leading to overlap and interpenetration. This damages the relative autonomy of separate institutional settings that are intended to form a system of checks and balances regarding the behaviour of power holders, particularly the president.

Any assessment of the quality of governance in the country at a national level over the last three decades would point to many shortcomings. Some of these have already been mentioned. In the remaining pages of the chapter, attention is focused on a few critical issues that deserve careful analysis. They are:

a. The role and nature of civil society.
b. Structure and composition of political parties.
c. Policy process.
d. State bureaucracy.
e. Public institutions.
f. The relationship between the state and the market.
g. Rule of law and the judiciary.
h. Corruption and abuse of power.
i. Media and the public discourse.

Each one of the above themes could be the subject for a whole separate paper, and cannot be dealt with in great detail in the context of this chapter. They are discussed here only briefly, in order to highlight the emergent trends.

It is often said that Sri Lanka does not have a vibrant civil society.[7] In modern societies, the size and the nature of civil society seem to depend on

---

[7] As is well known, there has been a wide-ranging discussion and debate on the notion of civil society involving many writers of diverse ideological persuasions.

the size of the middle class. Though Sri Lanka has a sizable middle class, it is fragmented along ethnic and political lines. A large part of the middle class is vulnerable to political pressure: as public servants, they are linked to the state sector. Many middle-class people belong to political parties and, when it comes to important issues, often stick to the party line rather than becoming independent civil society members. Those who belong to non-governmental organizations tend to be more vocal, but they often become the target of criticism by the powers that be and often do not enjoy wide popular support. The members of the middle class belonging to the private, corporate sector mostly remain cut off from popular movements due to the nature of their work, lifestyle and interests. Independent professional groups are not very large and are concentrated in the capital. Trade unions, student groups, university teachers, etc., often follow the political parties they are affiliated with.

Civil society organizations, which are highly fragmented, do not necessarily act as catalysts for social and political mobilization. Political parties and their leaders are able to ignore them and establish direct contact with their 'vote banks', mobilizing them from time to time through party networks. The party networks are maintained largely on the basis of personalized patron–client relationships.

Political parties have their constitutions, formal structures, election and selection procedures, etc., but informal and personal relationships seem to guide the internal decision-making processes. In other words, most parties are not open, democratic organizations. Nepotism and cronyism are often rampant in dominant political parties. Pragmatism often overrides longstanding ideological and policy positions, though leaders usually pay lip service to the latter from time to time. Endemic crossovers from the opposition to the government demonstrate this reality in no uncertain terms. As for party manifestos made public at election times, they tend to present mundane election promises along with vague policy statements. Such documents do not provide a basis for serious policy debates, which political leaders are in any case not keen to engage in.

It is, therefore, futile to look for a consensual view on the subject. Yet it is reasonable to say that for many, it denotes an arena outside of the family, the state and the market where people associate to advance common interests. See also Edwards (2004).

Political parties often do not help to articulate public policies through public discussion, either in the parliament or outside of it. However, it should be noted that, in the run-up to the 1994 parliamentary elections, the opposition parties at the time facilitated public discussion on the adverse impacts of open economic policies and the need to adopt appropriate policies to mitigate such adverse impacts. As mentioned earlier, the opposition parties also stressed the need for political reforms.

A coalition of oppositional political parties led by the SLFP swept the polls in 1994 and formed what was then called the People's Alliance government. The leader of this alliance, Chandrika Kumaratunga, won the presidential election in the following year and became the fourth executive president of the country. Under her leadership, many expert committees, commissions and task forces were appointed to draft public policies in a range of fields such as health, education, transport, local government, labour migration, political reforms, alcohol and drugs. Yet no concerted efforts were made to follow up on the recommendations of these various policy groups. For instance, the key recommendations of a 1998 report from the Presidential Commission on Local Government Reforms, although accepted by the government in principle, remained unimplemented more than a decade later. Pragmatic considerations seem to have dominated the political decision-making process. Politicians in recent years have tended to pay less attention to policy formulation than to the implementation of ad hoc political decisions. This tendency has had an adverse effect on the state bureaucracy, the implementation arm of the state. With increasing politicization of state institutions, public officials lost the considerable autonomy they enjoyed around the time of political independence.

The curtailment of the autonomy and independence of public officials can be traced back to the 1970s, when even district administration came under the direct control of political leaders.[8] The day-to-day functions of public officials could no longer be performed without the involvement

---

[8] It should, however, be noted that state bureaucracies also came under severe criticism from the people's representatives and the concerned members of the public for being elitist and conservative. Political leaders sought to contain their power by placing them under the control of political authorities. In the process, they have lost much of their authority and cannot often act as a check on over-reaching politicians at different levels.

and direction of political leaders. This was the result of the involvement in the activities of line ministries and public institutions of ruling party politicians at all levels. Any resistance on the part of public officials on account of long established rules, regulations and procedures could result in the removal of the official concerned. The general tendency today on the part of state bureaucrats is to follow instructions given by politicians. This often leads to irregularities, corruption, favouritism, injustice and discrimination. These practices undermine good governance, and an impartial state bureaucracy is supposed to prevent them. Ad hoc appointments to important positions in the state bureaucracy on a political basis, with little attention being paid to the suitability of the person concerned, have made the situation worse in recent years.

Public institutions constitute one of the most important pillars upon which modern democratic states rest. The term 'public institution' is used here to refer to any state agency wholly or partly financed by the state and managed by public officials. When defined so broadly, public institutions can include a whole range of institutions and agencies such as corporations, national commissions, state enterprises, statutory authorities, semi-government institutions, publicly funded universities and other educational institutions. Maintaining such institutions in an efficient and accountable manner not only contributes to good governance but also allows citizens to have access to them in an equitable manner. When rationally organized and managed, these institutions can also satisfy public demands efficiently and effectively.

Successive governments over the years have tended to use state institutions to give employment to ruling party supporters. Often heads of many such institutions have been appointed on the basis of political loyalty, and not necessarily on the basis of professional credentials. This has often led to inefficiency, corruption and decline. The appointment of unsuitable people as heads of institutions inevitably demoralizes efficient workers and qualified professionals within the organization. Any organizational analysis of a sample of public institutions in the country would attest to this fact. Meanwhile, badly managed public institutions often become financial liabilities for the state and create serious problems for the members of the public who rely on such institutions for various services. Yet political leaders, under whose purview such institutions come, are able to use them to achieve their narrow political and personal objectives.

The relationship between the state and the market is a crucial aspect of governance today. With the spread of neoliberal ideas, the state is increasingly perceived as the facilitator rather than the regulator of the market. In fact, many states with a liberal economy already in place find it difficult to rein in the market without being accused of undue interference. When market forces are operating in full swing, weak and dependent governments of developing countries may not take effective measures to prevent adverse effects of the market on the economy or on the people.

Though the market is often referred to as an invisible hand, the market actors are in fact not so invisible. The functioning of the market depends on the decisions that these actors make on a day-to-day basis. The actions of the business community, multilateral lending agencies and regulatory bodies like the World Trade Organization have an influence on capital flows, labour migration, exchange rates, prices and cost of living. If the state remains dormant, it is the actions of these actors that affect the life chances of the people.

Corruption, abuse of power and political interference in public institutions tend to undermine rule of law and the judicial process. As already mentioned, Sri Lanka's record regarding the above has not been exemplary. Political interference in the judiciary, by way of politically motivated higher level appointments and undue interference in the judicial processes have continued unabated over the last several decades, leading to the loss of faith in the judiciary on the part of the general public. Against this background, many people have tended to take the law into their own hands; instances of this phenomenon are frequently reported in the media.

Following economic liberalization, increasing private sector participation in the sphere of mass media led to an expansion of the media space in the country. Many new media institutions and products were established, enabling the general public to have access to a variety of media outlets such as newspapers, TV and radio stations. However, in more recent years, political influence over the media has become highly significant. State-run media institutions themselves have been highly politicized, leaving little room for media professionalism and independent and open public discussion. These institutions are largely used to distribute government propaganda, shape public opinion in favour of the regime and defend actions of leaders, irrespective of their merits or demerits (Herman and Chomsky, 1994). Private media institutions have also come under severe pressure due to politically motivated attacks on media institutions and journalists. Media institutions are not encouraged to promote political pluralism or tolerance of criticism and opposing views, two important aspects of the democratic way of life. The abolition of fees paid by the members of the public in the late 1990s not only made media institutions more dependent on commercial advertizing, but also removed any influence the media users had on these institutions.

What has been attempted above is to provide a brief account of the changes in the institutional fabric of the country over the last few decades, particularly in more recent years. Though this sketch is grossly inadequate for a fuller appreciation of the extent of institutional change, it nevertheless shows a broad outline of the emergent trends in recent years.

What is evident from post-independence political developments is that both horizontal and vertical inequalities in society have led to popular agitations and even violent political conflicts. Ethnic inequalities, in particular between the numerically and politically dominant Sinhalese community and the largest ethnic minority, the Sri Lankan Tamils, provided the key fault line within the Sri Lankan polity, at least from the time of independence. The steadily widening gap and the increasing tensions between the two communities prepared the ground for contentious policy debates, competition for resources, inter-community conflicts and finally the widely discussed ethnic war that had disastrous consequences. This conflict, its background and its consequences have received extensive treatment by many scholars and commentators including the present author.[9] No attempt is made here to expand on this theme. Meanwhile, the division between the socialist left and the liberal right underlined post-independence political debates over social and economic policy, eventually giving way to neoliberal reforms in the late 1970s. While the ethnic conflict led to an entrenchment of ethnic nationalism in the Sri Lankan polity, the left–right divide has shaped the state–society relationship in an unprecedented manner. Yet the egalitarian orientation of the state shows a high degree of resilience even under far-reaching neoliberal economic reforms. Persisting egalitarian policies in the areas of education, health and rural infrastructure attest to this fact.

[9] See, for example, Jayawardena (1985), Spencer (1990), Russell (1982), Tambiah (1986) and Hettige (2004).

The impact of neoliberal reforms on the economy and society has been far-reaching. In spite of agitations by the leftist parties against such reforms, the successive governments that have come to power over the last three decades have not been able, or at least not made much effort, to reverse the trends and policies. On the other hand, the state has not abandoned social sector programmes such as free health and education provision as well as some important state subsidies, in spite of the increasing impact of private sector participation in the economy and the social sectors. Given the persisting Sinhalese nationalist orientation of the Sri Lankan state, largely due to the rise of a pervasive Sinhalese lower middle-class dependent on state patronage, national reconciliation remains an unaccomplished national task. The growth of the lower middle class has been the result of social and economic policies in the recent past such as land reforms, food subsidies, free education, rural infrastructure development and basic health care services. These policies have compelled the state to spread public resources too thinly. For instance, expansion of education has not been matched by commensurate public investments, leading to a decline in educational standards. Only about 20 per cent of the country's secondary schools have facilities for science education. Universities and research institutes are poorly resourced and in turn contribute little to research and development. As is well illustrated by Southeast Asian countries such as Korea and Taiwan, investments in research and development are critical for economic development in a highly competitive global economic environment, particularly when there is no longer abundant cheap labour to attract foreign investors. This is the situation in Sri Lanka today.

The adoption of neoliberal policies facilitated the growth of a vibrant private corporate sector, largely confined to the Colombo metropolitan region and mostly concentrated in trade and service industries. But the escalation of the ethnic conflict in the country from the early 1980s onwards not only hampered the growth and further expansion of private investment, but also led to a diversion of finances into the defence sector, preventing much needed public investment in social sectors such as education. The conflict also persuaded many people to leave the country, in particular those who had excelled in diverse fields and would have provided the skills needed for the diversification of the economy away from the service sector and low-skilled industrial production. The current outflow of highly skilled individuals, in particular university graduates with professional qualifications in such fields as IT and engineering is also a reflection of the lack of attractive employment opportunities in the country.

The implementation of neoliberal policies, facilitating the emergence of a liberal, westernized urban middle class, threatened to undermine the material and ideological basis of the pervasive rural lower middle class that flourished under state-led development policies implemented from the mid-1950s onwards. The same state-led policies reinforced the relationship between the Sinhalese community and the Sri Lankan state. The steady expansion of the state sector in the late 1950s and the late 1960s at the expense of the private sector created opportunities for upward social mobility for the members of the rural lower classes, including the smallholding peasantry. The removal of English language competency as a prerequisite for upward mobility ensured that the educated Sinhalese youth could rise to very high levels in the public service, including the highest positions in state institutions. However, the curtailment of the state sector in a context of private sector expansion under neoliberal policies implemented from the late 1970s onwards, along with the massive challenge to the Sri Lankan state posed by the separatist Liberation Tigers of Tamil Eelam (LTTE), threatened to undermine the life chances of the members of the Sinhalese rural lower and lower middle classes. This was almost 'history repeating itself', a convergence of class and nationalist interests after a lapse of four to five decades since a very similar convergence in the mid-1950s.

The rise of a Sinhala nationalist[10] regime in 2005 and its increasing popularity in the years that followed cannot be attributed entirely to its military triumph over the LTTE. Its rhetoric, which criticizes previous regimes' explicitly neoliberal policies for shrinking the state sector, appeals to marginalized sections of the population, particularly the upwardly mobile, rural Sinhalese youth. In fact, the leaders had the full backing of the JVP at the 2004 general elections and 2005 presidential elections.

---

[10] The leader of the regime hails from the Sinhalese-Buddhist heartland of Hambantota in southern Sri Lanka, a region also known as Ruhuna, the name of a medieval Sinhalese kingdom located in the region. He hails from a political family connected to the post-1956 Sinhala nationalist regime led by S.W.R.D. Bandaranayake who spearheaded pro-Sinhala Buddhist social and political reforms after 1956.

As mentioned before, the JVP has been the main political party representing the interests of rural Sinhalese youth since the early 1970s. The rapid expansion in state sector employment—from about 800,000 state employees in 2004 to about 1.3 million in 2010—due to new recruitment during the period is very much a reversal of the trend of the two previous decades, under structural adjustment policies. Most of these jobs were given to educated Sinhalese youth hailing from rural lower and lower middle-class backgrounds. Some of these youths have also been elevated to very high positions in the state sector, almost in contrast to the practice under earlier regimes that preferred Western educated individuals hailing from privileged urban backgrounds for such positions, apparently due to their belief in a meritocratic state. Many other state interventions are also aimed at sustaining the rural lower middle-class support base. These include generous subsidies to farmers, and rural infrastructure and development projects. Many of these measures are often contrary to the policy prescriptions of development assistance agencies such as the WB.

Sri Lanka is once again at a crossroads, 60 years after achieving independence. The Sri Lankan Tamil community that agitated for non-discriminatory public policies and regional autonomy for the northeast threw up a violent separatist movement in the late 1970s. It faced an unprecedented backlash in 2009 when the LTTE was decisively defeated by the Sri Lankan security forces. The government in doing so also mobilized the Sinhalese nationalist forces in an unprecedented manner. The regime managed to mobilize Sinhalese nationalist groups for its political campaign as well as a subsequent military campaign against the separatist movement. The resultant political polarization in the country has made national reconciliation following the war more difficult.

On the economic front, the regime has made a significant effort to prop up the state sector, which stagnated under structural adjustment policies. This is being done by creating mostly unproductive jobs in state institutions. Nevertheless, the result has been the recruitment of many people to public service jobs with regular salaries and other privileges. Most of these new recruits would have otherwise remained unemployed for prolonged periods, swelling the ranks of opposition parties, in particular more militant ones. On the other hand, the maintenance of an overstretched state sector is a major challenge in view of the country's deteriorating public finances, largely due to growing foreign and domestic public debts.

The inflationary pressures exerted by a large, mostly unproductive public sector are felt by a wide cross section of the population, in particular those in non-agricultural employment. The continuing exodus of hundreds of thousands of people seeking overseas employment is the result. As Table 4.4 shows, although there was a slight decline in 2009 due to the global economic crisis, migration of all categories of labour from Sri Lanka has otherwise continued unabated in recent years.

As mentioned earlier, the ethnic war which raged for over three decades diverted public funds away from critical sectors such as education. The large public education system remained underfunded and stagnant,

Table 4.4
Annual Departures for Foreign Employment,
by Source, Gender and Manpower Category

Employment	2007		2008		2009*	
	Number	Per cent	Number	Per cent	Number	Per cent
Total placements	218,459	100.0	250,499	100.0	247,119	100.0
By source						
Licensed agents	146,515	67.1	160,973	64.3	156,720	63.4
Other	71,944	32.9	89,526	35.7	90,399	36.6
By gender						
Male	103,482	47.4	128,232	51.1	119,276	48.3
Female	114,977	52.6	122,267	48.9	127,843	51.7
By manpower category						
Professional	1,653	0.8	2,835	1.1	2,820	1.1
Middle level	3,962	1.8	8,727	3.5	6,392	2.6
Clerical and related	4,551	2.1	6,791	2.7	6,706	2.7
Skilled labour	50,263	23.0	59,718	23.8	61,230	24.8
Semi-skilled labour	3,499	1.6	5,326	2.1	6,036	2.4
Unskilled labour	52,176	23.9	59,239	23.6	50,158	20.3
Housemaid	102,355	46.9	107,923	43.1	113,777	46.0

* Provisional.

Source: Central Bank, Sri Lanka Annual Report, 2009.

without being reformed in order to respond to new demands emanating from the corporate sector. This forced the individuals emerging from the system to depend on the state sector for employment. The lack of investment in research and development prevented any diversification of the economy, particularly in its industrial sector. This was not a conducive environment for new foreign investment either. As a result, Sri Lanka continues to export the same traditional commodities as it did about three decades ago. While imports continue to expand faster than exports, the widening trade gap is increasingly filled by private remittances sent by Sri Lankans employed overseas (see Table 4.5 and Figure 4.1).

On the economic front, Sri Lanka's future remains highly uncertain. Political uncertainties in the Middle East are a serious concern due to the country's extreme dependence on both imported oil and private remittances originating from there. Persistent tensions in bilateral and multilateral relations between Sri Lanka and the West, owing to domestic governance issues such as human rights violations, are also likely to affect trade and aid relations to the detriment of Sri Lanka's development prospects. Under the weight of domestic and international pressures, Sri Lanka's incumbent nationalist regime is likely to become more defensive in the twin areas of governance and development. Whether liberalism, which

Table 4.5
Value of Exports, Imports and Trade Gap in Sri Lanka, by Year ($ thousands)

Year	Exports	Imports	Trade gap	Remittances
1950	296.5	246.3	50.2	–
1960	377.2	421.2	–44	–
1970	338.7	391.8	–53.1	–
1980	1,064.7	2,051.2	–986.5	–
1990	1,983.9	2,686.4	–702.5	444
2000	5,522.3	7,319.3	–1,797	1,157
2010*	8,307	13,512	–5,205	4,116

*Annual Report 2010, Ministry of Finance and Planning Sri Lanka.

Source: Central Bank (2007).

Figure 4.1
The Size of the Trade Gap in Sri Lanka, by Year ($ thousands)

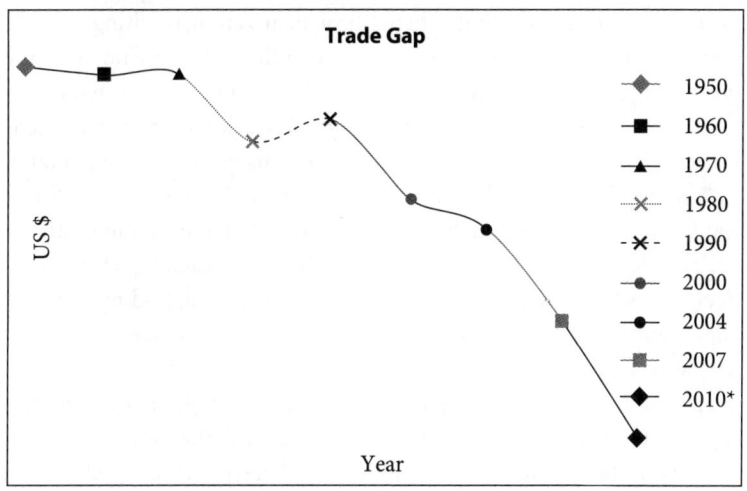

*Annual Report 2010, Ministry of Finance and Planning Sri Lanka.

Source: Central Bank (2007).

has faced a major setback in recent years, will triumph anytime soon in Sri Lanka remains a difficult question to answer. The ideological and class groups that have captured state power are unlikely to loosen their grip on power unless they are forced to do so by a more powerful popular force.

CONCLUSIONS

The main purpose of this chapter has been to offer a broad overview of the nexus between development and governance in post-independence Sri Lanka. Given the broad canvas that the chapter has covered, the issues concerned have not been covered in great detail.

The developments after 1977 in particular clearly point to the symbiotic nature of the relationship between governance and development. The radical shift in economic policy in 1977 reinforced some of the government's authoritarian and anti-democratic tendencies, while the introduction of open economic policies created social and economic conditions conducive to the spread of all forms of rent-seeking behaviour, abuse of power and election-related violence. The evident decline in standards of governance in the recent past has contributed to political polarization, resulting in intolerance of dissent and political instability, conditions that are not ideal for promoting self-sustaining development. Poor economic performance has perhaps increased popular pressure on the political leaders and made them vulnerable, encouraging them to be more defensive and less democratic.

The implications of the ethnic conflict that culminated in an all-out war between the LTTE and the Sri Lankan security forces, ending with the decisive defeat of the LTTE in 2009, have been far-reaching. One consequence has been the triumph of Sinhalese nationalism, leading to a new alignment of ideological and class forces among the Sinhalese. Another has been the restructuring of the state itself. The nationalist forces have supported the incumbent regime not only to defend the state against the separatists but also to promote the interests of the Sinhalese lower middle class, which became marginalized under neoliberal policies. The liberalism that thrived under neoliberalism has been a major casualty of the war and continues to face serious challenges.

The economic and social policies of the post-2005 regime appear to be guided by a desire to maintain its key support base among the Sinhalese lower middle class, which is largely village based. However, given Sri Lanka's high degree of integration with the global economy through external trade and aid relations, the management of external finances is a major challenge. The strategy adopted to do so appears to be dominated by short-term measures such as promotion of the export of labour and tourism, rather than longer term policies aimed at restructuring the domestic economy and creating sustainable livelihoods in the country. The increasing inflationary pressures exerted by foreign remittances and an overstretched, largely unproductive state sector continue to contribute to increasing cost of living, persuading more and more low-income groups to consider foreign employment as a coping strategy. Exodus of labour in turn leads to wage pressures in almost all sectors of the economy, making Sri Lanka a less attractive destination for foreign direct investment. In other words, Sri Lanka's development future is not any more certain than its political future.

REFERENCES

Abeyratne, S. 2000. 'Policy and Political Issues in Economic Growth in Sri Lanka', in Hettige, S.T and Mayor, M. (eds), *Sri Lanka at Crossroads*. New Delhi: Macmillan, pp. 19–49.

De Silva, K.M. 1998. 'Sri Lanka: Electoral Politics and Resilience of Democracy', in Richardson, J.M. and Samarasinghe SWE De S. (eds), *Democratization in South Asia*. Kandy, Sri Lanka: ICES.

Edwards, M. 2004. *Civil Society*. Cambridge: Polity Press.

Esping-Andersen, G. 1990. *The Three Worlds of Welfare Capitalism*. Princeton, NJ: Princeton University Press.

Herman, E.S. and N. Chomsky. 1994. *Manufacturing Consent: The Political Economy of Mass Media*. London: Vintage.

Hettige, S.T. 1995. 'Economic Liberalization and the Emerging Patterns of Social Inequality in Sri Lankan', *Sri Lanka Journal of Social Science*, 18(1): 89–115.

———. 2004. 'Economic Policy, Changing Opportunities for Youth and the Ethnic Conflict in Sri Lanka', in D. Wislow and M. Woost (eds), *Economy, Culture and Civil War in Sri Lanka*. Bloomington: Indiana University Press.

———. 2008. 'Public Policies and Ethnic Relations in Sri Lanka', in Terling, N. and Gomez, E.T. (eds), *The State, Development and Identity in Multi-ethnic Societies*. London: Routledge.

———. 2011. *Impact of Protective Discrimination in Sri Lanka*. Paper presented at the International conference of Protective Discrimination, DCRC, University of Delhi, India.

Hyden, G. Court, J. and Mease, K. (eds). 2004. *Making Sense of Governance: Empirical Evidence from Sixteen Developing Countries*. Boulder, CO: Lynne Reviewer.

Jayasuriya, D.L. 2010. *Taking Social Development Seriously*. New Delhi: Routledge.

Jayawardena, K. 1985. *Ethnic and Class Conflict in Sri Lanka*. Dehiwala: Centre for Social Analysis, Sri Lanka.

Kelegama, S. 1999. 'Economic Costs of Conflict in Sri Lanka', in Robert, R.T. (ed.), *Creating Peace in Sri Lanka*. Washington: Brookings Institution, pp. 71–88.

Kollmayer, C.J. 2001. *Globalization, Democracy and American Exceptionalism, Political Change in 16 Advanced Capitalist Countries*. Paper presented at the ISA RC 28 meeting on Inequality, Global and Local Perspectives, August 14–16. Berkeley, CA, USA.

Lakshman, W.D. 1977. 'Dilemmas of Development: Fifty Years of Economic Change in Sri Lanka, Colombo: Sri Lanka Association of Economists,' in Manor, J. (ed.), *Sri Lanka in Change and Crisis*. London: Croom Helm.

Moore, M. 1990. 'Economic Liberalization versus Political Pluralism in Sri Lanka'. *Modern Asian Studies*, 24(2): 345–83.

Marga Institute. 1974. *Welfare and Growth in Sri Lanka*. Colombo: Marga Institute.

Overseas Development Institute. 2006. *Governance, Development and Aid Effectiveness: A Quick Guide to Complex Relationships.* ODI Briefing Paper, ISSN 0140-8682, London.

Rizvi, G. 2008. *Democracy and Development; Restoring Social Justice at the Core of Good Governance.* Neelan Thiruchelvam Memorial Lecture, Colombo (July 27).

Ranugge, S. 2000. 'State, Bureaucracy and Development', in Hettige, S.T. and Mayer, M. (eds), *Sri Lanka at Crossroads.* New Delhi: Macmillan.

Russell, J. 1982. *Communal Politics under the Donoughmore Constitution 1931–1947.* Dehiwala: Tisara Prakashakayo.

Sarvananda, M. (ed.). 2005. *Economic Reforms in Sri Lanka.* Colombo: ICES

Snodgrass, D.R. 1963. *Ceylon: An Export Economy in Transition.* Illinois: Richard D. Irwin Inc.

SPARC. 2010. *National Youth Survey, 2009.* Colombo: Social Policy Analysis and Research Centre, University of Colombo.

Spencer, J. (ed.). 1990. *Sri Lanka History and the Roots of Conflict.* London: Routledge.

Strategic Foresight Group. 2004. *Cost of Conflict in Sri Lanka.* Mumbai: Strategic Foresight Group.

Tambiah, S.J. 1986. *Sri Lanka: Ethnic Patricide and the Dismantling of Democracy.* Chicago: University of Chicago.

UNDP. 2010. *Human Development Report.* New York: UNDP.

Chapter 5

Rituals of Democracy and Development in Nepal

DAVID N. GELLNER

INTRODUCTION

Critiques of development are many and various, and Nepal could provide plenty of ammunition for most of them.[1] Development as building useless infrastructure? Unused, locked, and eventually decaying offices and training centres were built in many places around the country in the 1970s–80s. Development as education? Nepal has more and more high-school and university graduates but nowhere for them to go, with a widening gap between state and private provision. At the same time, the vast majority of rural students either fail to make it to the final class ten of high school, or if they do, fail their School Leaving Certificate, thus creating a vast reserve army of aspiring, semi-educated, unemployed rural youth who are no longer content to live from agricultural labour as their parents did. Training projects inappropriately designed so that they violate local expectations about gender? Take the assistant nurse midwife programme, for example, which expected new nurse midwives to head off for the hills and work on their own in areas where they had no friends or relatives (Justice, 1986). Seminars in big hotels in the capital

---

[1] I would like to thank the following for comments on this chapter: Stephen Biggs, Eva Gerharz, Siri Hettige, Deborah James, Ravinder Kaur, Lola Martinez, Dilip Menon, Chaitanya Mishra, Joanna Pfaff-Czarnecka, John Whelpton, Nira Wickramasinghe and other participants in the Kandy and Bristol conference sessions in 2006 where it was presented. I have certainly not been able to do justice to the all insightful criticisms and suggestions, which it was my privilege to provoke.

at which experts demonstrate their ignorance of what actually goes on in villages? Judith Justice found that her reports of peons administering healthcare at many rural health posts were greeted with frank disbelief (Justice, 1986: 104–06). Development peddled as empowerment of the disadvantaged, while actually serving to create a new middle class, not to mention a wealthy over-class of Western experts living a life of luxury that they could not for a moment aspire to back home (Hancock, 1989)? Just spend a little time in Kathmandu and see how five-star hotels survive even without tourists on development seminars, society weddings and visiting experts, and listen to local complaints about the 'Pajero culture' that has grown up in the capital (Tuting, 1986; Pye-Smith, 1990; Pandey, 1999).

Fashions in development and ideas of their relation to democracy have come and gone. In the 1980s both the official Nepali view (that of the Panchayat regime which lasted from 1960 to 1990) and the dominant donor viewpoint increasingly began to be criticized for taking a much too naïve view of development, for failing to see how expanding education, improving healthcare and building infrastructure would on their own do nothing to address pre-existing political and social inequalities, and might indeed exacerbate them. Development practice has responded to numerous critiques and dissatisfactions by evolving towards much greater involvement of beneficiaries in determining targets and deciding how to achieve them, much greater emphasis on governance, empowerment and inclusion at all levels, and much greater emphasis on targeting the poor and the disadvantaged in development initiatives—though it should immediately be pointed out that there is, and perhaps has always been, great divergence in styles, aims and philosophies between different national and multilateral agencies. Yet despite all the emphasis on pro-poor policies and on empowerment, on democratic modes of organizing as an integral part of development, development is still a relationship between the powerful and the rich, on the one side, and those who are in a much less powerful position on the other.

Pigg (1992), in a well-known account of the way in which villages and lower castes were associated with underdevelopment whereas towns and the mores of urbanized high-caste Nepalis were associated with development, anatomized the Panchayat mode of development at the very moment when it had just come to an end. But the idea of development, its allure and dominance, as well as its association with towns, continued, perhaps even stronger, in the new multiparty political dispensation after 1990. Pigg took her inspiration from an earlier version of Escobar's critical analysis (1995) which views development as a powerful and seductive idea, with coercive and constraining effects both on the way people perceive and, concomitantly, on how they can act.

Other influential analyses have also argued that the idea of development has been constructed in such a way as to remove all politics, history and contestation (Ferguson, 1994). On this line of thinking, development initiatives conceptualize change in a non-political way and induce people to adopt these new and non-political solutions and self-definitions. It is true that these effects are neither so seamless nor so universal as the Foucaultian approaches often seem to imply (Mosse, 2005: 14). Yet effects there certainly are. In the words of W.I. Thomas with which Robert Merton began his classic essay, 'The Self-Fulfilling Prophecy': 'If men define situations as real, they are real in their consequences' (Merton, 1957: 421).

One important way in which development initiatives achieve their effects is through ritual or rather ritualized performance. The same is true of the idea of democracy; it is through participation in elections that the idea of democracy becomes real for most people. Though there is some literature on democracy as a performative process,[2] development as performance has received insufficient attention. Ethnographic study is particularly well placed to reveal this crucial aspect of the development process. I shall therefore outline the major periods of recent Nepali history and try to trace the different ways in which development and democracy have been performed in each of them.

THE PANCHAYAT ATTEMPT 'TO MOBILIZE THE NATION FOR DEVELOPMENT'

Development in the Panchayat period (1960–90) was closely tied to King Mahendra's project to energize the country through a form of democracy and mobilization that was supposedly 'true to the soil' of Nepal, that is, through local councils called panchayats. Strong claims were made that

---

[2] On South Asia, see Hauser and Singer (1986), Banerjee (2007) and Michelutti (2007).

these institutions stretched right back to the Lichhavi period (5th–10th century CE) or even earlier, that they were a valid and authentic expression of local communities, and that they overcame, bypassed or somehow subsumed both foreign concepts of difference such as class and ethnicity and more local ones like caste. Mahendra's Panchayat ideologues shared that much, at least, with Gandhi's vision of village republics, though Gandhi never hankered for a return to Hindu monarchs whereas in Nepal the word 'republic' was taboo. King Mahendra managed to make his notion of directed development and democracy stick for a considerable period. It required considerable political cunning and a willingness to use force. But at the same time he managed to use his not inconsiderable charm and force of personality to persuade many former opponents of his regime to abandon their opposition and to join his self-declared mission to 'build the nation' (Joshi and Rose, 1966; Hoftun et al., 1999; Whelpton, 2005: Chapters 4–6).

It is significant that the term adopted for 'democracy', *prajatantra*, translates, etymologically, as something like 'rule by subjects', *praja* being a word for the subjects of a king or queen. These monarchical implications remained implicit in the 1940s–50s, with even the communists using and accepting the word. However, in the three and a half years from October 2002 to April 2006, anti-monarchical activists (including those who favoured a ceremonial monarchy) campaigned under the banner of a new translation of 'democracy', *loktantra*, which has no such monarchical implications.[3]

Mahendra's vision of a nation united under the King was not just expressed through partyless political institutions, but also permitted a kind of corporatist representation by profession. Thus, there were 'class organizations' (*sangathan*) for ex-soldiers, women, peasants, (university) graduates, workers and youth, each of which selected (or in the case of the graduates elected) between two and four members of the National Panchayat (Hoftun et al., 1999: 76). In this way it was recognized that different professions, as well as women and young people, might have different voices that needed representation. What was explicitly denied

---

[3] It would appear that, because democracy has become so much more embedded in the culture there, terms such as *loktantra*, *prajatantra* and *jansatta* are used pretty much interchangeably in north Indian languages.

and rejected was any claim that different ethnic, caste or linguistic groups deserved protected representation or special measures. Nor were regional identities—for example, those of the far northern regions, or the far West, or, most sensitive of all, the Tarai plains bordering India—accepted as worthy of constitutional or legal recognition, even though in some cases they were targeted for development as 'remote areas'. There was a concerted effort to 'build the nation' by discouraging other languages (for example, removing Newari and Hindi from Radio Nepal in 1965), by encouraging Nepali and expanding school attendance and by encouraging a single national identity based, to all intents and purposes, on high-caste Parbatiya culture and a modernized Hindu identity. This homogenized (and for many minority Nepalis quite discordant) cultural identity was propagated by school textbooks that promoted development (*vikas*) and encouraged a conflation of urban ways and Parbatiya culture with development/civilization/forward-looking attitudes.[4] In the Tarai, where Hindi had long been used for education, and in the Kathmandu Valley, with its literate Newar tradition, these impositions were particularly resented.

The attempt to build national unity meant that census figures for ethnic groups and castes were not released under the Panchayat regime, but only figures for language and religion. Minority ethnic and religious activists argued vociferously that the figures were manipulated to exaggerate the numbers of Nepali-speakers and the number of Hindus (Gurung, 1998: 94). The proportion of high castes—especially Bahuns (Brahmans)— in elite positions, as compared to their proportion in the general population, could only be guessed at. The absence of positive discrimination, or 'reservations' as they are called in India, meant that in practice Dalits (ex-untouchables) and other minorities benefited only marginally from the advantages of education. All this became clear after 1990 when census figures were finally released. It became obvious just how much the

---

[4] As noted above, Pigg (1992) is the *locus classicus* for this argument; see also Fujikura (2001) and Ahearn (2001). Textbooks written since 1990—reflecting the much more multicultural ethos of the post-Panchayat era—demonstrate considerably more subtlety than this, and no longer invariably take Parbatiya (Bahun-Chetri) identity as given and modular (Gellner, 2004: 13). On ethnicity in Nepal generally, see Gellner et al. (1997); and on the Panchayat era's attempts to deal with it, see Whelpton (1997), Pfaff-Czarnecka (1997), Gellner (2001) and Guneratne (2002).

Bahun–Chetri–Newar—here meaning high-caste Newar—group domi-
nates politics, the judiciary, the civil service, tertiary education and so on.[5]

Mahendra's ideology was also expressed in the 'Back to the Village
Campaign', begun in 1967. Initially this was an attempt to spread the
ideas behind the Panchayat regime to all the villages, modelled on Mao's
Little Red Book and China's Cultural Revolution. The idea was that the
Panchayat system should be a radical and modernizing one, in line with
the Land Reforms carried out in 1963 and 1964 and the abolition of the
legal recognition of caste with the new law code in 1963. In practice, the
campaign turned into a method of surveillance and control by the palace.

From 1974, all students doing Master's degrees in Nepal had to spend
a year in a village, producing a 'village study' as part of the National
Development Service (NDS). Apparently, most saw this as no more than
a 'jolly picnic in the countryside' (Hoftun et al., 1999: 236). But for some it
was a genuinely motivating experience, both for themselves and for those
they were teaching in local schools. They organized youth clubs, carried
out public health education and mobilized people for local infrastructure
projects. 'Despite its short life, it provided a vital and significant learning
experience both for the participating youth and their host communities.
In the opinion of many, it was an unquestionably successful student study
service program' (Yadama and Messerschmidt, 2004: 107). Nonetheless,
the programme fell victim to the politics of the Panchayat. After King
Birendra called a referendum on whether or not to continue with the
Panchayat system, the supporters of the Panchayat regime managed to
have the programme suspended in order to prevent the students from
radicalizing villagers and persuading them to vote for the multiparty
system. When NDS was revived for a few years in the 1980s, it was a much
watered-down programme, with the students spending only one month
in a village (Yadama and Messerschmidt, 2004: 107).

The actual practice of local government between 1960 and 1990 was,
of course, a far cry from the rhetoric about 'unleashing a wave of development'. There were attempts to devolve power to 'development regions' in
the 1970s but little came of these efforts (Whelpton, 2005: 126). Rather,
local units of government were dominated by those who were already
powerful: high-caste landowners and moneylenders with pre-existing links

---

[5] See Gurung (1998: 121–28), Neupane (2000: 82) and Lawoti (2005: 104–5).

to the centre (Ramirez, 2000). In certain areas, where particular ethnic groups were numerically dominant (in some districts or parts of districts one group forms the only inhabitants of the area, with the exception only of Dalits and a few incomers), they were able to resist domination by Bahuns and Chetris, the two top castes of the Parbatiya hierarchy. In some rare cases, they could even use their domination of the new political apparatus locally to improve their position economically and buy out Bahuns and Chetris. But in most cases, and in most of the country, it was the Bahuns and Chetris who benefited from their higher rates of literacy, their closer relationship to the state and the state's need to base itself on a firm foundation in rural areas. Caplan (1970) described how processes of land alienation from the 'indigenous' Limbus of east Nepal to Brahmans worked. In other cases, especially where people had no education and no links to the centre, as with Tamangs, there was considerable and blatant exploitation (Holmberg, March and Tamang, 1999; Shneiderman, 2010).

As far as local people were concerned, the state was legitimated by a combination of factors—the continuity of a royal family intimately linked with religious sites, the simple fact of the state/government (*sarkar*) as overarching and unquestioned authority, and ultimately the link of democracy and development. Development was understood—and still is primarily understood—in terms of material benefits: roads, schools, hospitals, electricity, access to manufactured goods; but many grasped that it had to do with changes in attitudes, habits and general culture as well. Graham Clarke, who followed Pashupati Shamsher Rana on the electoral stump in the mid 1980s in one of the poorer regions just east of the Kathmandu Valley, described how his electors looked at it as a kind of cargo cult promising manna from heaven.[6]

It is true that the state had become much less oppressive than in the Rana period before 1951. Taxes and corvée labour were no longer extracted (land tax had dwindled to the merely nominal). The terms of trade between the rural and urban areas were moving so that rural-dwellers could barely afford the amenities of the town. In fact, retired Gurkha soldiers who once would have settled in their ancestral village and bought land there

---

[6] Clarke (1997: 584) cites an election poster from 1986 which read 'What is an election for? 1. To select one's representative. 2. To make use of one's democratic right. 3. For development'.

(Ragsdale, 1989) were now settling in Pokhara, Kathmandu and other cities (Pettigrew, 2000; Macfarlane, 2001). The same movement to towns and cities, away from villages and old hill-top bazaars, was happening throughout Nepal. In times of political instability and uncertainty (for example, 1980 and 1990), very large numbers would rush in and squat on land in Pokhara, for instance, where the price of land was now beyond what any poor rural Nepali could afford (Yamamoto, 2007).

During the Panchayat period development came to be identified, as we have seen, with the towns. Villages were the places to which development needed to be brought.[7] There were several key places where development and modernity were enacted. In villages, the primary site was the school: the lines of children singing the national anthem, the recitation of the school textbook by heart (the verb *padhnu*, 'to read', means both reciting and studying) and repeated inculcation of the view that the old ways (resorting to shamans, not farming rationally, behaving in an unclean manner) were backward and reprehensible.[8] From time to time political rituals or development meetings took place, very often in the school grounds, which in the hills is often the only extended flat place. These activities were key sites where new structures and hierarchies were demonstrated and wrapped up in exhortations to be modern and nationalistic.

One important ritual of modernity is the worship of statistics. Numerous examples could be cited from the Nepalese context. Let me cite only two. Tod Ragsdale, in his brilliant ethnography of education in a Gurung village in the 1970s, wrote as follows:

> In Kaski during 1974 one might wonder whether statistics had not been made into a new religion. The supervisor who was supposed to visit the Lamnasa middle school treated his job as a sinecure; his chief activity was making impressive statistical charts for display. These were shown to visiting dignitaries as well as to villagers, the latter duly impressed by the air of mystery emanating from them. [...] The supervisor whom the author accompanied on his two-week walk to schools in Kaski spent much of his time instructing teachers how to make statistical charts for their office walls. [...] Privately, this supervisor assured the author he thought the charts nonsense and little related to what was really going on. (Ragsdale, 1989: 180–1)

---

[7] For a rich and detailed ethnography of literacy and ideas of development in a village in west Nepal, see Ahearn (2001).

[8] On this last, see the discussion in Gellner (2004).

Meanwhile, in the capital, there is a torrent of statistics but no certainty about numbers. As Jagannath Adhikari points out, 'In five decades of aid dependence if nobody can tell us anything about the precise quantum of aid flows into Nepal, other than quoting the discrepant figures offered by various official sources, it clearly points to a dearth of independent economic research into donor activity' (Adhikari, 2003).

THE END OF THE PANCHAYAT SYSTEM

The Panchayat regime would finally collapse in 1990 under King Mahendra's son, Birendra, who had succeeded his father to the throne in 1972. No one had ever been in any doubt where Mahendra stood, at least after 1960, when he threw the elected Prime Minister B.P. Koirala in jail, banned political parties and decided, finally, to rule by himself. As mentioned above, Mahendra was able to persuade many people who had originally been supporters of either the Nepali Congress or the Communists to accept positions in his government, in the Royal Nepal Academy, in university think tanks, or in some other institution associated with the regime. King Birendra was different. For a start he was educated abroad, at Eton and Harvard, which meant that he was much less at home linguistically in Kathmandu, where three languages—Nepali, Newari and English—are needed to really have your ears to the ground. Thanks to this British education, Birendra was always able to give the impression, to interlocutors who were predisposed to interpret his views in that way, that he personally preferred the British model of purely ceremonial monarchy. If that was in fact so, he was never able to outmanoeuvre those in the palace who believed that a Hindu king should not be purely ceremonial.

Birendra was a very different character from his father, much less political and certainly much less cunning. After riots in Kathmandu and elsewhere in 1979, following the death of Zulfikar Bhutto in Pakistan (protests against a dictatorship abroad were transparently protests against authoritarianism at home), Birendra allowed a referendum, in 1980, on whether or not the partyless Panchayat regime should be allowed to continue. The party side lost the referendum by 45 per cent to 55 per cent, but it was a Pyrrhic victory for the Panchas: the parties, once allowed to operate openly in order to campaign in the referendum, could only with great difficulty be repressed and removed from the public sphere. The people now knew who stood for what. Morally, many felt that the Panchayat system had lost, as the urban and more developed areas all voted for the party system and it was widely believed that the palace had bought votes to support the Panchayat side.

In the years after 1980 the Panchayat regime lost its figleaf of a radical and authentically Nepali justification for its existence, and even some of its early ideologues (Tulsi Giri, Mohammed Mohsin) began to criticize the way it had turned out in practice. Early on, the idea had been that all should serve the nation and there had been a fair amount of genuine enthusiasm for this idea. Parties were seen as instantiating sectoral (class and ethnic) differences, differences that set Nepalis against Nepalis, sometimes in violent conflict. Now, the legitimacy of the Panchayat system gradually drained away as more and more corruption scandals, not to mention murder, sex and drug-running scandals reaching right up to the royal palace, became known to the general public, if not written about.[9] As revolts broke out in eastern Europe against the Soviet and communist yoke, similar demonstrations gradually spread in the Kathmandu Valley in 1990. After 44 people had died (according to the later, official figures— the true figure may have considerably higher than this), King Birendra conceded defeat and summoned the leaders of the political parties to form a government and oversee the writing of a new constitution.

In one sense the days of the Panchayat regime belonged to a different world. The United States and the Western powers were happy to back any regime that was anti-communist and to take talk of local understandings of democracy at face value. India was and remains the single most important external power for Nepal, because the border between the two countries is completely open and citizens of either country may live and work freely in the other (and hundreds of thousands of Nepalis have worked as police and soldiers for India and many have subsequently settled in India). The only restriction is that Indian citizens cannot buy land, set up businesses without a Nepali partner, or become a Nepalese government servant—restrictions

---

[9] 'It was the rampant corruption within the Panchayat system and even within the palace itself that caused the educated population to become deeply disillusioned with the political system' (Hoftun et al., 1999: 232). Exactly the same could be said of their experience of the political parties between 1990 and 2002.

which are no more severe than in some parts of India itself (for example, Kashmir or some of the northeastern states).[10] India always operated on the twin pillar theory of support both for the King and for political parties until King Gyanendra's own actions in 2004 and 2005 persuaded the Indian foreign policy establishment to abandon him.

During the Panchayat period, the idea of democracy involving people's participation in elections for both local and national levels took firm root. The form those elections should take was far from uncontested, however. The 1980s brought these political differences out in the open; and besides, many were aware of communist alternatives or at least of general leftist critiques both of the status quo and of liberal variants of multiparty democracy. Likewise, the idea that development should include community participation was increasingly stressed by all those involved in the process; but just how that participation should be ensured and enacted was far from universally agreed.

NEOLIBERALISM AFTER 1990

With the fall of the Panchayat regime, twelve years of multiparty government followed. The final few years were dominated by the Maoist insurgency and the instability following the royal massacre of June 2001. Before that, however, there was a genuine attempt to introduce a new mode of development, a new relationship between democracy and development, and—surprisingly, perhaps, for those used to analysing and explaining Nepalese failure and backwardness—some considerable signs of economic health and growth. There were also high levels of participation in, and enthusiasm for, democracy, even if disillusion with particular politicians and with parties in general grew.

Politicians now began to accept the new global orthodoxy that the state could not provide employment, that loss-making state industries should be sold off, that at best what the state could do was to set the legal framework and encourage its citizens to make money.[11] In the Nepalese

---

[10] Nepal began to introduce work permits in 1988 for Indians working in the Kathmandu Valley, in breach of treaty obligations, a move which was rescinded after 1990 (Hoftun et al., 1999: 266; Whelpton, 2005: 112).

[11] Economic liberalization had already begun in the 1980s.

case, that meant, in many cases, facilitating travel abroad by providing passports. Nepalis were in increasing demand as labourers in the Gulf and Southeast Asia, and were perceived as hardworking, reliable and compliant. Enormous numbers—probably over a million—were already working in India, where official statistics did not immediately distinguish them from more long-standing residents who had migrated from Nepal one or even more generations previously.[12] Even the UML (Unified Marxist-Leninist), the principal opposition party for most of this period, who formed a minority government in 1994–95, for the most part accepted the neoliberal world context, despite their communist background (Hachhethu, 2002: 228).

Nepalis might still understand development largely in terms of new infrastructure, but development fashion had moved on. Now it was about targeting disadvantaged groups, enacting pro-poor policies, encouraging gender sensitization and above all, spreading something called empowerment. As part of this trend, aid projects—often funded by international donors and run by local non-governmental organizations (NGOs) which had learned to design projects in the approved language—sought to encourage the poor to help themselves by, for example, setting up rotating savings groups. At the same time the government sought to encourage similar 'empowerment' by decentralizing measures. The Panchayat regime had talked about decentralization, but in fact had retained more and more power at the centre.[13]

The one outstanding success of the Panchayat period, continued after 1990, was the institutionalization of Forest User Groups. It was widely agreed that the nationalization of the forests by King Mahendra in 1957 had been a disaster, and had led—since they now belonged to everyone and therefore to no one—to massive privatization, that is, individuals clearing areas and registering them in their own name. The international donors interested in forestry persuaded the government to reverse this

[12] Indians of Nepali descent in Darjeeling and elsewhere in India have long had fierce debates about whether to call themselves 'Nepali', 'Gorkhali' or 'Gorkha'. The latter, which attempts to cut the link with Nepal, became the official designation in Darjeeling following the success of Ghising's Gorkhaland movement (Subba, 1992).

[13] In Knall's words (1993: 28), it 'made decentralization the task of its highly centralized political structure, a system-immanent *contradictio in adjecto*'.

move and hand over control to local user groups starting in 1978 (Gilmour and Fisher, 1991). Although there have been claims that the user groups are dominated by local members of the elite (Harper and Tarnowski, 2003), nonetheless, overall, the Forest User Groups have presided over a resurgence in forest cover and resource conservation at a time of rising population. The very weakness of the Nepalese state (as compared to India, for example) has led to greater powers, in this sphere, being available to local people. In 1995 a national organization of Forest User Groups, Federation of Community Forestry Users Nepal, was founded, with funding from the Ford Foundation. It has rapidly grown into a powerful pressure group, claims five million members in all 75 districts of Nepal, and, despite the foreign funding initially, is by no means a mere cypher of foreign conceptualizations.

By contrast with forestry, in other areas, as noted, decentralization has only been piecemeal. There have been genuine legislative attempts to devolve power to the local level by making local bodies responsible for their own budgets, for example. Yet the struggle for power at the centre, and the need for politicians at the centre to maintain their own support networks by rewarding followers, have meant that in practice the centre is wary of removing its hands from the levers of control. Thus even measures which on paper were designed to enhance local autonomy—such as the short-lived UML government's Build Your Village Yourself campaign, which gave ₹300,000 a year for development projects to each Village Development Committee (VDC)—were in practice delivered through UML party channels, thereby undermining autonomy (Hachhethu, 2002: 254–55; 2008).[14]

The rules of 'empowerment' are clearly those of participation as a 'modern' citizen. In the words of Henkel and Stirrat:

> [I]n the case of many if not all participatory projects it seems evident that what people are 'empowered to do' is to take part in the modern sector of 'developing' societies. More generally, they are being empowered to be elements in the great project of 'the modern': as citizens of the institutions

[14] Martinussen (1995) argued that local democracy was also undermined by NGOs and foreign donors who preferred to deal direction with 'user groups'.

of the modern state; as consumers in the increasingly global market; as responsible patients in the health system; as rational farmers increasing GNP; as participants in the labour market and so on. Empowerment in this sense is not just a matter of 'giving power' to formerly disempowered people. [...] [T]he attempt to empower people through the projects envisaged and implemented by practitioners of the new orthodoxy is always an attempt, however benevolent, to reshape the personhood of the participants. It is in this sense that we argue that 'empowerment' is tantamount to what Foucault calls subjection. (Henkel and Stirrat, 2001: 182)

In practice, many development projects do not in fact go so far as to reshape anyone's sense of personhood. The project may be framed in terms of empowerment, its reporting and milestones try to measure empowerment, but the actual practice of it is far more expressive and, in some ways, more traditional. The rural people whose participation is sought in trainings will always want to know 'what do we get out of this?' (Heaton Shrestha, 2002: 27). What they often get is a monetary incentive to attend for a day, plus other incentives in kind. Numbers attending workshops can be taken as a measure of empowerment imparted. One estimate (Biggs et al., 2005) is that there are 400,000 sponsored groups—that is, groups called into existence by NGO encouragement—in Nepal. Another study (Dhakal, 2006) in Morang in the eastern Tarai found 351 Community-Based Organizations in 28 VDCs, that is, more than 12 per village. Thirty-five of these were children's clubs and 191 were management committees of various sorts.

For the villagers subjected to myriad NGO development programmes, the modernity to which rural people aspire is acted out and embodied by the NGO workers with their baseball caps, relatively free male–female interaction and 'bracketing' of caste differences (Heaton Shrestha, 2002, 2006). This enactment of modernity is equally visible in the towns, of course. In the early sixties, men who wore trousers, or what the Americans call pants, were considered very daring and modern. By the time I was doing my first fieldwork in the early 1980s, modern young women were wearing them. But even today married women do not normally wear them, rather they adopt saris or the Punjabi salwar kameez for work and the office. Liechty's work on consumption in Kathmandu in the early 1990s reveals just how much the practice of 'doing fashion', that is, wearing the right clothes and having the right hair styles, is built around the tradition–modernity dichotomy:

> Noting the stylish ready-made clothes of a seventeen-year-old college student, my research co-worker asked him, 'What do you think about *fashion*?'
>
> 'Listen,' the student replied, 'these days the world has become very modern. So, about *fashion*, it's like without *fashion* we can do nothing. Before now, it was a wild, savage age. People used to run around wearing tree bark! Actually, now, in a way, *fashion* has become a part of our bodies.'
>
> 'And are you personally interested in *fashion*?' my co-worker asked.
>
> 'That's for *sure*! Look, I'm a young man, so of course I am really into *fashion*. Today's *young people*, we are almost into the twenty-first century ... so we're interested in *fashion*, but also films, sports ... and the *romantic world*. (Liechty, 2003: 35; original emphases indicate English words used in a Nepali sentence)

In this kind of urban context, modernity and development are defined not just by new patterns of consumption, as described by Liechty, but also by patterns of behaviour and practice in the workplace. Heaton Shrestha (2002) shows how NGO offices define themselves in opposition to government offices: by the timing of arrivals, by the way in which work is organized, by the styles in which offices are decorated, and by styles of personal interaction. The same opposition may apply to some extent to independent research NGOs as opposed to Tribhuvan University.

What one would like to know for rural contexts—and only detailed ethnography from varied Nepalese contexts will provide the answers—is how far the language of empowerment is actually used to manage and extend patron–client and other forms of dependent relationships. That they can be so is evident from many anecdotal cases, as related by Tamang (2003) when she writes of the 'disempowering manner in which ostensibly "democratizing" principles or objectives are actually applied in Nepal's development world. Clearly, society to be civil must also be obedient to the strictures of civil society patrons'. Pfaff-Czarnecka's (2008) study of the way local politicians, NGO workers and bureaucrats posted to the district work together as 'distributional coalitions' to cream off advantages is suggestive of the ways in which development bureaucracy (and in the case of the far Western region, bureaucracy involved in famine relief) works against the interests of the intended beneficiaries. Evans' work with Bhutanese refugee youth in camps in southeast Nepal shows how empowerment rhetoric can be taken up and understood by youth in a way very different from what development organizations intend (Evans, 2008, 2009).

THE CRITIQUE AND IMPACT OF THE MAOISTS

The Maoists launched their 'People's War' in 1996. After 10 years, they realized that they would not be able to achieve military victory, despite controlling to varying degrees most of the rural areas of the country. From 2002, King Gyanendra's foolish attacks on the parties eventually drove them into alliance with the Maoists, a combination that eventually led to the monarch's overthrow.

At the most sophisticated level, the Maoists' leaders uphold a classic Marxist critique of neoliberalism, of the sham nature of bourgeois democracy and of the way in which the elite in Kathmandu operate to further their own interests and those of global and regional capitalism—notwithstanding their rhetoric about nationalism, development, or democracy (Bhattarai, 2003a, 2003b). By the early 2000s, that critique had been tempered by an acknowledgement that military insurgency may be able to hold the countryside and inspire terror, but cannot capture the cities; and after 2006, when the party came above ground and entered parliamentary politics, there was a rapid evolution of Maoist thinking. At the level of ordinary cadres, it is apparent that the ideology is understood in simpler terms: the old must be uprooted in order to establish the new, and it is worth dying as a martyr in this cause. Maoists have a desire just as strong as that of ordinary rural Nepalis more generally for the infrastructural side of development: roads, electricity, bridges, factories and hospitals. In order to build this new Jerusalem, sometimes brutal methods have to be employed against moneylenders, landlords and representatives of the 'old power'.[15]

---

[15] On the Maoist movement in Nepal, see Thapa (2003), Thapa and Sijapati (2004), Hutt (2004), Karki and Seddon (2004), Leve (2007), Ogura (2007, 2008), Lecomte-Tilouine (2009b), Manandhar and Seddon (2010), and for a pro-Maoist viewpoint, see Onesto (2005). See also references in footnote 19.

On more than one occasion I have heard anecdotes about NGO trainings being given. The importance of gender equality and female empowerment is stressed. The need for development and new ways of thinking and education is emphasized. On the last day of the training workshop a group of Maoist cadres turns up and asks to address the meeting. They explain what they are about and say that if the trainees want true empowerment, they should come with them, and a few do indeed leave for the hills with them.... There can in fact be no doubt that many Maoist cadres, who otherwise would have to seek long-distance labour migration and menial jobs, do feel empowered by embarking on a mission which simultaneously assures them that what they are doing is supremely altruistic and gives them a gun and the authority to give orders to ordinary villagers, whom they would normally have to respect as their seniors. This applies a fortiori to female Maoists, who make up a third or more of cadres even within the People's Liberation Army (the only exception to this is at the very highest levels of the movement, where men do predominate) (Pettigrew and Shneiderman, 2004). The explanation for this astonishingly high level of female participation in the Maoist movement may have to do with the position of women in the Nepalese hills.[16] On the one hand, women are definitely and clearly disadvantaged compared to men; regardless of regional and cultural differences, within the household economy the young daughter-in-law is most disadvantaged of all. By providing an alternative to marriage, a career, a way—as it appears—to make use of and sense of what education they have received, and a way to serve their nation and the people, the Maoists have tapped into a strong vein of altruistic motivation. On the other hand, though disadvantaged in comparison to men, Nepali hill women have a lot more freedom and autonomy than women of the Indian plains, so that once an organized alternative to subordination in marriage and lifelong labour in the fields is offered to them, large numbers are evidently keen to seize it with both hands.[17]

---

[16] Classic works here would include Bennett (1983), Watkins (1996), Cameron (1998), Des Chene (1998) and March (2002). Cf. Leve (2007).

[17] One should note that many are also motivated by a desire for revenge for wrongs done either to themselves or to their immediate families (Onesto, 2005: 156–60; Ogura, 2008: 438–40).

It is striking that the Maoists share a common ritual vocabulary with the state and the NGOs, whom they are fighting. They too mobilize people through meetings that the people themselves may not be keen to attend (though they often include dance and song entertainment in order to sweeten the pill). Where NGO meetings have to pay people to be present, the Maoists more often use force or the threat of force. During such meetings people have to sit and listen to interminable speeches using poor-quality amplifying equipment. Only occasionally is the speaker inspiring or witty. A shared and well-understood etiquette means that there must be a master of ceremonies, who himself (or herself) is introduced at the beginning and thanked at the end. There must be a large number of speakers. The main guest either speaks last or—if they have to depart for more pressing business—near the beginning. Everyone with an expectation of being asked to speak must be allowed to speak. No one must be forgotten.

There is in the Maoist case the same concern with infrastructure projects. Important in this regard is the construction of the 'Martyr's Road' to their 'capital' Thabang in Rolpa district through what is claimed to be voluntary labour, with some additional (no doubt largely symbolic) help from international brigades of volunteers. Other ways in which modernity is enacted include the construction of memorial gardens for martyrs, collectivized production for tailors and the instigation of 'factories' in Maoist-controlled areas. Initially, when they were still unsure of themselves and keen to win people's hearts and minds, nothing was done against religion. But as they have gained power, local Maoist activists have started to ban the observance of religious festivals, or alternatively insist on the inclusion of Dalits at temples where heretofore they had been excluded. Their opposition to 'superstition' is as strong as, and more forceful than, that of any NGO worker's, even where it makes the Maoists unpopular with local people.[18]

Where they were able to exert control, the Maoists set up local 'people's governments' to replace the VDCs (Ogura, 2008), though these were dismantled as part of the peace agreement after 2006. Very often, people who were not in fact Maoist supporters were chosen to be members and

---

[18] On the Maoists' activities in the areas they controlled during the People's War, see Lecomte-Tilouine (2009a), de Sales (2009) and Manandhar and Seddon (2010).

even leaders of these bodies. In the years between 2001 and 2005, when the government security forces claimed that so many Maoists had surrendered or been killed, it was often these imposed and unwilling Maoists who were being counted. In some cases the Maoists permitted VDC elections to take place with candidates explicitly standing as non-Maoists, though 'bourgeois' parties, such as the National Democratic Party and Congress, were banned.

The cult of historical and political martyrs began in the 1950s with memorials to those who were hanged by the Rana regime in their campaign for democracy. The Panchayat regime continued to honour those martyrs, though in a low-key way, because it too claimed legitimacy from the revolution of 1950–51. It was the Maoists who raised the cult of martyrs to a new height, and with good reason, because so many of their members died in the struggle. Martyrs' ceremonial gates, regular memorial biographies in the Maoist newspaper *Janadesh*, and frequent remembrance services function to keep their memory alive and to inspire new generations of fighters and political workers to be willing to risk their lives for the cause.[19] The use of song and poetry to express and instil a love of death and a yearning of sacrifice in the great cause of freedom, love of the Motherland and revenge against evil class enemies is well understood by the leaders of the Maoist movement.

It is noticeable how often Maoist cadres—and not just the military—are on the move. As a political and cultural movement it appears to be kept alive by constant campaigns, which involve members being 'in movement', performing and meeting each other. Despite the authoritarian structure, with the need for secrecy and discipline of a typical Leninist party, the etiquette of meetings is largely the same as described above.

Furthermore, the Maoists also share in the political vocabulary of protest with other political actors: marches, *bandh*s (strikes in which shops, schools and offices must close, and wheeled transport is banned), burning of effigies, rallies. This modernist political repertoire goes back to Europe of the eighteenth century and the aim, in Tilly's summary, is to demonstrate four kinds of claim: worthiness, unity, numbers and commitment (what

---

[19] See de Sales (2003a [2001]) and Ramirez (1997) for the original publications which started off the analytical academic study of Maoist martyrdom. See also de Sales (2003b) and Lecomte-Tilouine (2004, 2006).

he calls WUNC: Tilly, 2004). Repeated and credible claims of WUNC, publicly performed, can be translated into political influence. This kind of political action demonstrates the Maoists' belief, now shared with the avowed aims of most development agencies, that development is not just a technical fix but is about changing attitudes and adopting new forms of governance. Performing these kinds of public actions, along with the internal meetings and the party hierarchy that they inform, is understood to be the practice of democracy by those involved.

ALTERNATIVE SOCIAL MOVEMENTS: THE CASE OF BASE

There are some organizations which neither share the Maoists' use of violence nor seem to be embroiled in the 'dollar farming' (*dolar kheti*) that characterizes so many other big NGOs in Nepal. One of the most interesting of these is BASE or 'Backward Society Education'. It grew out of a young men's club in the inner Tarai valley of Dang, started in 1985. Initially, it carried out vegetable gardening and literacy programmes. From 1988, when Dilli Chaudhuri, leader of BASE, attended a workshop in Thailand and learned the international discourse of indigenous rights, it began to call itself the Workers' Liberation Organization (Shramik Mukti Sangathan). When, after 1990, it was able finally to gain formal registration as an NGO, it took the less political name of BASE. The term 'backward' is a specifically Indian-English usage, referring to disadvantaged minority groups. The group was initially, and to a large extent remains, a movement of Tharus, the indigenous 'tribal' group that is found right across the Nepalese Tarai, as well as over the border in India. But, for strategic reasons, as with the change of name to avoid leftist overtones, no reference is made to ethnic attachments (Krauskopff, 2003).

With financial support from the Danish International Development Agency, BASE grew to become the largest NGO in the Tarai. It ran literacy classes and campaigned against bonded labour, still a prevalent practice in the Nepalese Tarai in the 1990s. Dilli Chaudhuri has remained a modest figure, eschewing the political influence that could have been his and refraining from opening expensive offices in Kathmandu or buying the four-wheel-drive vehicles that would normally go with it. The fact that he won the Reebok Human Rights Award in 1994 for his work with bonded labourers (*kamaiyas*) gave him a visibility and an international access that has been invaluable to BASE.

By 2000, BASE had expanded to 30,000 members with members paying one rupee per year as a membership fee, which gave them the right to vote and participate in all decision-making. All those taking their night literacy classes were encouraged to join. For the most part decisions are taken by consensus, in line with traditional expectations:

> Those who prefer open debate and votes in relation to one issue or another, appear to have often labeled the preference for consensus and unanimity as a sign of backwardness, or an outcome of a history of oppression. One BASE member told me: 'There are people who prefer to simply obey, rather than speak up. There is still a problem of 'culture of silence' [he used the English phrase]. This is not just a problem among us Tharus. This is also a problem for the Nepali society as a whole. But in this time and age, everyone should be able to express their own opinion even if they are in the minority'. (Fujikura, 2007: 354)[20]

Nepalese government rhetoric has always been against bonded labour, ever since Chandra Shamsher Rana 'abolished slavery' in 1923. However, it is one thing to pass a law in Kathmandu, another to ensure that conditions on the ground are such that people can take advantage of their new freedoms. As Fujikura (2007) describes, a combination of strategic action by BASE and interested NGOs from Kathmandu in 2000 meant that a national liberation of bonded labourers was declared that had seemed impossible in previous years, in spite of many localized protests against the institution. The BASE-backed *kamaiyas* made use of rituals of opposition—marching, standing outside parliament with black bands over their mouths—and they linked up with well-connected human rights organizations in the capital (Fujikura, 2007).[21] This combination of locally rooted activists and globally connected organizations illustrates one of the

---

[20] A similar reluctance to put things to a vote and a preference for face-saving consensus has, until recently, characterized most ethnic organizations in Nepal (Gellner and Karki, 2007).

[21] Unfortunately, many of the freed *kamaiyas* have not been able to obtain the compensation and support they were promised.

typical modes of action of the new global activist networks identified by Keck and Sikkink (1998).

The Maoist insurgency hit BASE hard. Its members were attacked and intimidated by the Maoists who did not like—and often expelled or even killed—any rural activists who did not accept their leadership. At the same time BASE members also faced severe harassment from the security forces, who suspected any Tharu and all bonded labourers and their sympathizers of being Maoists.

CONCLUSION

In drawing attention to the symbolic and ritual aspects of development and democratic action, I do not mean to imply that the programmes and movements that I have mentioned are *merely* symbolic, *merely* ritual or *nothing but* a performance, a claim that would reproduce modernist and Protestant assumptions. In saying that these actions are, to a greater or lesser degree, ritualized, one is not implying that they are in any way fake, unreal, 'just play-acting', etc., as implied by the Protestant quest for inner authenticity. What I am claiming is that *all* social institutions involve 'acting out' or 'enacting' values and assumptions. Building new institutions necessarily involves introducing people to new ways of acting; democracy must be performed before it can be simply enjoyed.

Thus, in advocating the ethnographic study of the emergent modernity, I am not advancing the claim that 'we have never been modern' (Latour, 1993), nor I am saying that the distinctions introduced by modernism have no validity. I do not deny that Nepalis suffer from appalling levels of mortality and poverty, and I certainly oppose any methodology advocating a soggy blancmange of random hybrid notions in place of a rigorous analysis of social change. The point is rather that the distinctions—fundamental to the organization of political and social life in modern Nepal as elsewhere—between politics, economics, religion and so on, between collective action that is acceptable and exclusionary behaviour that is not, have to be worked at and have to be worked out. This cannot only be done by learning them by rote in school. Quite as much as traditional forms of cohesion-generating religious ritual, modern institutions and values have also to be performed publicly. When village Panchayats (or today VDCs), Forest User Groups, Maoist cells, or members of BASE hold formal meetings, vote and keep minutes of their decisions, or when they hold annual public celebrations memorializing their achievements and their martyrs, they are both performing and creating these new institutions. Inevitably, actual social processes frequently transgress the neat distinctions of modernity (between public and private, between political and religious, for instance), but the distinctions, insofar as they correspond to spheres of activity and are instantiated in legal and other institutions with transnational backing, have a life of their own and are increasingly coming to organize the life of Nepalis.[22]

In studying these social processes, ethnography has a key and irre placeable role to play (Paley, 2002; Mosse, 2005). In the 1960s, Adam Kuper set out to show—contrary what was claimed at the time in South Africa—that Africans, in their everyday life, could be deeply democratic. In doing this, he produced an exemplary early study of local democracy in practice (Kuper, 1970, 1992). He pointed to the paradox that, although the village processes he had studied in fact formed 'a highly democratic system', they were bolstered by authoritarian values. Locals represented 'their political system in formal terms as authoritarian and traditional' (Kuper, 1970: 170) because that was what was expected at the time. What I have been examining in Nepal is often the reverse: cases of development organizations that aim to 'empower' the powerless and to be democratic in their processes. A legitimating discourse of egalitarianism coexists with highly unequal access to resources and, therefore, the continuation and creation of what are in fact unequal patron–client relations. By now, I would hazard a guess, similar development rhetoric about empowerment has also reached the Botswana villages where Kuper did his Ph.D. and is probably as equally enmeshed in transnational patron–client linkages. Paradoxically, an unequal set of translocal relationships is today probably represented as democratic, just as once actual, everyday democracy was represented as hierarchical.

I have suggested that practices of democracy and development need to be seen as public performances. As in a recent attempt to distil and describe

---

[22] I have explored the roles of activists in creating and mediating these modernist distinctions in the introductions to two collections on activism in South Asia (Gellner, 2009, 2010).

modern anthropology (James, 2003), I propose that there be an ineluctable ceremonial aspect to all purposive human activity. What is conventionally called 'a ritual' is an extreme case of action, and rituals are in fact often not so fixed as usually imagined (contemporary scholars of liturgical ritual like to counter the association between ritual and fixity by emphasizing how much ritual changes). Most action is ritualized to some degree, and this is an inherent part of its meaningfulness. Sometimes, inevitably, public performance is carried out cynically, with a large gap between what must be done to satisfy the funders and what the participants believe in 'backstage' contexts. But in other cases 'doing' democracy and/or development is a large part of participating in and appropriating modernity. Paying attention to these processes of ritualization may help development practitioners to understand why they are so often dissatisfied with the results of their programmes. Accepting the performative nature of much of what they actually do may help them to plan and to enact it more effectively.

REFERENCES

Adhikari, J. 2003. 'Aid in Developing Nepal', *Himal Southasian*. Retrieved from www.himalmag.com/2003/july/review.htm (accessed on 2 August 2006).

Ahearn, L. 2001. *Invitations to Love: Literacy, Love Letters, and Social Change in Nepal*. Ann Arbor: University of Michigan Press.

Banerjee, M. 2007. 'Sacred Elections'. *Economic and Political Weekly*, 42(17): 1556–62.

Bennett, L. 1983. *Dangerous Wives and Sacred Sisters: Social and Symbolic Roles of High-Caste Women in Nepal*. New York: Columbia University Press (reissue Himal Books 1983).

Bhattarai, B. 2003a. *The Nature of Underdevelopment and Regional Structure in Nepal: A Marxist Analysis*. New Delhi: Adroit.

———. 2003b. 'The Political Economy of the People's War', in A. Karki and D. Seddon (eds), *The People's War in Nepal: Left Perspectives*. New Delhi: Adroit, pp. 117–64.

Biggs, S.D., S.M. Gurung and D. Messerschmidt. 2005. 'An Exploratory Study of Gender, Social Inclusion and Empowerment through Development Groups and Group-Based Organisations in Nepal: Building on the Positive'. Report submitted to the Gender and Social Exclusion Assessment (GSEA) Study, National Planning Commission, World Bank and DFID, Kathmandu (Version 2, March 2005). (http://www.prgaprogram.org/IAWFTP/IA%20 WEB/resources.htm)

Cameron, M. 1998. *On the Edge of the Auspicious: Gender and Caste in Nepal.* Urbana/Chicago: University of Illinois Press.

Caplan, L. 1970. *Land and Social Change in East Nepal.* London: Routledge & Kegan Paul.

Clarke, G. 1997. 'Development (*Vikās*) in Nepal: Mana from Heaven', in S. Karmay and P. Sagant (eds), *Les Habitants du Toît du Monde: Hommage à Alexander Macdonald.* Nanterre: Société d'Ethnologie, pp. 583–608.

de Sales, A. 2003a. 'The Kham Magar Country: Between Ethnic Claims and Maoism', in D.N. Gellner (ed.), *Resistance and the State: Nepalese Experiences.* New Delhi: Social Science Press, pp. 326–57.

———. 2003b. 'Remarks on Revolutionary Songs and Iconography'. *European Bulletin of Himalayan Research,* 24. 5–24.

———. 2009. 'From Ancestral Conflicts to Local Empowerment: Two Narratives from a Nepalese Community'. *Dialectical Anthropology,* 33: 365–81.

Des Chene, M. 1998. 'Fate, Domestic Authority, and Women's Wills: Bhauju's Story', in D. Skinner, A. Pach III, and D. Holland (eds), *Selves in Time and Place: Identities, Experience and History in Nepal.* Lanham: Rowman and Littlefield, pp. 19–50.

Dhakal, S. 2006. *Politics Beyond the Political Sphere: Community-Based Organizations and the Local Democracy.* Paper presented at the 19th European Conference on Modern South Asian Studies, Leiden.

Escobar, A. 1995. *Encountering Development: The Making and Unmaking of the Third World.* Princeton, NJ: Princeton University Press.

Evans, R. 2008. 'The Two Faces of Empowerment in Conflict'. *Research in Comparative and International Education,* 3: 50–64. Retrieved from http://www.wwwords.co.uk/rss/abstract.asp?j=rcie&aid=3238 (accessed on 2 August 2006).

———. 2009. '"Innocent Children" or "Frustrated Youth"? The Impact of Political Conflict and Displacement on Bhutanese Refugee Concepts of Childhood and Youth'. *Studies in Nepali History and Society,* 14(1): 143–78.

Ferguson, J. 1994. *The Anti-Politics Machine: 'Development,' Depoliticization, and Bureaucratic Power in Lesotho.* Minneapolis/London: University of Minneapolis Press.

Fujikura, T. 2001. 'Discourses of Awareness: Notes for a Criticism of Development in Nepal'. *Studies in Nepali History and Society,* 6(2): 271–313.

———. 2007. 'The Bonded Agricultural Labourers' Freedom Movement in Western Nepal', in H. Ishii, D.N. Gellner and K. Nawa (eds), *Political and Social Transformations in North India and Nepal.* New Delhi: Manohar, pp. 319–59.

Gellner, D.N. 2001. 'From Group Rights to Individual Rights and Back: Nepalese Struggles with Culture and Equality', in J. Cowan, M. Dembour and R. Wilson (eds), *Culture and the Anthropology of Rights.* Cambridge: Cambridge University Press, pp. 177–200.

Gellner, D.N. 2004. 'Children's Voices from Kathmandu and Lalitpur, Nepal'. *Journal of Asian and African Studies*, 68: 1–47. Retrieved from http://www. aa.tufs.ac.jp/book/journal/journal68.pdf (accessed on 2 August 2006).

———. 2009. 'Introduction: How Civil are "Communal" and Ethno-National Movements?', in D.N. Gellner (ed.), *Ethnic Activism and Civil Society in South Asia*. New Delhi: SAGE Publications, pp. 1–24.

———. 2010. 'Introduction: Making Civil Society in South Asia', in D.N. Gellner (ed.), *Varieties of Activist Experience: Civil Society in South Asia*. New Delhi: SAGE Publications, pp. 1–14.

Gellner, D.N. and M.B. Karki. 2008. 'Democracy and Ethnic Organizations in Nepal', in D.N. Gellner and K. Hachhethu (eds), *Local Democracy in South Asia: Microprocesses of Democratization in Nepal and its Neighbours*. New Delhi: SAGE Publications, pp. 105–27.

Gellner, D.N., J. Pfaff-Czarnecka and J. Whelpton (eds). 1997. *Nationalism and Ethnicity in a Hindu Kingdom: The Politics of Culture in Contemporary Nepal*. Amsterdam: Harwood. 2nd edition [2008] by Vajra Books, Kathmandu, as *Nationalism and Ethnicity in Nepal*.

Gilmour, D.A. and R.J. Fisher. 1991. *Villagers, Forests and Foresters: The Philosophy, Process and Practice of Community Forestry in Nepal*. Kathmandu: Sahayogi.

Guneratne, A. 2002. *Many Tongues, One People: The Making of Tharu Identity in Nepal*. Ithaca, NY: Cornell University Press.

Gurung, H. 1998. *Nepal: Social Demography and Expressions*. Kathmandu: New Era.

Hachhethu, K. 2002. *Party Building in Nepal: Organization, Leadership and People, a Comparative Study of the Nepali Congress and the Communist Party of Nepal (Unified Marxist-Leninist)*. Kathmandu: Mandala Book Point.

———. 2008. 'Local Democracy and Political Parties in Nepal: A Case Study of Dhanusha District', in D.N. Gellner and K. Hachhethu (eds), *Local Democracy in South Asia: Microprocesses of Democratization in Nepal and its Neighbours*. New Delhi: SAGE Publications, pp. 45–70.

Hancock, G. 1989. *Lords of Poverty*. London: Papermac.

Harper, I. and C. Tarnowski. 2003. 'A Heterotopia of Resistance: Health, Community Forestry, and Challenges to State Centralization in Nepal', in D.N. Gellner (ed.), *Resistance and the State: Nepalese Experiences*. New Delhi: Social Science Press, pp. 33–82.

Hauser, H. and W. Singer. 1986. 'The Democratic Rite: Celebration and Participation in the Indian Elections'. *Asian Survey*, 26(9): 941–58.

Heaton Shrestha, C. 2002. 'NGOs as *Thekadar* or *Sevak*: Identity Crisis in Nepal's Non-governmental Sector'. *European Bulletin of Himalayan Research*, 22: 5–36.

———. 2006. '"They Can't Mix Like We Can": Bracketing Differences and the Professionalization of NGOs in Nepal', in D. Lewis and D. Mosse (eds), *Development Brokers and Translators: The Ethnography of Aid and Agencies*. Bloomfield, CT: Kumarian, pp. 195–216.

Henkel, H. and Stirrat, R. 2001. 'Participation as Spiritual Duty: Empowerment as Secular Subjection', in B. Cooke and U. Kothari (eds), *Participation: The New Tyranny?* London: Zed, pp. 168–84.

Hoftun, M., W. Raeper and J. Whelpton. 1999. *People, Politics and Ideology: Democracy and Social Change in Nepal.* Kathmandu: Mandala Book Point.

Holmberg, D., K. March and S. Tamang. 1999. 'Local Production/Local Knowledge: Forced Labour From Below'. *Studies in Nepali History and Society,* 4(1): 5–64.

Hutt, M. (ed.). 2004. *Himalayan 'People's War': Nepal's Maoist Rebellion.* London: Hurst & Co.

James, W. 2003. *The Ceremonial Animal: A New Portrait of Anthropology.* Oxford: Oxford University Press.

Joshi, B.L. and L.E. Rose. 1966. *Democratic Innovations in Nepal.* Berkeley, CA: University of California Press.

Justice, J. 1986. *Policies, Plans, and People: Foreign Aid and Health Development.* Berkeley, CA: University of California Press.

Karki, A. and D. Seddon. (eds). 2004. *The People's War in Nepal: Left Perspectives.* New Delhi: Adroit.

Keck, M.E. and K. Sikkink. 1998. *Activists Beyond Borders: Advocacy Networks in International Politics.* Ithaca, NY: Cornell University Press.

Knall, B. 1993. 'Economic Development, Participation, and Decentralization in Nepal'. *European Bulletin of Himalayan Research,* 5: 26–9.

Krauskopff, G. 2003. 'An Indigenous Minority in a Border Area: Tharu Ethnic Associations, NGOs, and the Nepalese State', in D.N. Gellner (ed.), *Resistance and the State: Nepalese Experiences.* New Delhi: Social Science Press, pp. 199–243.

Kuper, A. 1970. *Kalahari Village Politics: An African Democracy.* Cambridge: Cambridge University Press.

———. 1992. 'Postmodernism, Cambridge, and the Great Kalahari Debate'. *Social Anthropology,* 1(1A): 57–71.

Latour, B. 1993. *We Have Never Been Modern.* New York: Harvester Wheatsheaf.

Lawoti, M. 2005. *Towards a Democratic Nepal: Inclusive Political Institutions for a Multicultural Nepal.* New Delhi: SAGE Publications.

Lecomte-Tilouine, M. 2004. 'Regicide and Maoist Revolutionary Warfare in Nepal: Modern Incarnations of a Warrior Kingdom'. *Anthropology Today,* 20(1): 13–19.

———. 2006. '"Kill One, He Becomes One Hundred": Martyrdom as Generative Sacrifice in the Nepal's People's War'. *Social Analysis,* 50(1): 51–72.

———. 2009a. 'Terror in a Maoist Model Village, Mid Western Nepal'. *Dialectical Anthropology,* 33: 383–401.

———. 2009b. *Hindu Kingship, Ethnic Revival, and Maoist Rebellion in Nepal.* New Delhi: Oxford University Press.

Leve, L. 2007. '"Failed Development" and Rural Revolution in Nepal: Rethinking Subaltern Consciousness and Women's Empowerment'. *Anthropological Quarterly,* 80(1): 127–72.

Liechty, M. 2003. *Suitably Modern: Making Middle-Class Culture in a New Consumer Society*. Princeton/Oxford: Princeton University Press.

Macfarlane, A. 2001. 'Sliding Down Hill: Reflections on Thirty Years of Change in a Himalayan Village (new preface to Macfarlane 1983)'. *European Bulletin of Himalayan Research*, 20(1): 105–10.

Manandhar, P. and D. Seddon (eds). 2010. *In Hope and in Fear: Living Through the People's War in Nepal*. New Delhi: Adroit.

March, K. 2002. *"If Each Comes Half Way"*: *Meeting Tamang Women in Nepal*. Ithaca, NY: Cornell University Press.

Martinussen, J. 1995. *Democracy, Competition, and Choice: Emerging Local Self-Government in Nepal*. New Delhi: SAGE Publications.

Merton, R. 1957. *Social Theory and Social Structure*. Glencoe: The Free Press.

Michelutti, L. 2007. 'The Vernacularisation of Democracy: Popular Politics and Political Participation in North India'. *Journal of the Royal Anthropological Institute* (N.S.), 13: 639–56.

Mosse, D. 2005. 'Global Governance and the Ethnography of International Aid', in D. Mosse and D. Lewis (eds), *The Aid Effect: Giving and Governing in Global Development*. London: Pluto, pp. 1–36.

Neupane, Govinda. 2000. *Nepalko Jatiya Prasna: Samajik Banaut ra Sajhedariko Sambhavana*. Kathmandu: Centre for Development Studies.

Ogura, K. 2007. 'Maoists, People, and the State as seen from Rolpa and Rukum', in H. Ishii, D. Gellner and K. Nawa (eds), *Political and Social Transformations in North India and Nepal*. New Delhi: Manohar, pp. 435–75.

———. 2008. 'Maoist People's Governments, 2001–05: The Power in Wartime', in D.N. Gellner and K. Hachhethu (eds), *Local Democracy in South Asia: The Micropolitics of Democratization in Nepal and its Neighbours*. New Delhi: SAGE Publications, pp. 175–231.

Onesto, L. 2005. *Dispatches from the People's War in Nepal*. London: Pluto.

Paley, J. 2002. 'Towards an Anthropology of Democracy'. *Annual Review of Anthropology*, 31: 469–96.

Pandey, D.R. 1999. *Nepal's Failed Development: Reflections on the Mission and the Maladies*. Kathmandu: Nepal South Asia Centre.

Pettigrew, J. 2000. '"Gurkhas" in the Town: Migration, Language, and Healing'. *European Bulletin of Himalayan Research*, 19: 7–39.

Pettigrew, J. and S. Shneiderman. 2004. 'Ideology and Agency in Nepal's Maoist Movement', *Himal Southasian* (January: pp. 19–29).

Pfaff-Czarnecka, J. 1997. 'Vestiges and Visions: Cultural Change in the Process of Nation-Building in Nepal', in D.N. Gellner, J. Pfaff-Czarnecka and J. Whelpton (eds), *Nationalism and Ethnicity in a Hindu Kingdom: The Politics of Culture in Contemporary Nepal*. Amsterdam: Harwood Academic Publishers, pp. 419–70.

———. 2008. 'Distributional Coalitions in Nepal: An Essay on Democratization, Capture, and (Lack of) Confidence', in D.N. Gellner and K. Hachhethu (eds),

Local Democracy in South Asia: Microprocesses of Democratization in Nepal and its Neighbours. New Delhi: SAGE Publications, pp. 71–104.

Pigg, S.L. 1992. 'Inventing Social Categories through Space: Social Representations of Development in Nepal'. *Comparative Studies of Society and History*, 34: 491–593.

Pye-Smith, C. 1990. *Travels in Nepal: The Sequestered Kingdom.* London: Penguin.

Ragsdale, T.A. 1989. *Once a Hermit Kingdom: Ethnicity, Education and National Integration in Nepal.* New Delhi: Manohar.

Ramirez, P. 1997. 'Pour une anthropologie religieuse du maoïsme népalais'. *Archives des Sciences Sociales des Religions*, 99: 47–68.

———. 2000. *De la Disparition des Chefs: Une Anthropologie Politique Népalaise.* Paris: CNRS.

Shneiderman, S. 2010. 'Creating "Civilized" Communists: A Quarter of a Century of Politicization in Rural Nepal', in D.N. Gellner (ed.), *Varieties of Activist Experience: Civil Society in South Asia.* New Delhi: SAGE Publications, pp. 46–80.

Subba, T. 1992. *Ethnicity, State and Development: A Case Study of Gorkhaland Movement in Darjeeling.* New Delhi: Har-Anand/Vikas.

Tamang, S. 2003. 'Civilising Civil Society: Donors and Democratic Space in Nepal', *Himal Southasian* (July). Retrieved from www.himalmag.com (accessed on 2 August 2006).

Thapa, D. (ed.). 2003. *Understanding the Maoist Movement of Nepal.* KTM: Martin Chautari.

Thapa, D. and B. Sijapati. 2004. *Kingdom under Siege: Nepal's Maoist Insurgency, 1996 to 2004.* London: Zed Books.

Tilly, C. 2004. *Social Movements, 1768–2004.* Boulder & London: Paradigm.

Tuting, L. 1986. *Bikas Binas: Development or Destruction: The Change in Life and Environment in the Himalaya.* Munich: Geobuch.

Watkins, J. 1996. *Spirited Women: Gender, Religion and Cultural Identity in the Nepal Himalaya.* New York: Columbia University Press.

Whelpton, J. 1997. 'Political Identity in Nepal: State, Nation, and Community', in D.N. Gellner, J. Pfaff-Czarnecka and J. Whelpton (eds), *Nationalism and Ethnicity in a Hindu Kingdom: The Politics of Culture in Contemporary Nepal.* Amsterdam: Harwood Academic Publishers, pp. 39–78.

Whelpton, J. 2005. *A History of Nepal.* Cambridge: Cambridge University Press.

Yadama, G.N. and D. Messerschmidt. 2004. 'Civic Service in South Asia: A Case Study of Nepal'. *Nonprofit and Voluntary Sector Quarterly*, 33(4) (supplement): 98s–126s.

Yamamoto, Y. 2007. 'The Sukumbasi Transformation from Communitas to Community: The Birth and Death of "Proto-Charisma" among Squatters in Pokhara', in H. Ishii, D.N. Gellner and K. Nawa (eds), *Nepalis Inside and Outside Nepal: Social Dynamics in Northern South Asia* (Vol. 2). New Delhi: Manohar, pp. 115–58.

PART III
GOVERNANCE, CONFLICT AND DEVELOPMENT: EXPERIENCE AT THE GRASSROOTS

Chapter 6

Negotiating a Dual Governance System during the Conflict in Nepal

NATALIE HICKS

The Maoist rebellion in Nepal formally started in February 1996 and concluded with the signing of the Comprehensive Peace Agreement (CPA) on 21 November 2006. During the conflict, over 13,000 predominantly rural Nepali people lost their lives. All 75 districts that surround the Kathmandu Valley were subject to varying degrees of contestation between Maoist and government forces. By May 2002, the Maoists were considered to be in effective control of about 25 per cent of the country and have significant influence over the rest (Karki and Seddon, 2003: 43). From 2003 onwards, the dividends of control between the two contending powers were distributed between the government of Nepal, which largely retained control of the district headquarters, and the Maoists, who controlled many of the villages. Therefore, during the latter stages of the conflict, people in many of the districts throughout Nepal lived under two conflicting systems: Maoist People's Governments (*jan sarkar*) and His Majesty's Government of Nepal.[1] This dynamic is referred to in this chapter as a dual governance system.

This chapter will examine three questions related to the development of a dual governance system during the conflict in Nepal. First, what factors led to the establishment of two competing governance systems? Second, did the Maoists and villagers share the same vision for a radical agenda of change in Nepal? Finally, how did rural people living outside

[1] This chapter is written from the perspective of events prior to the changes wrought by the April Revolution in 2006 (*jan andolan II*).

the Kathmandu Valley negotiate this dual governance system in their daily lives? These three questions are examined by looking at historical and contextual factors that ignited and sustained the conflict in Nepal and also by using theoretical perspectives on rural revolution in Asia.

Initially, this chapter explores the factors that contributed to the rise of the Communist Party Nepal-Maoists (CPN-Maoists). Key attention is given to the dynamics of Maoist mobilization at a local level and the contrasting inability of successive national governments to connect purposefully with the political and social realties outside Kathmandu. It is proposed that the Maoists' skill in adapting their ideological message at a grassroots level constituted what Race (1973) has referred to as a 'revolution within a revolution', or what Scott (1977) describes as the contrast between 'little tradition' and 'great tradition'. Writing on the communist revolution in Vietnam, Scott (1977: 1–10) suggests that at a little tradition level, peasant aspirations and motivations for protest might be quite different from the communist leadership, or great tradition. Race (1973) sought to provide an empirical basis for this theory through his research on the conflict in the Mekong Delta (Vietnam) between the Communists and the Government of the Republic of Vietnam, where he found that most people supported the revolution for personal and immediate reasons rather than because of grand ideological goals. The context for Maoist recruitment in the rural areas of Nepal was ripe; and this chapter proposes that Maoist mobilizers were successful because of their ability to adapt to the local context, while the top leadership retained a flexible approach to Maoist ideology and strategy.

After the formation of the People's Liberation Army (PLA) in September 2001 and the declaration of a state of emergency in November 2001, the intensity of the conflict increased. It was at this time that ordinary people became increasingly trapped between the national security forces and Maoist combatants. The voices of Dalits in Dang District and porters in Sankhuwasabha District, whose livelihoods and lives were imperilled as a result of these opposing combatant forces, are well captured in first-hand accounts (Biswokarma, 2004; Rai, 2004). Literature on the Maoist conflict in Nepal has tended to highlight the lack of agency that many Nepalis had when trapped between two armies and two contending political forces. Hutt (2004: 19) describes this scenario as a zero sum game for

Nepali villagers: 'It really was a case of two regimes, in which villagers had to choose between support, acquiescence, opposition or flight'.

This chapter suggests a greater agency for people than the majority of the literature on the conflict in Nepal has allowed for thus far; it explores how people were able to negotiate their daily lives through making logical choices to work and cooperate with the two regimes simultaneously. Through a series of three case studies, it is suggested that on some occasions, rural people found modes to work both systems, in particular the Maoist government, to their minimum disadvantage. They were able to do this through what Scott (1976, 1986) describes as acts of 'everyday politics' such as corporate bargaining and the enactment of subtle compacts with local cadres. Scott explored the individual and corporate agency of peasants caught in revolution and attempted to dispel hegemonic notions of peasants as 'history's losers', subject only to the manipulation of political operators (Scott, 1986). He observed, 'However partial or imperfect their [the peasants'] understanding of the situation, they are gifted with intentions and values and purposefulness that condition their acts' (Scott, 1986: 38). This perspective is also found in some literature on Nepal exploring the anthropology of political violence. Judith Pettigrew observed in her 2002 research in Nepal that 'fear remains a way of life but agency provides a possibility of creative resistance' (Pettigrew, 2004: 283). Pettigrew identified three key survival strategies adopted by villagers to resist the vicissitudes of armed violence from both sides: 'tracking,' 'silence' and appealing to cultural norms (Pettigrew, 2004: 272, 273, 283). However, while Pettigrew's research focuses almost exclusively on strategies employed to cope with the Maoists, this research provides illustrations of how communities were able to broker agreements between the Maoists and state officials to facilitate a best case outcome, such as enhancing local security. This chapter is most keenly focused on the events taking place at the grassroots level during the conflict in Nepal. This focus derives, in part, from Joel Migdal's analysis on social transformation in third world countries (Migdal, 2001). Migdal states, 'For those interested in how third world societies are ruled and the influence of politics on social change, the local level often holds the richest and most instructive hints' (2001: 88). The attention to social change at the grassroots level also builds on the previous work of this author on revolution and transformation in rural

China and Vietnam. The revolutionary lens that was applied to conflict in East and Southeast Asia is transposed to better answer the three research questions in this chapter.

METHODOLOGY

This account of the development and realities of dual governance, like the anthropological study of the conflict in Dolakha District by Shneiderman and Turin, was partially 'accidental' (Shneiderman and Turin, 2004: 84). The research was undertaken in 2005–06 when the author was the director of Friends for Peace (FFP), a Nepali conflict research institute based in Kathmandu. In 2005, it was the first job of the author to review recent field data collected by the research institute from 14 districts in Nepal. The data were based on extensive interviews with community members on their perception of the impact of conflict at a grassroots level.[2] Through regular interaction with the international and political elite in Kathmandu, it was apparent that perspectives on these issues were often very different between Kathmandu and the villages covered during that research. The apparent disconnect between Kathmandu and the rest of Nepal inspired me to commission two further community-based research studies at FFP. These research publications examined peace agendas and human security from grassroots perspectives and aimed to bridge the gap of understanding between the centre and periphery in Nepal (Bharadwaj et al., 2007a, 2007b). It is from this research conducted by the author and FFP staff that the case studies and observations of this chapter are taken.

This methodology was mostly qualitative in nature, and it applied research tools used in development research and appraisal—such as focus groups, formal interviews and informal interviews—in order to capture perspectives on the most significant change stories. The methodology had some advantages, such as the benefit of a large team of well-trained researchers covering all the development regions in Nepal. The major drawback was that the research design was not specific to exploring dual governance in Nepal. Instead, data pertaining to this specific area were collected in a largely ad hoc fashion. The theme of this research was driven

[2] This research was never published.

by conversations that took place in the field in 2005–06, and which inspired the author to explore the topic later in this chapter.

BACKGROUND TO THE CONFLICT IN NEPAL

It is not the objective of this chapter to delve critically into the historical antecedents of the conflict in Nepal, but rather to give a brief contextual overview. The prime focus of this chapter is the theoretical and practical modalities of how rural people find space to live within a conflict situation that forces many communities to live between two contesting local government systems. The analysis and data explicate the conflict context prior to the People's Revolution of April 2006, which generated dramatic changes in the political landscape throughout Nepal. While this chapter only focuses on Nepal, there will also be comparative value for other countries in conflict in Asia, who face similar dilemmas with competing rural administrations in certain regions of their countries.

In 1990 a people's movement (*jan andolan I*) swept through Nepal, fuelled by grievances against the governing Panchayat system and a worsening economic situation caused by India's closure of border points in the southern Terai region. By November 1990, the reigning monarch, King Birendra, agreed to institute multiparty democracy and a constitutional role for the monarchy. This was a critical period for the left wing parties in Nepal. In November 1990, the Communist Party of Nepal-Unity Centre was formed and Prachanda was appointed as the General Secretary. The Party then passed a resolution to begin 'a people's war to bring about new democratic revolution in Nepal' (Thapa, 2004: 34). By 1995, the Unity Centre party had abdicated any place in the democratic system in Nepal, renamed itself the CPN-Maoists and in September made the following declaration.

> [...] formulation of the plan for initiation of the process that will unfold as protracted people's war based on the strategy of encircling the city from the countryside according to the specificities of our country, the Party once again reiterates its eternal commitment to the theory of people's war developed by Mao as the universal and invincible Maoist theory of war.
> (Thapa, 2004: 36–7)

The people's war began on 13 February 1996. Nepal (2003: 406) observed that 'the violent movement launched by the Maoists cannot be separated from its historical context and background'. Indeed, the culture of armed violence, coupled with a vision for socio-economic transformation was not new to Nepal. Armed insurrections led by communist groups such as the All Nepal Revolutionary Coordination Committee were launched in eastern Nepal in the early 1970s. Successive Kathmandu-centric state regimes had served to dislocate the national leadership from the rest of Nepal, and this lack of decentralization meant that the government had not been effective at recognizing or addressing societal needs and grievances. This situation in turn created space for insurgent groups outside of the capital to try to address local aspirations for change. The CPN-Maoists were arguably the most successful group to opportunistically exploit what Hutt (2004: 17) has described as the ruling elite's lack of 'nerve endings in the districts'.

The Maoists chose to launch their people's war from the isolated mid-western districts of Rolpa and Rukum. The terrain of these districts was conductive to fighting a guerrilla-style war. Equally significant was what Ramirez (2004: 230) described as the convergence of 'autonomous political networks and the presence of fairly numerous ethnic minorities'. This region had an established history of rejecting Kathmandu rule and was, therefore, fertile for local Maoist mobilizers. Furthermore, the frustrations at social and political isolation experienced by many of the ethnic minority groups provided the Maoists with a ready-made energy and will to change the status quo.

The will to enact social transformation existed throughout the 75 districts of Nepal. There were longstanding grievances, which provided a clear context for the armed conflict. These included discrimination on the grounds of gender, caste and ethnicity; poverty and unequal development; poor governance and dissatisfaction with exploitative agreements with India. These multifarious and diverse grievances required skilful political entrepreneurs to harness the sentiments into a cohesive revolution. This chapter asserts that it was the Maoists' skill in adapting, at a grassroots level, a theoretical vision of communist transformation into more immediate and palatable localized visions of change that was the key to their support in Nepal. Eck (2007) highlighted locally and culturally appropriate mass meetings and cultural shows which generated a sense of empowerment for the populace. Even Maoist detractors, such as Kattel (2003: 60) acknowledge:

> If the government of the day is now far away from the people and has completely failed to maintain any positive relations with the mass of the rural people, the people will obviously be closer to the Maoists who are around them, for better or for worse, and familiar with their needs and demands.

The chronology of the people's war was marked by a transition from low-intensity to high-intensity conflict by 2002. The Maoist leadership plotted their revolution through three defined stages. The first of these was 'strategic defence', which lasted from February 1996 until 2001 and involved six defined substages. It was launched in Rukum, Rolpa, Jajarkot, Salyan, Gorkha and Sindhuli Districts. The objective of this stage of revolution was to build a core of support and establish temporary base areas in the mid-western and centre-east of Nepal (Karki and Seddon, 2003: 22). The end of this stage was heralded by a new strategy known as the 'Prachanda Path' which focused efforts on urban insurrection and redoubled efforts on building support in the rural areas.

The second phase, which lasted from 2001 to 2004, was known as 'strategic balance'. In this phase alternative governments-in-waiting were built. By 2002, the elected governments at the village level (Village Development Committees, or VDCs) in many areas of the country had been replaced by Maoist structures. Thus, in effect, there was no properly elected government system. The government in Kathmandu reacted to this situation with heavy-handed military attacks on Maoist positions such as the infamous Operation Romeo, which did not significantly dent the Maoists' hold in the villages but did serve to alienate ordinary people who were killed and injured in the assaults. As with many guerrilla insurgencies around the world, when cadres 'move like fish through water', it is impossible to identify insurgents and, thus, ordinary civilians bear the brunt of violence which heightens discontent and fuels further conflict. Most official government VDC chairmen, state officials and the armed forces retreated to the district headquarters which stood like island fortresses in a sea of Maoist controlled villages.

The third and final phase was launched in 2004 and was referred to as the 'strategic offensive' stage. In this phase, the Maoists had moved into the final stage of the armed campaign to capture state power. However, in October 2005 political and military observers were doubtful as to whether the Maoists had the strength to defeat the Royal Nepal Army and, thus, capture state power (International Crisis Group, 2005: 25–26). At this point, the Maoists again revealed their skill for strategic flexibility and sought a political alliance with the Seven Party Alliance. In concert with these political partners, the CPN-Maoists helped to inspire a second people's revolution, which forced the King to relinquish power and initiated a formal process to end the conflict with the CPA in November 2006.

THE RAISON D'ÊTRE OF THE MAOISTS

It is clear that in 1995 and 1996 there were serious ideological debates and intra-Party schisms regarding the correct ideological path of the Maoist movement. There were two important outcomes from these debates. The first of these was a rejection of the scientific determinism of Marxist–Leninism that predicted revolution through a progression of social changes driven by capitalist exploitation. Instead, Prachanda's clique favoured change through direct military means. The second outcome was the social change agenda envisaged by the Maoists, referred to as 'ascending three mountains to achieve liberation'. This meant the 'over-throw of the bureaucratic-capitalist class and the state system, and an end to feudalism and imperialism'.

The Maoist agenda for change was most clearly and simply articulated in the '40-Point Demand' that was submitted to the Prime Minister, Sher Bahadur Deuba, by Baburam Bhatteri on 4 February 1996.[3] Although these demands were to some degree aspirational, they clearly set out the Maoist position in simple terms. These demands were categorized into three themes relating to nationalism, the public and its well-being, and people's living conditions. Some of the notable demands are as follows:

 I. *Demands related to nationalism:*
     Demand 1.   Regarding the 1950 Treaty between India and Nepal, all unequal stipulations and agreements should be removed.

---

[3] http://www.humanrights.de/doc_en/archiv/n/nepal/politics/130299_40demands_Maoist.htm (accessed on 30 August 2012).

Demand 2.   His Majesty's Government should admit that the anti-nationalist Tanakpur agreement was wrong, and the Mahakali Treaty, incorporating the same, should be nullified

Demand 9.   Regarding non-governmental organizations (NGOs) and international non-governmental organizations (INGOs): Bribing by imperialists and expansionists in the name of NGOs and INGOs should be stopped.

II. *Demands related to the public and its well-being:*

Demand 10.   A new Constitution has to be drafted by the people's elected representatives.

Demand 11.   All the special rights and privileges of the King and his family should be ended.

Demand 12.   Army, police and administration should be under the people's control.

Demand 13.   The Security Act and all other repressive acts should be abolished.

Demand 19.   Girls should be given equal property rights to those of their brothers.

Demand 20.   All kinds of exploitation and prejudice based on caste should be ended. In areas having a majority of one ethnic group, that group should have autonomy over that area.

Demand 21.   The status of Dalits as untouchables should be ended and the system of untouchability should be ended once and for all.

Demand 22.   All languages should be given equal status. Up until the middle-high-school level arrangements should be made for education to be given in the children's mother tongue.

Demand 25.   In both the Terai and hilly regions there is prejudice and misunderstanding in backward areas. This should be ended and the backward areas should be assisted. Good relations should be established between the villages and the city.

Demand 26.   Decentralization in real terms should be applied to local areas which should have local rights, autonomy and control over their own resources.

III. *Demands related to the people's living:*

Demand 27.   Those who cultivate the land should own it. (The tiller should have right to the soil he/she tills.) The land of rich landlords should be confiscated and distributed to the homeless and others who have no land.

Demand 32.   Poor farmers should be completely freed from debt. Loans from the Agricultural Development Bank by poor farmers should be completely written off. Small industries should be given loans.

Demand 35.   All should be given free and scientific medical services and education. Education for profit should be completely stopped.

Demand 39.   Corruption, black marketing, smuggling, bribing, the taking of commissions, etc., should all be stopped.

In regard to the demands for nationalism, the treaties with India were not largely known to the rural populace when they were asked about this issue during the author's fieldwork in Solukhumbu and Morang Districts in 2005–06. However, the Maoist nationalist agenda was transposed at a local level to have resonance with many Nepalis. Shneiderman (2003: 44) observed that

> the emphasis is on an alternative nationalism, one that recognizes the value of indigenous participation and local sacrifice. By proposing a counter-hegemonic national vision where indigenous needs and local sacrifices are acknowledged, the Maoists cleverly deployed the symbol of the Nepali nation to take advantage of existing local sentiments.

The Maoist attitudes towards INGOs and NGOs were mixed, and at times contradictory. This author found Maoist cadres in all the districts where this research was conducted to be cooperative to the research agenda of FFP. The Maoists tacitly accepted that international aid projects could deliver much needed public services in rural areas that the Maoists simply could not provide to people. On the other hand, Shneiderman and Turin (2004: 82) recount that in Dolakha District, aid workers were asked to leave, 'some more forcefully than others'. The fact remains that taxation from INGOs and NGOs was a source of income to feed the Maoist machine.[4]

---

[4] It should be noted that despite the fact that Basic Operating Guidelines stated that no levies of this nature should be paid by aid organization in Nepal, a number of INGOs did pay these taxes to continue their project work in parts of Nepal.

Demands 10–13 related to the public and its well-being. These demands were subject to dialogue with the ruling elite at various stages of the conflict. In the case of the demands relating to the abolition of the monarchy, at times the Maoist position on this issue appeared to be flexible. When the fieldwork for this chapter was conducted in the latter stages of the conflict, a majority of respondents—and importantly those from diverse ethnic groups—were not in favour of a republic. Despite the evident autocracy of King Gyanendra in Kathmandu, in remote districts such as Solukhumbu, some people felt that the King was an important symbol of national unity for Nepal and forged an identity that few were willing to sacrifice.

Demands 19, 21, 22, 25 and 26 addressed the historical exclusion and discrimination that had fuelled years of latent discontent with the Nepal politic. Gender discrimination was an important and appealing part of the Maoist agenda for change. The commitment to equality and improved well-being for women was evident in the Maoist machine (including the front organizations, political wing and military wing). It was estimated that women constituted 30–40 per cent of the guerrilla force (International Crisis Groups, 2005: 16). In many districts visited by the FFP fieldwork teams, women reported that the Maoist ban on alcohol in some areas had a positive impact on reducing domestic violence. The Maoists served to raise expectations for gender equality in a way that no movement had done before. FFP researchers conducting a study into community security mechanisms in Makwanpur District in 2006 were reminded just how far gender equality expectations had risen. A group of female ex-combatants informed the team that should gender equality not be part of the New Nepal, they would 'go back to the jungle and fight'.

The demand to end the system of untouchability was a rallying call to many Dalits throughout Nepal, regardless of their geographic location. However, the end to this form of discrimination was not a new initiative to people in Nepal. National and international development organizations had been attempting to empower this group in communities for a number of years. Despite these efforts, Dalits still remained excluded socially, politically and economically at the start of the twenty-first century. Community empowerment is a delicate and iterative social change initiative. As a Dalit community near Saleri in Solukhumbu District pointed out to the author in December 2005, they were not ready yet to be 'forced' to share wells with Brahmin and Chettri families.

The Maoists' agenda for better inclusion along ethnic and geographic lines struck a chord with many of Nepal's ethnic minority groups. Some of these groups, such as the Kirats in northeastern Nepal, had been vocally demanding autonomy and the right to self-determination long before the initiation of the people's war (Shrestha, 2004: 19). At a grassroots level, Ramirez (2004: 230) has observed how effective festering ethnic tensions can be to mobilizing people to actively join an armed uprising. Cynically, Maoist attempts to forge alliances with well-established anti-establishment groups could be viewed as a traditional communist tactic predicated upon the Dimitrov Line, whereby strategic alliances are formed as a means to swallow any potentially competing political groups.[5] The call for the creation of autonomous ethnic regions is a radical vision for a new Nepal that continues to reverberate in the post-conflict context, as an International Crisis Group report of 2005 prophetically suggested, 'Regardless of the success or failure of their own movement, they have changed the environment in which future governments will have to work' (Ramirez, 2004: 30).

In common with communist and Maoist revolutions elsewhere in Asia, the question of 'land to the tiller' was a central platform of the people's war in Nepal. Although the issue of land reform was not new in Nepal, observers such as Kattel (2003: 53) observed that the Maoists were the only party to back up this slogan with actions. As the momentum of the conflict spread throughout the districts in Nepal, so did the Maoists' confiscation of land from wealthy landlords. This had a significant impact on poorer Nepalis in rural areas. Although these acts were not often seen firsthand, stories of these activities were spread through grassroots mobilizers and depicted in Maoist cultural shows. A folk culture developed around the Maoist redistribution of both land and financial assets that conceived the Maoist cadres as Robin Hood type figures. As such, the impact of land confiscation and land distribution became a large part of rural consciousness.

The Maoist attitude to government schools was highly interventionist. Schools were a key forum for Maoist recruitment and indoctrination. As Bohara's research (2004) highlighted, the Maoists kidnapped entire classes

---

[5] The Dimitrov Line is named after Georgi Dimitrov who pioneered the tactic of 'popular front movements' at the 1935 Seventh Congress of the Comintern.

of children, conducted re-education classes at school and insisted that some school syllabuses include Maoist ideology. The personal histories collected by Bohara indicate that hundreds of children escaped to India as a strategy to avoid forced recruitment by the Maoists (Bohara, 2004: 51–57). For the most part, villagers did not approve of Maoist interference in government schools. FFP community-based research in 2005 in Jhapa, Solukhumbu, Nawalparasi, Kailali and Parbat Districts found that all respondents in these districts felt that the conflict had a negative impact on education (Bharadwaj et al., 2007a).[6] The issue of education was, therefore an arena in which local people and Maoist cadres were at odds. It was also an area in which people did negotiate with the Maoists to try to bargain for the continuance of basic education services in their communities. This issue is explored in more detail in a case study, 'Negotiating for education in Dhankuta District', later in this chapter.

The raison d'être of the Maoists was grounded in communist ideology but, most significantly, it needs to be understood in the context of localized realities. To a large extent, the philosophy was reactive to a longstanding prevailing status quo that marginalized many social and ethnic groups. The top leadership were ideologues but they were also pragmatists in recognizing that in order to be successful 'political entrepreneurs' and create a mass movement, they must directly address the grievances of their rural constituencies. However, the need for Maoists to recruit, sustain and grow also put their local agenda for change at odds with local people, most clearly in the case of education.

THE RAISON D'ÊTRE OF THE GOVERNMENT OF NEPAL

The government of Nepal experienced a number of transitions after the 1950s. Until the *jan andolan* of 1990, Nepal was governed by a royalist system in which political parties were illegal and the monarch stood at the apex of government. After 1990, political parties were legalized and

---

[6] Respondents were asked how they felt the conflict had affected given aspects of their everyday lives on the following issues: caste and gender discrimination, access to health services, access to education, family relationships and the culture of hospitality.

were able to participate in the government at all levels of the state administration based on electoral processes. From 1990 to 2005, the successive
national governments failed to pursue an agenda that would improve
rural lives and end entrenched discriminatory practises. From a grassroots
perspective, their self-interest stood in stark contrast to the radical transformative agenda of the Maoists. Policies that were inaugurated by the
national government tended to be a slow reaction to Maoist policies and
mired in political infighting. One such example was the announcement of
a new land reform policy by the Nepali Congress government in August
2001. A failure to reach political accord over key definitions relating to
the division of holdings left this policy floundering in the political mire
(Kattel, 2003: 53).

On 1 February 2005, King Gyanendra enacted a royal coup, disband-
ing the parliament and seizing autocratic powers. Governing positions in
the national government and in the District Development Committees
(DDCs) were essentially positions of royal patronage. If we may talk of a
raison d'être of the royal governing system at that stage, it was primarily
to defeat the Maoist insurgency and sustain royal autocracy. This is not to
say that lip service was not paid to the reinstating of free and fair electoral
practises or recognizing the importance of local service delivery. However,
the practicalities of the conflict meant that the government simply didn't
have the capabilities, or indeed the genuine will, to address these objectives.

THE MAOIST PEOPLE'S GOVERNMENTS

For the Maoists, institutionalizing an effective grassroots administration
in the rural areas was the key to the success or failure of the revolutionary campaign in Nepal. In accordance with the second 'strategic balance'
phase of the conflict, the Maoists needed to develop people's governments (*jan sarkar*) in order to effectively administer controlled areas and
prepare a government-in-waiting for when the prevailing regime was
overthrown. Mao Zedong's revolutionary prescriptions, coupled with
the geographic realities of the territory captured by the Maoists, meant
that they approached the building of their people's government from the
lowest administrative level first. Shneiderman and Turin (2004) observed

that by 2001 Dolakha District had a fledgling Maoist government. They recounted villagers' perspectives on this:

> The villagers now know what the democracy movement must have felt like, since we are seeing and living another such movement in our villages and inside our homes. There is a Nepali proverb: *'gaun nabanikana desh banna sakdaina'* (without building the village, the country cannot be built). All politicians make use of this saying, but none have acted upon it. In contrast, the Maoists have worked according to this rule. (Shneiderman and Turin, 2004: 88)

The process of building people's governments was quite organic and reflected a degree of autonomy granted to lower levels of the Party to initiate this process (International Crisis Group, 2005: 14). Common to all the people's governments were local tax collection, the establishment of people's courts, and the initiation of land reform and collectivization. The mass meetings and presence of Maoist cadres in the villages lent a strong local flavour to the *jan sarkars* which was notably lacking in the administration of the VDCs by national government officials.

Local dispute resolution was an integral element of the Maoist governing system. People's courts were established to administer swift justice, in contrast to the lengthy and corrupt processes of state-administered justice. In a community research programme conducted in 20 districts in 2004 and 2005, approximately 90 per cent of community respondents in the villages said that they used and trusted the Maoist courts to resolve any legal disputes.[7] The main reason for this was the speed at which justice was administered in comparison to the tardy and unreliable government legal system. Maoist provision of justice was a logical extension of their social change agenda. Cases relating to social ills such as domestic violence and inappropriate sexual relations were frequently put before the courts. Critics of these courts say that Maoist justice was not meticulous and intruded into areas, which had nothing to do with the law, such as sexual relations between adults and other family matters.[8]

---

[7] This research was not published by FFP.

[8] Reported at http://news.bbc.co.uk/2/hi/south_asia/6048272.stm, accessed on 30 August 2012.

One impact of the people's courts has been to diminish the role of traditional forms of dispute resolution across Nepal. For example, in research conducted by this author in 2005, members from the Tharu community in Kailali explained that prior to the conflict, disputes had been resolved by the Bhalmansa, a respected member of the community who would administer a resolution to local disputes. One community respondent commented that 'the Bhalmansa used to solve any problems but now the people from the jungle do it' (Bharadwaj et al., 2007b: 20). This situation was mirrored in Solukhumbu District where the traditional village courts (*pancha bhela* and *kachahari*) had been replaced by Maoist judicial mechanisms (Bharadwaj et al., 2007b: 21). It is a curious disjuncture of Maoist strategy that they should render certain elements of ethnic culture defunct while simultaneously promoting indigenous rights to linguistic and cultural freedom.

THE FUNCTIONS OF THE ROYAL GOVERNMENT OF NEPAL

By the start of the twenty-first century, the Royal Government of Nepal had very minimal control over the VDCs. The provision of governance in terms of justice, public security forces, public services and the state bureaucracy was centred in the district capital towns. The DDC, usually appointed on royal patronage (after 1 February 2005), was seldom native to the district and their loyalty belonged to their national masters in Kathmandu rather than to the local constituency. This was not a favourable position from which to provide good governance to people.

The Royal Government in the district headquarters had the advantage of having, relative to the Maoists, more resources at its disposal in terms of public service provision and bureaucratic infrastructure. This situation placed people living outside of the district centre in a very difficult position, because to gain access to these services meant leaving Maoist-controlled areas and entering into government-controlled areas, which generated great mistrust from the Maoists against any individual trying to negotiate the dual governance system to survive. One community member in Solukhmbu recounted to the author the great difficulties that he had faced in getting a passport to enable him to work in Qatar. Since passports were then issued by the DDC he had to walk for several days through areas contested by the PLA and Royal Nepal Army. He risked not only being caught in the crossfire, but also the consequences of mutual suspicions from both sides. Considering the fact that every year, thousands of Nepalis leave their villages to work overseas for economic and conflict-related reasons, it is possible to imagine just how many people faced this dilemma. Before we delve deeper into how ordinary Nepalis have managed to negotiate this system, it is necessary to shed some further light on the question of whether the Maoist insurgency in Nepal constitutes a 'revolution within a revolution'.

REVOLUTION WITHIN A REVOLUTION

As mentioned earlier in this chapter, a number of the senior leaders of the CPM-Maoists that led the people's war in Nepal were well-educated intellectuals. The complex internal ideological debates that took place during the mid and latter parts of the 1990s indicated that Marxist–Leninist–Maoist doctrines were not simply ideological hatstands to build and justify a military campaign, but were central to the functionality of the senior leadership. Ideological indoctrination campaigns, such as those described by Eck (2007), were the vehicle to carry these philosophies to the wider population. Indoctrination was most extremely employed in regard to students at government schools. For example, in 2004 in Achham District alone, 700 students were abducted by the Maoists and compelled to attend Maoist programmes (Bohara, 2004: 52).

The central question is whether the base support of the Maoist movement derived from a commitment to ideology or more personal and localized concerns. Research conducted by this author with FFP in 2005–06 indicated the latter was the case. Overwhelmingly, people in rural communities throughout Nepal stated that what was most important to them was to have enough food to feed their family, to send their children to school and to live a life free from fear and extortion. Even interviews with lower level Maoist cadres suggest that their support for the movement stems more from immediate and self-interested goals, such as a woman having the right to choose her own husband. The CPN-Maoists are pragmatic and recognize that their ideological modus vivendi must be flexible enough to match the aspirations of a diverse population. As Shneiderman and Turin (2004: 93) observed, 'It may be useful to differentiate between the theoretical ideology advanced by the Maoist leadership at a national level, and the practical ideology employed at the village level.'

Despite the flexibility of the Maoist leadership, there was a clear dislocation between the ideologues who lead the Maoist movement and ordinary people who supported the Maoists at a grassroots level, willingly or tacitly, because of their more personal and immediate needs. This constitutes a revolution within a revolution, where the aspirations of the masses are not necessarily congruent with the guiding principles of the Maoist doctrine.

This chapter was initially written before the end of the conflict in Nepal. It was hypothesized by the author at that time that, owing to a distance between the 'great tradition' (Maoist leadership) and 'little tradition' (the groundswell of supporters in rural areas), it was possible that in the event that the Maoists controlled the national government, it could evolve into a form of 'quasi-democratic state'. A theory of this kind was developed and tested by Brantly Womack during the 1980s, with a focus on post-revolutionary political contexts of China and Vietnam. Womack believed that the rationale of the communist cadres changed dramatically after victory. During the revolution, the communist leadership was attentive to the preferences of the masses. After victory, however, the incentive for mass-regarding politics was lost and the dogmatic ideological stance of the Party dominated (Womack, 1987). Although the Nepali Maoists did not achieve the total victory of a people's war, they did enter multiparty politics and led a national coalition government from August 2008 to May 2009. During this time, the Maoist leadership was noticeably quiet and passive on key elements of its reform agenda, such as 'land to the tiller' and renegotiating the treaties with India. The logic of enticement demonstrated by the Maoists during the conflict had been replaced; their priorities were now negotiating the multiparty system and holding on to the seat of power.

EVERYDAY POLITICS AND NEGOTIATING A DUAL GOVERNANCE SYSTEM

Coercion, fear and violence became a part of everyday life for many rural people, as Pettigrew (2004) has highlighted in her research into the 'culture of terror' in Nepal's villages. The dual governance system, alongside open combat between two opposing military forces, made it increasingly difficult for people to access basic services like education and also acquire official documentation such as passports. However, sometimes through small everyday acts people were able to work both government systems to their minimum disadvantage. On a basic level, this may be thought of as employing coping strategies. Pettigrew (2004) observed three key coping strategies for villagers in 'Maurigaun' village.[9] First, silence was widely used when interacting with both sides. Pettigrew cites a female village respondent who commented that 'nowadays you cannot be sure of whom you are talking to and so you must know when to be silent' (Pettigrew, 2004: 273).

The second strategy was 'tracking' of Maoist cadres by the village as a whole as a way to enhance community security and confidence. Pettigrew (2004: 282) recounts:

> When Maoists arrived in the village during one of my visits, under the guise of making a visit to a shop a neighbour and her young son did a reconnaissance to estimate the numbers and possible destinations of the insurgents so that she and her neighbours could be prepared. Another woman went on a supposed errand to a different part of the village to acquire information about the movements of the insurgents there. These women could not prevent the visits to their homes but by anticipating them, they acquired a measure of control over their immediate destiny.

The third coping mechanism that Pettigrew describes relates to villagers exploiting cultural norms to extract small compromises from the Maoists. She explains that 'by appealing to cultural boundaries of hierarchy and indebtedness [of a guest in the home], villagers can symbolically 'dis-arm' their youthful invaders' (Pettigrew, 2004: 283).

This chapter proposes that the ways in which people negotiated the dual governance system and opposing military forces during the conflict in Nepal were more sophisticated than reactive coping measures. While Pettigrew's research focuses almost exclusively on strategies employed to cope with the Maoists, this research provides illustration of how communities were able to broker agreements between the Maoists and state officials

---

[9] Maurigaun village was a pseudonym employed by Pettigrew (2005: 261).

to facilitate a best case outcome, such as enhancing local security. The three case studies, taken from the author's own research and research conducted by staff at FFP, will help to illustrate the power that local people can gain from collective negotiation and from the making of subtle compacts with both local Maoist cadres and the opposing state regime.

Negotiating for Education in Dhankuta District[10]

This case study illustrates how parents in Siduwa village were able to facilitate an agreement with the Maoists to ensure that the government high school was able to remain open and operate on state rather than Maoist guidelines.

Sagarmatha English Medium High School is situated in Siduwa village in Dhankuta District (eastern Nepal). Despite providing reasonably good quality education to 400 local students, the Maoists decided that the founder of the school was operating the facility for personal financial gain and they decided to close down the school and confiscate the entire property in cash and kind. The local parents agreed that they could not tolerate the hampering of their children's education, so after one month they formed an informal lobbying group and requested that the Maoists open the school.

The parents decided that they would ask for a member of the Federation of Nepalese Journalists, Ramesh Adhikari, to facilitate the negotiation process. The Maoists bargained that they would allow the school to resume only if it followed the Maoist calendar and the Maoist education policy. Thus, began a process of discreet talks between the local parents and Maoist cadres facilitated by Mr Adhikari. After long deliberations, arguments and compromise on both sides, the Maoists decided to let the school reopen on the condition that the monthly fees were significantly reduced. It was agreed that the school would be operated as per the government regulations and not those of the Maoists. After this agreement, the Maoists also agreed to return the property that they had confiscated. The successful resolution of this local problem illustrates the sophisticated

---

[10] This community research was conducted by FFP in 2004 and 2005. The research was conducted with the objective of understanding community peace agendas in the districts outside the Kathmandu Valley.

level of collective action that local communities are able to take in difficult circumstances.

Brokering an Agreement for Agricultural Services in Morang District

This case study provides an insight into how people have been able to negotiate between both Maoist and state district authorities to access the services they need to continue with their agricultural livelihoods.

Most rural people in Nepal rely on agriculture to sustain their livelihoods, but in Maoist-controlled areas there is very little technical support in terms of inputs and agricultural extension facilities. At the same time, the Maoists have refused to allow the government's agricultural support services and personnel into Maoist villages to help people. This impasse has served to further retard the economic well-being of many farmers throughout Nepal. However, in Morang District the local farmers were able to broker an agreement between the Maoists and the District Agriculture Development Office to allow government agricultural extension officers to support farmers in Maoist-controlled villages.

At the District Agriculture Development Office in Morang, agricultural officers introduced a successful System of Rice Intensification (SRI) and publicized this programme on the radio and in newsletters. This led many farmers to start demanding training in SRI methods in their localities. However, the Maoists refused to allow government vehicles on the roads to their villages (outside the district headquarters), which greatly curtailed movement for SRI training. The farmers recognized the fact that this problem was denying them vital services and because they wanted to learn SRI methods (at any cost), they contacted the local Maoist leaders and requested that technicians' mobility not be interfered with. The farmers were able to collectively convince the Maoists of the importance of receiving SRI support to improve their livelihoods and a compromise was brokered amongst the government, local farmers and the Maoists. The Maoists agreed to allow motorcycles with private number plates—not government number plates—to travel freely. The colours of the project motorcycle number plates were changed, and the agricultural extension staff were able to start visiting farmers' fields to give SRI training.

Finding a Solution to Crime on the Indian Border in Jhapa District[11]

The following two case studies take place in Jhapa and relate to how people can find solutions to their insecurities generated by the border with India. The first case study illustrates how people were able to co-opt local Maoist leaders to bring an end to the sex trade in their community. The second study more closely resembles the precious case studies and highlights how people were able to facilitate an agreement between the Maoists government forces to improve border security.

Jhapa is a district in the east of Nepal which shares a long open border with India. In 2005, the developing sex trade in a town bordering India was flourishing under the control of local elites. Most people in this area did not approve of the industry and approached the local Maoist leaders to help them close down the business. In this instance, the Maoists and local communities were able to cooperate together to peacefully pressurize the local elites to end the sex industry in this area.

There are various permutations regarding the modalities of how local communities can negotiate to live within a dual governance system. Another example of this from Jhapa also relates to seeking better local security mechanisms with regard to the problems posed by the open border to India. In the south of Jhapa District, cross-border raids and daylight robberies committed by Indian dacoits (armed bandits) were severely endangering the lives of local people. Local communities judged that the Maoist forces could not provide them adequate protection from this growing problem. Therefore, the local communities entered into negotiations with both the local Maoist forces and the Royal Nepal Army to seek a solution. The result of these negotiations was a request presented to the Maoists, asking them to allow the government security forces to set up a camp in the area. Surprisingly, the Maoists granted this request and a limited measure of protection was provided to the communities from the government security forces.

---

[11] This community research was conducted by FFP in 2005. The research was conducted with the objective of understanding community peace agendas in the districts outside the Kathmandu Valley.

Despite the violent conflict and dual governance system that prevailed in the rural areas of Nepal during the latter stages of the conflict, there were occasions where local communities found mechanisms to live within both systems. These mechanisms went beyond simple coping strategies and demonstrated sophisticated community negotiation and bargaining techniques, allowing people to work both systems to their minimum disadvantage. This is not to suggest that such negotiations were widely prevalent throughout Nepal. However, the research conducted by Pettigrew and this author (in conjunction with FFP staff) suggests that people trapped in 'cultures of violence' are not passive victims but agents, able to creatively forge compromises with more powerful forces to gain access to human rights such as security and basic public services.

CONCLUSION

This chapter began by asking a series of three questions. The first question asked about the factors contributing to the development of a dual governance system during the conflict in Nepal. This research has identified three main causes leading to the development of Maoist people's governments. The first of these relates to a fundamental principle of Maoist strategy, which is that political and military activities cannot be divorced. The establishment of village people's governments enabled the Maoists to consolidate and control their base areas as a sound foundation to conduct military operations and spread revolution into the urban areas, with the objective of surrounding and strangling Kathmandu. The tax collection by the new governments was also an important way to fund the Maoist machine. The creation of a government-in-waiting was one of the key elements of the 'strategic balance' phase of the Maoists' revolution. Through Maoist prescription and necessity, these governments were built from the grassroots upwards and, thus, provided a contrast to the Kathmandu-centric multiparty and royalist governments (from 1990 onwards).

The radical vision of change envisioned by the Maoists required mechanisms to bring this new agenda to life. Maoist people's governments were a way to systematically administer social, political and economic change. Arguably, the people's courts were one of the most effective mechanisms to demonstrate to rural people the superiority of swift Maoist justice versus the lengthy and corrupt state justice system. The people's courts were also able to drive through Maoist agendas on curbing social ills such as domestic violence.

The development of people's governments benefitted greatly from a politically enabling environment. The failure of successive state administrations to develop 'nerve ends' in the districts and villages outside Kathmandu left a vacuum of power for the Maoists to step into. Furthermore, the lack of serious intent on the part of any national government to address the diverse grievances in many Nepali villages created a socially enabling environment for the Maoists. In the case of both the social and the political factors, the Maoists took little time to seize these opportunities to build and sustain their revolution.

The second question explored in this research was whether the Maoists and villagers shared the same vision for change in Nepal. The lofty ideology espoused by the senior Maoist leadership, or what Scott (1976) terms the 'great tradition', did not resonate deeply with the majority of villagers, or 'little tradition'. For the most part, people were interested in having their basic needs met through a more responsive and less self-interested governance system. However, by looking at the lower level Maoist cadres it is clear that they had a degree of autonomy from the higher ranking party members. This degree of autonomy enabled lower level cadres to transpose communist ideology into a local context that resonated with many villagers. The Maoist demands for an end to ethnic, gender and Dalit exclusion tapped into a strong well of support in a number of diverse communities throughout Nepal.

Some local cadres demonstrated high levels of political entrepreneurship through their use of cultural shows which depicted Maoist confiscation of land and assets from wealthy landlords. This helped to form a popular folklore around Maoist cadres that could counterbalance the stories of violence that contributed to the culture of fear in many villages. Many Maoists did try to exact maximum social capital from their perceived status as Robin Hood type figures.

Even at a local level, the Maoists and villagers did clash over certain issues. This was most notable over the question of education, whereby the Maoist strategy of indoctrinating and recruiting students was clearly at odds with their own demand for a universal education for all. Certain hypocrisy can also be observed in the Maoist approach to ethnic and cultural freedom. This type of freedom was promoted in the Maoists' '40-Point Demand', but was partially undermined by the institution of a new governance system which attenuated traditional community justice mechanisms.

Finally, this chapter asked how people were able to negotiate a dual governance system in their everyday lives. It was highlighted in Pettigrew's research (2004) that people can employ reactive coping strategies, such as silence and the tracking of Maoist forces, to garner a degree of control over their personal safety. However, this chapter sought to show that villagers were capable of sophisticated corporate bargaining to gain access to public services and security from both the Maoists and the national government of Nepal. The case studies presented in this chapter may not represent a universal phenomenon during the conflict in Nepal, but they do point to the fact that many villagers had the skill and will to mobilize around a cause and negotiate successfully with more powerful forces. The individual and corporate agency of people in rural Nepal, witnessed during conflict, may still yet prove a potent force for change in post-conflict Nepal.

REFERENCES

Bharadwaj, N., R. Crozier, S. Dhungana and N. Hicks (eds). 2007a. *Voices from the Villages: People's Agendas for Peace*. Kathmandu: Friends for Peace Publications.

Bharadwaj, N., R. Crozier, S. Dhungana, N. Hicks and C. Watson (eds). 2007b. *Nepal at a Crossroads: The Nexus between Human Security and Renewed Conflict in Rural Nepal*. Kathmandu: Friends for Peace Publications.

Biswokarma, B. 2004. 'Dalits and the Conflict', in M. Mainali and R. Dahal (eds), *People in the 'People's War'*. Kathmandu: Centre for Investigative Journalism, pp. 1–10.

Bohara, K. 2004. 'Out of Nepal and into India', in M. Mainali and R. Dahal (eds), *People in the 'People's War'*. Kathmandu: Centre for Investigative Journalism, pp. 51–57.

Eck, K. 2007. *Recruiting Rebels: Indoctrination and Political Education in Nepal*. Paper presented at the 36th Annual Conference on South Asia and the 2nd Annual Himalayan Policy Research Conference, 10–14 October 2007, Madison, WI.

Hutt, M. (ed.). 2004. *Himalayan 'People's War': Nepal's Maoist Rebellion*. London: C. Hurst & Co.

International Crisis Group. 2005. *Nepal's Maoists: Their Aims, Structures and Strategy.* Asia Report No. 104, Brussels/Kathmandu: International Crisis Group.

Karki, A. and D. Seddon. 2003. 'The People's War in historical Context', in A. Karki and D. Seddon (eds), *The People's War in Nepal: Left Perspectives.* New Delhi: Adroit Publishers, pp. 3–48.

Kattel, M. 2003. 'Introduction to the People's War and Its Implications', in A. Karki and D. Seddon (eds), *The People's War in Nepal: Left Perspectives.* New Delhi: Adroit Publishers, pp. 49–74.

Migdal, J.S. 2001. *State in Society: Studying How States and Societies Transform and Constitute Each Other.* Cambridge: Cambridge University Press.

Nepal, P. 2003. 'The Maoist Movement and Its Impact in Nepal', in A. Karki and D. Seddon (eds), *The People's War in Nepal: Left perspectives.* New Delhi: Adroit Publishers, pp. 405–37.

Pettigrew, J. 2004. 'Living between the Maoists and the Army in Rural Nepal', in M. Hutt (ed.), *Himalayan 'People's War: Nepal's Maoist Rebellion.* London: C. Hurst & Co., pp. 261–83.

Race, J. 1973. *War Comes to Long An: Revolutionary Conflict in a Vietnamese Province.* Berkeley, CA: University of California Press.

Rai, S. 2004. 'Porters in the Crossfire', in M. Mainali and R. Dahal (eds), *People in the 'People's War'.* Kathmandu: Centre for Investigative Journalism, pp. 77–81.

Ramirez, P. 2004. 'Maoism in Nepal: Towards a Comparative Perspective', in M. Hutt (ed.), *Himalayan People's War: Nepal's Maoist Rebellion.* London: C. Hurst & Co., pp. 225–42.

Scott, J. 1976. *Moral Economy of the Peasant: Rebellion and Subsistence in South East Asia.* New Haven, CT: Yale University Press.

———. 1977. 'Protest and Profanation. Agrarian Revolt and the Little Tradition: Part One'. *Theory and Society,* 4(1): 1–38.

———. 1986. *Weapons of the Weak: Everyday Forms of Peasant Resistance.* New Haven, CT: Yale University Press.

Shneiderman, S. 2003. 'Violent Histories and Political Consciousness: Reflecting on Nepal's Maoist Movement from Piskar Village'. *The Journal of the Association for Nepal and Himalayan Studies,* 23(1): 39–48.

Shneiderman, S. and M. Turin. 2004. 'The Path to Jan Sarkar in Dolakha District: Towards and Ethnography of the Maoist Movement', in M. Hutt (ed.), *Himalayan People's War: Nepal's Maoist Rebellion.* London: C. Hurst & Co., pp. 79–111.

Shrestha, D.M. 2004. 'Ethnic Autonomy in the East', in M. Mainali and R. Dahal (eds), *People in the 'People's War'.* Kathmandu: Centre for Investigative Journalism, pp. 19–40.

Thapa, D. 2004. 'Radicalism and the Emergence of the Maoists', in M. Hutt (ed.), *Himalayan People's War: Nepal's Maoist Rebellion.* London: C. Hurst & Co., pp. 21–37.

Womack, B. 1987. 'The Party and the People: Revolutionary and Post-revolutionary Politics in China and Vietnam'. *World Politics,* 59(4): 479–507.

Chapter 7

Empowerment of Excluded Groups

Local Democracy and Social Change in Rural Odisha, Eastern India[1]

B.B. MOHANTY

INTRODUCTION

One of the striking features of Indian rural society is the glaring inequality in the distribution of power. The literature provides various different accounts of power structures in rural India. According to one group of scholars, the inequality in the distribution of power is structured in terms of caste relations. In their view, the higher castes dominate the power structure due to their possession of major power resources such as a high ritual status, greater control over land and other economic assets, and relatively higher levels of education, (Mayer, 1958; Srinivas, 1959; Laxminarayana, 1970; Berreman, 1972; Carter, 1974). Another group of scholars holds that thanks to the modernization of agriculture through the expansion of irrigation, cash crop cultivation, mechanization and adoption of high yielding crop variants, a class of rich peasants has emerged in the countryside, which has taken all the village-level institutions into their control (Frankel, 1971; Dasgupta, 1977; Byres, 1981). Yet another group has argued that power is no longer subsumed by the structure of caste or class. Power has deviated from the caste and class model; instead,

[1] This chapter is derived from the Odisha part of an all-India study, 'Inclusion and Exclusion in Local Governance' sponsored by the Institute of Social Sciences, New Delhi.

it depends upon a plurality of factors including contact with the politicians and party bosses outside of the village, position in an elaborate system of patronage, numerical support and personality attributes (Oommen, 1970; Beteille, 1971).

The views expressed by these three groups of scholars are based on studies mostly undertaken in the early phase of the introduction of the *panchayati raj* (literally, rule by local councils) system, at which time there was no provision for the inclusion of members of scheduled castes, tribes and women in the *panchayati raj* bodies. Given their inferior position in rural society, the members of these excluded groups were hardly able to participate in local decision-making processes. Shortly after the implementation of the three-tier *panchayati raj* system in accordance with the recommendation of the Balawantrai Mehta Committee, Moore (1967: 408) commented that, '[…] democracy does not yet exist in the Indian countryside […] The Panchayat "revival" […] is mainly romantic rhetoric'.

To generate participatory grassroots democracy, the *panchayati raj* was restructured in 1993 through the enforcement of the 73rd Constitutional Amendment, which made provisions for the inclusion of members of the scheduled castes, tribes and women by reserving a specified percentage of elective seats for them. Hence, it is imperative to examine how far this new, experimental inclusion of the members of hitherto excluded groups in rural local bodies has contributed to their empowerment and affected the dominance of the privileged groups. However, early studies have indicated that the elected members belonging to these hitherto excluded groups are representatives in name only, unable to effectively participate in governance owing to the dominance of privileged groups (Lieten and Srivastav, 1999; Mathew and Nayak, 1996). Of course, there are success stories (Lieten, 1996; Pai, 2000). However, the findings of these studies may not fit neatly with the situation in Odisha, where the initial conditions of *panchayati raj* and the socio-economic and historical features are different.

ODISHA POLITICS IN PERSPECTIVE

At the time of independence, Odisha was under the control of the feudal *zamindar*s (landlords) and princes of the native states who enjoyed the reverence usual in a feudal society (Jena, 1966). Subsequently, the members of the higher castes, who expanded their social and economic base during the British Raj—by taking advantage of its land revenue system, caste-based bureaucratic arrangement, and the limited opportunities for modern education—emerged as the dominant political force through the rhetoric of the anti-feudal drive and the politics of nationalism among the Oriya-speaking people. The upper castes maintained hegemonic control of state politics by accommodating the ex-rulers of the feudatory states, while the lower castes were unable to come up as competing forces, given their perpetual struggle for subsistence owing to backward agriculture, high food grain prices, low wage rates, indebtedness and frequent occurrences of floods, cyclones and droughts.

In the post-planning era (from the 1950s onwards), a systematic attempt was made to modernize agriculture and maximize agricultural output. As these measures were introduced without removing the prevailing inequalities, their advent generated further inequalities (Baboo, 1992; Mohanty, 2000). As a result, the landowning higher castes emerged as a class of rich farmers. Thus, a class structure emerged within the framework of a caste society. Caste and class became intertwined and mutually buttressed each other (Pathy, 1981: 180). The effects of modern agriculture and programmes of economic development also pushed a section of the middle castes to the forefront, which generated a mild stream of consciousness among them and created new pressures. However, the upper castes adjusted themselves well to the new situation by co-opting potential challengers (Mohanty, 1990). Bailey (1963: 106) observed that,

> the members of these [...] castes, together with an increasing number of lower castes [...] with the few members of the Princely families, constitute Orissa's very small middle-class *elite*, and it might be more correct to regard their dominance in politics and the administration as a class phenomenon, rather than a caste phenomenon.

Today, all the major political parties of the state are dominated by the higher castes (Mohanty, 1990, 2001; Harriss, 1999; Manor, 2000). Though the political necessities and democratic processes set into motion by the constitution forced the political parties to enrol and train some lower caste members for the reserved constituencies, these elected representatives have remained the followers of the leaders of the higher castes. Their success has been attributed to the influence of prominent higher caste leaders and their political parties (Mohanty and Bahidar, 1993). The failure of caste associations or opposition parties to pave the way for the autonomous politicization of the lower castes has facilitated the continuation of upper caste control over the major political parties. Moreover, the dominance of the higher castes has remained unchallenged due to the absence of strong social movements against them, as happened in states such as Maharashtra, Tamil Nadu and Karnataka. There have been no strong caste-based parties or associations, as there were in Uttar Pradesh and Bihar, to generate awakening among the disadvantaged castes. The lower caste organizations, under the leadership of Shri Shantanu Das of Jajpur and Shri Mohan Das of Ganjam, have had hardly any influence (Mohanty and Bahidar, 1993). The state also does not have a sustained leftist movement, as in West Bengal and Kerala. Although caste is socially present, it is not politically mobilized (Sahu, 1998). Stated simply, the situation has left enough spaces for the upper castes to dominate society and politics. Since the very first election, the state assembly and the ministry have been dominated by the members of the higher castes.[2] So far, the position of the chief minister has alternated solely between higher caste leaders.[3] Though there is rivalry among the leaders of the upper castes, resulting in several splits and mergers of political parties as well as the growth of new forces, this has not encouraged the lower castes to emerge as a powerful alternative. All of the major political parties appear to share the same position regarding the advancement of the lower castes. This is evident from the indifferent attitude displayed by all parties when the state witnessed violent protests in 1990 over the issue of the adoption of the recommendations of the Backward Classes Commission. The then Chief Minister, Biju Patnaik, lambasted the former Prime Minister V.P. Singh for accepting the Commission's recommendations (Sengupta, 2001).

[2] An analysis of the composition of the Odisha Assembly and its Ministry since 1952 clearly shows greater representation of the higher castes, particularly the Brahmins and the Karans. See the Election Commission website: http://www.eci.nic.in (accessed on 17 September 2012).

[3] Though the Congress Party has made tribal leaders as the chief ministers of the state thrice, they have done so only for a very short time just before the elections in order to woo the tribal population.

Politics at the state level also operates within a strong patriarchal framework. All the political parties are dominated by men (Mohanty, 1990). The representation of women in the state assembly and the ministry is negligible,[4] notwithstanding the temporary ascendancy of a female chief minister in the 1970s. Though a handful of women participate in state politics, they belong to the wealthy segments of the higher castes and ex-royal families. The majority of them are closely related to the powerful higher caste leaders. Despite the widespread atrocities against women which often hit media headlines, there have been no organized protests against male dominance.

The privileged groups—given their advantageous position in society, structured in terms of unequal class–caste–gender relations and dominance over the political parties—find it easier to mobilize the masses, who are overwhelmingly rural, poor, illiterate and uneducated, in their favour. Their political and economic power is rooted in rural socio-political institutions, mainly the panchayats and cooperatives through which the state-sponsored, subsidized agricultural inputs and other developmental schemes are usually launched. In such a context, it is difficult to alter the power structure because the groups who have entrenched privilege are not likely to surrender their power to underprivileged people.

Against this background, an attempt is made here to analyze how far these new provisions for the inclusion of members of hitherto excluded groups in rural local bodies have contributed to their empowerment and challenged the dominance of privileged groups. In order to analyse the nature of the representation and participation of women and scheduled caste members in the *panchayati raj* institutions, and the consequent impact that is made on the decision-making process at the local level, three panchayats—namely, Marshaghai, Dashipur and Silipur, all of Kendrapara district[5]—have been selected for comparative study. All three

---

[4] Analysis of the composition of the State Assembly since the 1952 elections shows that women currently make up 3–4 per cent of all members. However, in 2000 the number increased to 8 per cent. Meanwhile, the proportion of women in the council of ministers has always been negligible.

[5] Kendrapara is overwhelmingly rural with a relatively high concentration of the scheduled castes in its population. The scheduled castes are mostly landless, and the bulk of the population consists of agricultural labourers with minuscule holdings, sharecroppers or other types of insecure tenants. The district is also known

of these panchayats come under Marshaghai Block. They are similar in terms of caste structure, agricultural practices and livelihood pattern, although the relative demographic strength of the caste groups varies considerably. While the sarpanches of Marshaghi and Dashipur include scheduled castes and women, respectively, Silipur panchayat is headed by a sarpanch belonging to an open or unreserved category. Data were collected from these panchayats using the participant observation method between January and June 2001. The required secondary information was collected from the respective panchayat offices.

Marshaghai Panchayat

There are 921 households in this panchayat with a total population of 6,254. The higher castes (the Brahmins, Karans and Khandayats) constitute 43 per cent of the total population and 40 per cent of the voters. The Khandayats are more numerous in the panchayat as a whole and they account for 37 per cent of the population. The 'backward' or intermediary castes constitute over 25 per cent of the population and 28 per cent of the voters. Among them the Gaudas are dominant. Over 32 per cent of the population and 31 per cent of the voters of the panchayat belong to scheduled castes. The major scheduled caste communities are the Kandaras, Kewats, Dhobas and Panas.

Agriculture is the principal source of income and employment for the population. However, a significant number of people are engaged in petty business and trading. The cultivable land of the panchayat is unequally owned by various castes. While the higher castes control 76 per cent of

---

for a high rate of atrocities perpetrated against women. Some of the more recent incidents reported by the media generated frantic debates in the State Assembly. Like the other districts of coastal Odisha, this district is also patriarchal and the upper castes are more numerous and powerful. An analysis of the profile of the Members of Parliament and Members of the Legislative Assembly of the district since the first general elections for the Lok Sabha and the State Assembly reveals that these leaders mostly belong to the Karan, Bramhin and Khandayat castes. The representatives belonging to scheduled castes are mainly from the reserved constituencies. The same can be said for the *panchayati raj* bodies. Until the 1992 panchayat elections, there were hardly any sarpanches who were female or from the scheduled castes.

the total land of the panchayat, the 'backward' castes and the scheduled castes own only 14 and 9 per cent, respectively. Landlessness is more pronounced among scheduled castes. While the Hadi caste does not figure in the landholding picture at all, the ownership of land among the Panas and Kandaras is negligible. The Kewats are the major landowners among the scheduled castes. They are a relatively well-off and advanced community because of their association with petty business and trading. Traditionally, they were not untouchables, and only in the 1970s were they included in the scheduled caste list. Many of them have prospered through their business activities in Marshaghai market. It is estimated[6] that in the last 20 years they have acquired over 30 acres of land sold by the other castes in the panchayat.

Previously, the panchayat was mostly under the control of the higher castes. Prior to the enforcement of the reservation rules as per the 73rd Constitutional Amendment, elections for this panchayat were held in 1961, 1967, 1970, 1975, 1984 and 1992. In all these years, a Brahmin or a Khandayat was elected to the position of sarpanch. Each time, the contest was mostly among the members of these two higher castes. The panchayat was headed by a Brahmin sarpanch up to 1970, and thereafter the Khandayats occupied the position. All these sarpanches, along with the ward members, were mostly upper caste males. However, in 1992 when the provision of reservation was introduced, female and scheduled caste ward members emerged.

As specified by the reservation rules of 1997, the sarpanch's position was reserved for the members of scheduled castes. The members of upper castes across the panchayat were disappointed with this development, and initially there was mild resistance. A former Khandayat ward member said,

> This is a prestigious panchayat and the government officials give this panchayat a lot of importance. When he (a Brahmin) was the *sarpanch*, he challenged the government officers. Who would care for a Kandara or Pana *sarpanch*? True, the earlier *sarpanches* were misappropriating funds but they were also doing something good and their words had some weight.

---

[6] This estimate was made by the secretary of the panchayat and his assistant (who are from the same locality) in consultation with the ward members and some senior persons of different villages, who are often consulted on matters of special importance.

A *harijan sarpanch* could neither feed himself nor others. We were thinking of boycotting the election.

Having realized that it was difficult to change the decision, attempts were made by the local leaders of all the political parties (who were mostly from the upper castes) to elect a candidate who would be acceptable to them. Though eight candidates contested for this position, the failure of most of the candidates was ensured because of the division of votes among the candidates having common support. A rich Brahmin landlord expressed his sentiments as follows:

> We do not mind their becoming the *sarpanchs* or *samitisabhyas* (members of panchayat). We have never prevented them from contesting for these positions. But they should remember their past. All of them were working in our land. After each festival and function whatever was left over, was given to them. Whenever there is a flood, cyclone, etc., we provide them shelter. Their children study in schools and colleges established by us. In return we do not need anything from them except the respect due to us.

At present the panchayat is headed by a sarpanch who belongs to the Kewat caste. He contested for this position way back in 1967 and claimed to be a candidate for the Praja Socialist Party. But prominent Praja Socialist Party leaders in Kendrapara remained indifferent to his candidature and supported a Brahmin candidate, who finally won the election. Subsequently, the Kewat sarpanch became a Congress Party worker. Realizing his potential, the local leaders offered him the position of the director of the Marshaghai Cooperative Society. Subsequently, with the support of the Congress Party workers, he became the vice-president (1985–90) and president (1990–95) of the same Cooperative Society. Over the course of his association with the society, he has reportedly gone out of the way to help the rich, higher caste farmers. In the process, his own economic position also improved. Now he is considered to be rich among the Kewat community. He owns three and a half acres of land and two shops in Marshaghai market. Consequently, he has become close to the leaders of the district, having influence over state politics. Hence, when the sarpanch's position was reserved for scheduled castes, he was the obvious choice. Similarly, the *samitisabhya* of the panchayat also went to another rich member of the Kewat caste, supported by the Janata Dal leaders.

The panchayat consists of 17 wards. Of these, 14 wards have ward members, and the other 3 wards (belonging to Juna village) remain vacant owing to strong opposition to the reservation of these positions for the women belonging to other 'backward' classes, scheduled castes and scheduled tribes. The members of the upper castes, who are considered to be knowledgeable about government rules in the village, mobilized the villagers for this protest. One of the former Khandayat ward members of the village remarked:

> Selecting a woman as a ward member is as good as not having a ward member. Reservation for a scheduled caste and scheduled tribe woman! It is an utter shame for the village as a whole and more so for the females as it is the prestige issue of their husbands, brothers and sons.

The rumour that the absence of protest might lead to the continuation of the reservation system in the future was widely circulated in the village. Even though the women of these communities showed interest, they were discouraged. A scheduled caste woman lamented:

> When the Brahmins and Khandayats of other wards are not opposing their women to become ward members, why were we stopped? Many of us were willing. For a ward member there is not much to read and write. Any one of us could have easily done it. We would have got at least the ward member's stipend and allowance.

In the case of some male ward member candidates belonging to the Khandayat and Gauda castes, there was no election and they were elected unopposed. Meanwhile, in some of the wards reserved for scheduled castes, the rich members of higher castes managed to get some of their labourers elected. For example, in Tulsipur, for ward number 17, the members of scheduled castes unanimously proposed a Kandara for the ward member position. To counter this, a rich Khandayat encouraged his attached labourer (also a Kandara of the same ward) to file the nomination paper. After this, the labourer was temporarily sent to Mumbai by the employer to help in his business. Though he was not in the village at the time of the election, his employer managed to get him elected.

As the sarpanch was male, the *naib*-sarpanch (female vice-head of the panchayat) position was reserved for a female candidate. Though there are four female ward members, the two of them belonging to higher castes were reluctant to occupy their positions because the sarpanch was from a lower caste. Finally, the contest was between two women, one from a scheduled caste (Pana) and one from a higher caste (Khandayat). While the scheduled caste woman worked as an agricultural labourer, the higher caste woman, though a housewife, belonged to a relatively poor family. Interestingly, a majority of the panchayat members supported the scheduled caste woman because of her docile behaviour. Moreover, her husband often worked as a labourer with many of the panchayat members.

Of the 15 panchayat members, the scheduled castes, the 'backward' castes and the higher castes have five members each. The members belonging to higher castes are mostly the Khandayats. Among scheduled castes, the Kewats have two members and the Panas, Kandaras and Dhobas have one member each. Four of the members including the *naib*-sarpanch are women. All the members have only been educated to the elementary-school level. Excepting the three (including the *naib*-sarpanch) who are landless labourers, the economic condition of most of the members of the panchayat is relatively good compared to the rest of the community. A large number of them depend on business as their major source of income. In terms of the class position of the members, while the sarpanch and one of the ward members are rich peasants, the female Brahmin member is a landlord. Five of the other members are middle peasants and the remainder belong to the category of small peasants and agricultural labourers. Some of the members of the small peasant category, those elected uncontested, are obliged to the rich landowners for their support. Five of the panchayat members (including the sarpanch) claim to be with the Congress Party, eight with the Janata Dal (now Biju Janata Dal—BJD), one with the Bharatiya Janata Party (BJP) and one is an independent candidate. The members belonging to the Pana and Kandara castes who are landless labourers are known to be the supporters of the Congress as they are guided by the sarpanch.

The panchayat has met 62 times during the tenure of the current sarpanch. Except for the occasional absence of two or three members, all meetings have been attended by all the members. The women and the scheduled caste members have regularly attended meetings. It was reported that the allowance of ₹30 per meeting has motivated them to do so. The meetings were held in the panchayat office and were presided over by the sarpanch. As a number of members have their business in the Marshaghai market, the meetings were convened at times convenient for them. The female members come with their husbands, sons or other male members of the family, who wait and watch from outside. The women (particularly those belonging to the Pana or Kandara communities) hardly participate in the discussion, instead remaining silent observers. When, on occasion, they do speak, they are ignored and discouraged.

At one meeting the *naib*-sarpanch proposed a discussion on the allotment of funds for the reconstruction of a non-formal school located in a *harijan basti* (slum of *harijan* or scheduled castes) which had collapsed in the cyclone, but nobody showed any interest in the matter. Some members said, 'Let us not open this issue now. It is already getting late. We have to go to the market'. The matter was deferred to the next meeting. There too it was discussed at the very end and no decision was reached. But proposals for the construction and renovation of the boundary wall of a temple, an approach road and other works were finalized. Finally, the school building was not repaired and the school had to be closed. The *harijan* children of that village had to go to another, more distant school.

The panchayat secretary, who is a Brahmin landlord, is as powerful as the sarpanch. He addresses most of the members by name only, and the members treat him respectfully. He participates actively in all the meetings and often influences the decisions made. Because of his long association with the panchayat, he claims to be the person with the most knowledge about government rules, often interpreting them in line with his own interests. He played a major role in preparing the list of beneficiaries for the Indira Awas Yojana (a housing scheme for rural families living below the poverty line), Antodaya Anna Yojana (a scheme for providing food grains to the poorest of the poor at highly subsidized rates) and other schemes. In a meeting which had been called to decide on Integrated Rural Development Programme (IRDP) beneficiaries, a scheduled caste member wanted to include a person from his community, but the secretary opposed him, and when the scheduled caste member gave an example of a beneficiary from an upper caste, the secretary reacted strongly:

> You were born only yesterday. What do you know about the government rules regarding this scheme? If anything happens, I will be held responsible. Who will come to you and who knows you? You should go home and ask

your father. He will tell you about my experience on panchayat affairs. He never talks like this. Are you his son or somebody else's?

None of the other members supported the scheduled caste member. Even the fellow scheduled caste members remained silent. Another time, the panchayat met to discuss the problem of low attendance in the *gram sabha* (village committee), and it was decided that they offer a special invitation to the prominent panchayat members for the *gram sabha* meeting, as their presence might increase the overall attendance. Interestingly enough, in the list of persons selected for the purpose, not a single woman or member of a scheduled caste was included.

Though the members are occasionally divided along party lines, such a division does not take place when development issues are raised by scheduled caste members. Usually debates and arguments are avoided. The proceedings are written up by the secretary, who systematically bypasses many important points. For example, the District Panchayat Officer once came to visit the panchayat while the meeting was going on. As soon as he arrived, the discussion was stopped and some members were asked to help the panchayat peon entertain the District Panchayat Officer and his assistants. The District Panchayat Officer delivered a speech emphasizing regular attendance, maintenance of proper office records, discipline and so on. Snacks were then served to all the members and the meeting ended without discussing the other points on the agenda. Nevertheless, the points not discussed were included in the minutes written up afterwards. It is also pertinent to note that the panchayat peon cleans the glasses and plates of all the members, including the sarpanch, except for those of the two scheduled caste members. Though untouchability is not practised in the sitting arrangement for the meeting, the only Brahmin woman member sits at a distance to avoid physical contact with the *naib*-sarpanch who belongs to the Pana caste. She does not take water in the glass used by the other members.

The *gram sabha* has met only 10 times during its present tenure, presided over by the sarpanch. People do not show an interest in these meetings and their lack of interest is such that meetings have often been held without the quorum. Many members prefer to go to the market rather than attend the meeting. The people belonging to the Brahmin community avoid these meetings. One of them frankly admitted, 'How could we attend the meeting when a *harijan* and a Paluni (the *naib*-sarpanch) at that sit on the chair and we are asked to sit on the floor?'

Apart from the *naib*-sarpanch, the female members never attend these meetings. However, some of the members of scheduled castes (mostly the Kewats) attend them. Fifty to sixty people attended the last three meetings, but two of them were cancelled following violent disturbances by some rich people belonging to the higher castes, as they were unhappy due to the exclusion of their names from the below poverty line (BPL) list. One of these meetings was called to discuss the Food for Work Programme and a large number of people belonging to the scheduled castes were present.

The *pallisabha* (village committee) has met four times in each of the villages of this panchayat. However, five meetings were held in the village of Juna. The sarpanch presided over the first *pallisabha* of each village and the IRDP beneficiaries were chosen. The subsequent *pallisabha*s were presided over by selected ward members from the villages where decisions relating to the identification of beneficiaries for the Indira Awas Yojana, the Annapurna Scheme, the BPL list and so on were taken up. Women were mostly absent from all the *pallisabha*s. However, the lower the caste, the greater the attendance of women. Women's attendance of public meetings along with men is viewed as a symbol of a family's low status.

The sarpanch presided over the *pallisabha* in Purusottampur village and only 10–15 people attended it in Tulsipur. Most of them were rich landowners and businessmen. The list of IRDP beneficiaries prepared by the residents of these two villages included the well-off households, many of whom are the beneficiaries of other schemes as well. However, in the case of the village of Juna where 116 people attended the meeting, the sarpanch found it difficult to select the beneficiaries of his choice. In the end, he included all the names proposed in the *pallisabha* but deleted some of them in the Block Office. Many recommendations made by the *pallisabha* have either been ignored or overruled. For example, the *pallisabha* of Tulsipur met in the Gateswari Thakurani temple to finalize the work order for the construction of a road in the *harijan basti*. The members of the scheduled castes who were sitting at a distance (as it was a temple complex) unanimously appealed for the work order to be given to them. Though some higher caste members were reluctant, the ward member who was presiding agreed. However, the final work order was given to a Khandayat by the sarpanch. In another Juna *pallisabha*, where

124 members were present to select the beneficiaries of the Antodaya Anna Yojana, the names proposed by the members of scheduled castes were changed. In almost all the *pallisabhas* held for the finalization of the BPL list, instead of inviting the people present to suggest names, the ward members and the panchayat secretary read out a list of names which they had already prepared. Though in some cases they went on to include additional households, the earlier names were all retained. In another *pallisabha* held in Purusottampur, a ward member and the panchayat secretary suggested a person's name to whom a work order could be issued and sought the opinion of the members. As the person in question is a rich and influential landlord of the village, nobody dared to oppose him. He spent a negligible portion of the estimated budget and got the bill approved.

Dashipur Panchayat

Dashipur panchayat consists of 719 households with a total population of 5,401. Compared to the other two panchayats, the scheduled caste population is relatively small (17 per cent). Higher castes constitute 56 per cent and 'backward' castes 26 per cent of the panchayat population. The distribution of voters' castes also follows the same pattern.

The economy of this panchayat is almost entirely dependent upon agriculture. The cultivable land of the panchayat is unequally distributed among the nine caste groups. The higher castes control 76 per cent of the land, while the 'backward' and the scheduled castes own 17 per cent and 7 per cent, respectively. Among the scheduled castes, there is a high incidence of landlessness, and this is particularly true of the Kandaras. About 87 per cent of their households are landless. However, the position of the Kewats and Dhobas is comparatively better. The Khandayats are the most privileged group in the panchayat, owing to their numerical strength as well as their land ownership.

Elections for this panchayat have been held twice only. The previous sarpanch was a Khandayat. The present female sarpanch also belongs to the same caste and the *naib*-sarpanch is a male of the Dhoba caste. Seven female candidates contested for the sarpanch's position and almost all of them were from the higher castes. Two of the ward members contested elections for the *naib*-sarpanch's position. As the Dhoba member was proposed by the sarpanch's husband, most of the members supported him.

As regards the socio-economic background of the panchayat members, seven (including the sarpanch) members out of the 18 belong to higher castes (Khandyats). The 'backward' castes have six members. While all the higher caste members are Khandayats, the 'backward' caste members are Gaudas. The scheduled castes have five members (including the *naib*-sarpanch): two Dhobas, two Kewats and one Kandara. Seven members are women, three are from higher castes, and the 'backward' and scheduled castes have two members each. All the members have studied up to elementary-school level, while the sarpanch is a university graduate.

The members belonging to scheduled castes are either tenants with miniscule holdings or landless labourers. The latter work with the landowners of the higher castes. The *naib*-sarpanch holds a lease on one acre of land and also works as a labourer with the panchayat secretary, who is a Gauda. The panchayat secretary is a staunch supporter of the sarpanch. The members belonging to 'backward' castes are mostly from the higher landowning group. In addition to cultivation, most of them are dairy farmers. All of them belong to the more well-off section of their community. Three of the higher caste members are also smallholders and tenants-cum-cultivators. Two of them were elected uncontested, thanks to support from their landlords. As regards their class position, the majority of the members, including the *naib*-sarpanch, are small peasants. The sarpanch belongs to a landlord family and four other members are rich peasants. The only member who belongs to the agricultural labourer category is from the scheduled castes. The division of members though takes place on the basis of the political parties their support does not correspond to either their caste or class position. While the sarpanch and the *naib*-sarpanch, along with another member of the Gauda caste, identify themselves with the BJP, five members identify with the Congress, eight members with the Janata Dal and one member with the CPM.

The sarpanch lives mostly with her husband (who is a government employee) in Marshaghai. He has connections with the BJP at the district level and he is close to a district BJP leader who is a minister in the state cabinet. The election of the sarpanch is attributed to her husband's political connections and the family's socio-economic base in the locality.

Most of the panchayat members are supporters of the sarpanch's husband. The panchayat has held 57 meetings; all of them presided over by the sarpanch except one, which was presided over by the Village Level Worker. All these meetings are held in the Dashipur Upper Primary School. The sarpanch attends the meetings mostly with her husband and the meetings are convened based on his convenience and availability. The meetings are held on Sundays or holidays on the pretext that this allows them to be held in the school. Though a majority of the male members attend almost all the meetings, many female members remain absent. The female members who do come do so with the male members of their families. Decisions are mostly taken by the sarpanch's husband in association with some members of the Khandayat and Gauda castes. The sarpanch's husband indicates his opinion on important matters beforehand, as a result of which other members find it difficult to oppose him. The secretary prepares the minutes and shows them to the sarpanch's husband for his approval. Though initially two rich peasants of the upper caste opposed the sarpanch and her husband, the sarpanch's husband pacified them by allotting them an IRDP loan and an Indira Awas house as well as distributing old age and widow pensions to their kith and kin even though they are rich. Though untouchability is not practised in the meetings, the female members sit separately. Some of them sit humbly with their heads down and covered with sarees to show respect to the elder males. The female ward members rarely participate in the discussion. One member pointed out:

> We feel uneasy saying anything in [the sarpanch's husband's] presence in the meeting. His wife also keeps quiet. He is a qualified person. When we propose something he listens carefully and asks thousands of questions, which makes our position embarrassing in front of the other men.

The *gram sabha* has met nine times during the tenure of the present sarpanch. It is held in the same school as the panchayat meetings. All the meetings are presided over by the sarpanch. The latter's husband remains present at all the meetings, from the beginning until the end. Only 10–20 people attend these meetings and the same people have attended almost all the meetings. The female members do not attend these meetings. Except for the *naib*-sarpanch, the scheduled caste members are absent.

However, one meeting which was called to decide upon the beneficiaries of the Indira Awas Yojana was attended by 50 people, many of them members of scheduled castes. Both the sarpanch and her husband were present. Though it was announced that the list of beneficiaries would be selected at the meeting, the sarpanch had finalized the list beforehand and she asked the panchayat secretary to read out the names for the approval of the *gram sabha*. A number of households included in the list were from the richer classes and even had concrete buildings. In some cases, two beneficiaries were from the same household but were treated as two families. Although a number of poor households were included among the beneficiaries from scheduled castes, many were relatively rich, belonging to the Dhoba and Kewat communities. Though many of the poor *harijan*s (scheduled castes) and other low-caste people felt the list was biased in favour of the richer classes, they were not able to publicly oppose the decisions as most of the beneficiaries were present at the meeting. One poor scheduled caste member (a Kandara) requested that the sarpanch include his name. Immediately, a number of rich people also suggested other names. The sarpanch's husband intervened:

> Compared to other panchayats our list is much bigger. This was possible because of my personal contact with the Block officials and higher authorities. The number can be decreased but it cannot be increased further. If any of the included names can be deleted, then I do not have any objection to including your [pointing to the scheduled caste member] name.

When the situation became noisy due to suggestions and counter-suggestions, it was decided that they would adjourn the meeting.

In the last five years, the *pallisabha* of each of the four villages has met four times. Less than five per cent of the village population attend these meetings. The women and the members of scheduled castes are absent from almost all of the meetings. While two of the meetings in each village were presided over by the *naib*-sarpanch, the other two meetings were presided over by the selected ward members of the respective villages. In all the villages, the *pallisabha*s called for the finalization of the list of BPL families (which serve as the guideline for the selection of beneficiaries for a number of schemes) were presided over by the *naib*-sarpanch. The BPL list was prepared by the Block Office but was referred to the *pallisabha* of each village for its approval. Many of the rich and well-to-do households mostly belonging to the higher castes managed to enrol themselves in the list through connections with the Block officials, and a large number of poor people were ignored. Though the *pallisabha* was given the power to modify the list in case of any irregularity, in most cases the original list was maintained. In a *pallisabha* meeting in Palaspur, the list was revised and some new names were included. But the sarpanch, in consultation with some influential and rich people, withheld the list and did not submit it to the Block Office within the prescribed time limit. After five months another *pallisabha* was called. Those present were informed that the revised list was not accepted by the Block Office.

The *pallisabha* was summoned for the finalization of the BPL list in Dashipur, but the panchayat secretary and the *naib*-sarpanch, who was to preside over the meeting, did not arrive even four or five hours after the scheduled time. In fact, they had gone to Marshaghai to consult the sarpanch's husband. Most of the people who came to attend the meeting were disappointed and returned home. Finally, the *naib*-sarpanch and the secretary reached Dashipur in the evening, called the people still present, and finalized the list. Only 13 people attended that meeting. Similarly, in another case, the list of beneficiaries of the Antodoya Anna Yojana prepared by the *pallisabha* was bypassed. As per the rule, the beneficiaries were to be chosen from among the BPL families. The panchayat secretary did not mention the rule and advised the *naib*-sarpanch to include the names of the *harijan*s who were not on the BPL list. But in the case of the upper castes, only the BPL families were included. Finally, in the Block Office the names of *harijan* families were deleted, as they did not belong to the BPL families. As well as this, not a single work order in any of these villages was issued with the consent of the *pallisabha*. Instead, the rich people had work orders issued in their names by colluding with the sarpanch's husband. The local officials forged the signatures of the *pallisabha* members and facilitated all of this.

In the first three years after taking up the position, the sarpanch was independently managing all of the panchayat's routine matters. But after the occurrence of the super cyclone in 1999—when the panchayat's activities increased owing to the distribution of relief materials, commencement of the reconstruction works and so on—and more particularly after the formation of a BJP–BJD coalition government in the state, the sarpanch's husband became more active. Even the local level government officials including the Block Development Officer bypassed the sarpanch and consulted her husband. She was only ever asked to give her signature.

As the sarpanch is from Dasipur, the majority of developmental work has been carried out in this village. Over 40 per cent of development grants have been utilized mostly for the benefit of the upper castes; for example, they have been used for the construction of a bathing complex, a sports house and a community centre. Although in other villages some road construction work has been undertaken, the approach roads in the *harijan basti*, particularly where the Kandaras are concentrated, have not seen any improvement. In the *naib*-sarpanch's own *basti* (slum), the approach road is also as bad as it was earlier. The work order for the *harijan basti* has been given to contractors from the higher castes. A comparison of the construction of an approach road in the *harijan basti* with that of the higher caste *basti* involving almost equal amounts of budget and which has been done by the same contractor shows that the quality of work in the former is extremely poor by comparison, and that the contractor has nonetheless been paid without any queries.

It is inferred from the analysis of both cases, the Marshaghai and the Dashipur panchayats, that inclusion of the members of scheduled castes and women in the panchayats has only helped the rich to consolidate their economic position. A poor Pana member of the Marshaghai panchayat made the following comments about the sarpanch:

> He is as bad as our earlier *sarpanches*. Though he belongs to a scheduled caste, he is not our *sarpanch*. He is the *sarpanch* of the rich. He does not look after the poor fellow-members of his own community and he's a long way away from attending to our problems. Our *basti* has not witnessed any notable improvement during his tenure. The only thing which has happened is that the numbers of beneficiaries of Indira Awas Yojana and old age/widow pension have increased. These days even rich people are getting such benefits. Besides, he has taken money from us for that.

Moreover, the inclusion of a woman sarpanch has created impediments and inconveniences for the poor sections of the community, particularly the scheduled castes. They have to wait for long hours to meet her and often get bad treatment. A person of the sarpanch's own caste lamented:

> For everything, she tells us to meet him [her husband]. Whenever she is there he is not there, and sometimes if he is there, she is not there. It is

difficult to get both of them. Unless it is unavoidable, we do not like to go to them. In the case of ordinary matters we just pay the *panchayat* secretary 20/30 rupees and get her signature.

The sarpanch herself remarked:

All the way they come bare foot and enter the house. I have told them to convey the matters through the secretary. Still they come. Even if they are told that my husband and I are not here, they wait for hours together. Sometimes my in-laws get irritated and shout at them.

Besides, the participation of women in local affairs has not freed them from their traditional duties and obligations. Their participation is accepted as long as it does not alter the existing order of gender relations and inequality. The husband of the *naib*-sarpanch of the Marshaghai panchayat commented:

Whatever she does and wherever she goes she informs me. She does all the household work. Of course, I help her in many ways. But I cannot do the household work, such as cooking, cleaning the utensils, washing clothes, etc. As it is, the people have started telling us that she dominates me, and if I do these chores, they will look down upon me.

Silipur Panchayat

The total population of Silipur panchayat is 4,067, consisting of 521 households. The higher castes form 37 per cent of the population, while the 'backward' castes and scheduled castes constitute 41 per cent and 21 per cent of the population, respectively. The Khandayats and Gaudas are the numerically dominant communities. Among scheduled castes, the Kewats are most populous. The caste-wise distribution of voters exhibits almost the same pattern.

Almost all the households of the panchayat depend upon agriculture for income and employment. Compared to the other two panchayats, the agriculture of Silipur panchayat is relatively advanced due to extensive irrigation facilities. The land distribution pattern closely follows the social hierarchy. The major landowning groups are the Khandayats, Gaudas and Brahmins. The scheduled castes, particularly the Kandaras and Panas, are the most disadvantaged communities. The Khandayats and Gaudas are the dominant groups in the village in terms of population as well as land ownership.

Since the panchayat is new, elections have been held only twice (in 1992 and 1997), and a Gauda has held the sarpanch's position consecutively for both terms. In the first election, he stood against a candidate of his own caste, but in the subsequent term the contest was with a candidate of the Khandayat caste. A majority of the members of scheduled castes voted for him. As the sarpanch is a male, the *naib*-sarpanch position has been given to a woman candidate. A Khandayat woman has been elected as the *naib*-sarpanch. Out of 13 positions, more than half are occupied by the Gaudas including the sarpanch, while the Khandayats have three positions including that of the *naib*-sarpanch. There are only two ward members from scheduled castes who are women. The *samitisabhya* of this panchayat is a Khandayat who has been elected as the chairman of the *panchayat samiti* (panchayat organization). On the whole, the Khandayats and Gaudas are the most powerful castes.

The sarpanch is a graduate and he belongs to a rich, progressive and innovative farming family. He owns a two-storey building in the village, 18 acres of land, a tractor, a pump set, a motorbike and other valuable household items. While three panchayat members belong to the rich peasant category (including the sarpanch and *naib*-sarpanch), the middle and small peasants have two and five members, respectively. The remaining two members are agricultural labourers who belong to scheduled castes. One of them works with the sarpanch as a labourer and the other is attached to the *samitisabhya*. Many of the small peasants work for the rich and middle peasant ward members as hired labourers. The panchayat secretary is a close relation of the sarpanch. The *samitisabhya* of the panchayat is also a rich landlord who owns a two-storey building, along with many assets and valuable household items. The sarpanch is a close associate of the chairman and both of them support the Congress Party. As the Congress Party ruled the state in the first three years of their tenure, all the local-level officials supported them. Eight ward members (including the *naib*-sarpanch) claim to be supporters of the Congress Party and many of them were elected with the support of the sarpanch and *samitisabhya*. Three of the four other members who identify themselves with the Janata Dal forgot their political differences and joined hands with the sarpanch after the election. The sarpanch enjoys the support of almost all the members because of his close association with the chairman of the panchayat samiti and Block administration.

The gram panchayat meeting has been held 63 times in the last five years. Excepting the occasional absence of the female members, particularly those from higher castes, all other members regularly attend the meetings. The scheduled caste members (both women and men) do not miss any meetings. In the beginning, female members were counted as having attended if an adult member of their family represented them. Subsequently, it was decided that they would have to come at least to sign in, but their male relations continued to be allowed to participate in the discussions.

The sarpanch encourages all the members to participate in the discussion but takes the final decision on the advice of a Khandayat member and the husbands of the *naib*-sarpanch and another female member. The sarpanch considers the opinion of other members if it suits him. While the higher caste members give their opinion freely on matters relating to the scheduled castes, the members of the lower castes are not allowed to participate in the discussion on issues relating to the higher castes. For example, when a scheduled caste member wanted to intervene in the argument between two higher caste members about the allotment of funds for the renovation of a temple, he was discouraged. One member of the high caste retorted: 'You keep quiet. We have not sought your advice. You have become a ward member but that does not mean that you will interfere in everybody's affairs'.

Whenever the female members suggest or recommend a matter for discussion, the opinion of their male family members is taken into account. When identifying the beneficiaries of the Indira Awas Yojana and Annapurna schemes, the names suggested by the female members were included in consultation with the male members of their families. However, in the case of the Pana female member, the sarpanch himself took the decision. Though the practice of untouchability is not observed in the panchayat meetings, caste- and class-based discrimination is certainly visible. While all the other members address each other with terms of respect or affection, the female Pana member alone is addressed by her name. Even the peon of the panchayat does this. Once, there were not enough chairs in the meeting space and she was asked to sit on the floor while all the other members sat on chairs.

The *gram sabha* has been called eight times during the tenure of the present sarpanch. No more than 20 people attended any of these meetings and the signatures of others were obtained afterwards to get the quorum. The attendance was higher for scheduled caste members than for members of other castes because the panchayat office is located near a *harijan basti*. The higher caste women did not attend these meetings. The sarpanch and the other members did not encourage free discussion. In a meeting after a cyclone, one scheduled caste member asked about the reasons for the unfair distribution of the blankets received by the panchayat from a non-governmental organization, annoying the sarpanch. Keeping this in mind, he asked that scheduled caste person to repay ₹250 taken on credit from him the next day. The sarpanch also deleted his name from the Antodaya Anna Yojana, under which he would have been given 20 kg of rice per month at a subsidized price.

The *pallisabha*s of the panchayat hardly meet. The panchayat secretary has maintained records of six *pallisabha* meetings. As the approval of the *pallisabha* is required when implementing various schemes and identifying their beneficiaries, many fictitious records are maintained for official purposes. It was revealed by some people, whose signatures are on record, that they have neither attended those meetings nor signed the papers. Most of the signatures are against the names of the members of the scheduled castes.

One way of assessing the nature of the participation of excluded groups in the decision-making process at the local level is to make a comparative analysis of their share in various developmental schemes implemented through the panchayats. It is found that in all the panchayats the dominant groups have appropriated the major share of the benefits of the developmental schemes (see Table 7.1). The women and the members of scheduled castes have not been able to enhance their share in the panchayat, even when the sarpanch belongs to their own groups. However, the scheduled castes' share is appreciably better in schemes such as Indira Awas Yojana. Nearly half of the beneficiaries of this scheme belong to scheduled castes. The greater number of beneficiaries from scheduled castes in the case of Indira Awas Yojana in Marshaghai panchayat is largely due to a greater concentration of BPL households from that category. Moreover, nearly

Table 7.1
Caste Distribution of Beneficiaries of Major Schemes Implemented in the Three Selected Panchayats between 1997 and 2000

		Panchayat		
Scheme		*Silipur*	*Dashipur*	*Marshaghai*
Indira Awas Yojana	Total beneficiaries	72	75	75
	Beneficiaries from scheduled castes	35	36	45
	Beneficiaries from scheduled castes (%)	48.61	48.00	60.00
Annapurna	Total beneficiaries	4	5	11
	Beneficiaries from scheduled castes	1	1	1
	Beneficiaries from scheduled castes (%)	25.00	20.00	9.09
Disabled Pension	Total beneficiaries	4	4	9
	Beneficiaries from scheduled castes	1	2	3
	Beneficiaries from scheduled castes (%)	25.00	50.00	33.33
Antodaya Anna Yojana	Total beneficiaries	53	58	75
	Beneficiaries from scheduled castes	17	17	21
	Beneficiaries from scheduled castes (%)	32.08	29.31	28.00
Old age and Widow Pension (State Govt.)	Total beneficiaries	92	111	189
	Beneficiaries from scheduled castes	9	8	11
	Beneficiaries from scheduled castes (%)	9.78	7.21	5.82
Old age and Widow Pension (Central Govt.)	Total beneficiaries	54	60	96
	Beneficiaries from scheduled castes	5	7	9
	Beneficiaries from scheduled castes (%)	9.26	11.67	9.38

(Table 7.1 Contd.)

(Table 7.1 Contd.)

Scheme		Panchayat		
		Silipur	Dashipur	Marshaghai
JRY	Total given (₹)	7,101,245	760,294	509,500
	Total given to scheduled caste members (₹))	620,000	70,000	20,000
	Proportion given to scheduled caste members (%)	8.73	9.21	3.93

half of these beneficiaries are Kewats. Though the number of beneficiaries is relatively high in the case of Antodaya Anna Jojana and Annapurna (a scheme that provides 10 kg of free foodgrains per month to those senior citizens who, although eligible, do not receive an old age pension), it is negligible in absolute terms. In case of both the union- and state-government-led old-age pension schemes, the members of scheduled castes have hardly benefitted. Although the majority of the poor senior citizens in these panchayats belong to scheduled castes, scheduled caste members only make up about 10 per cent of the beneficiaries of the old age pension schemes. The interests of women and scheduled castes have largely been ignored in the Jawahar Rojgar Yojana (JRY) scheme (a poverty alleviation scheme designed to generate supplementary employment opportunities for the rural poor during agricultural slack periods by creating social assets such as public roads, ponds and forests). Even in the panchayat that is headed by a scheduled caste sarpanch, only four per cent of the total JRY fund was given over to the development of scheduled castes. In the other two panchayats, the allocation of funds for scheduled castes was comparatively better.

CONCLUSIONS

The power structure in rural areas involves diverse interactions between different dimensions of inequality such as class, caste, gender and political party affiliation. It does not correspond neatly to any general model, but it operates broadly within a caste–gender-based class framework. The inclusion of the hitherto excluded groups in the panchayats led only to their formal empowerment not the real empowerment. The persisting class, caste and gender hierarchies and domination largely neutralize the potential effects of the constitutional amendment aimed at empowering hitherto excluded and marginalized groups. It is rightly argued that the provisions of inclusion of members of the hitherto excluded groups in the *panchayati raj* bodies has enhanced their participation in the decision-making process at the local level, but it is inadequate for their empowerment (Mohanty, 2009: 74). The dominant sections used several strategies to minimize the effective presence of women and the members of scheduled castes in the panchayats affairs in order to retain their traditional hegemony over the panchayats. They mostly followed the course of conciliation and manipulation rather than that of open confrontation. To meet the demands of the new constitutional amendment for inclusion of the members of hitherto excluded groups in the panchayats, the privileged groups have co-opted either the dominant members of those groups, who are able to protect their caste–class interests or the loyal and faithful members who can act as their agents in the panchayats. The female representatives are made as proxies for their male relatives and they are often representatives in name only. The phenomenon of proxy role played by women's husbands/sons is common across several states in India (Baviskar and Mathew, 2009: 14). Male domination, particularly in public spheres, inhibits women in coming forward.

However, this does not mean that the members of scheduled castes and women do not gain anything at all. There is a silver lining in this cloudy and gloomy scenario. Even symbolic gain has certain value. Participating in the election process, becoming representatives, attending meetings and expressing viewpoints at various levels are all signs of change in the lives of the members of hitherto excluded groups. The exposure to panchayats allowed them to become aware of many aspects of local governance and they are gradually learning the rules of the game. They acquire confidence and are asserting themselves to gain democratic rights as well as the benefits of development.

As the three studied panchayats are located in the heartland of upper caste dominance and patriarchy, it is difficult for the members of scheduled castes and women to assert their rights that openly challenge the existing social order however well-framed the constitutional provisions. As per the norms, the members of scheduled castes were expected to serve the higher castes and remained loyal to them. Barring a handful of few, they mostly work as landless agricultural labourers and depend on rich upper castes for their day-to-day employment and livelihood. Similarly, though differences exist among women in terms economic conditions they are invariably subordinate to their male counterparts across the groups. Any change in women's roles and responsibility are tolerable as long as it does not alter the existing gender relations. Moreover, as this region has not witnessed any kind of social transformation from below, the caste–class- and gender-based inequality and domination is deeply frozen in the social structure. Given this situation, changes initiated from above can never be smooth and the unwillingness of the dominant groups to surrender their power to the members of hitherto excluded groups is not something unusual.

Though the response of the members of scheduled castes and women to the new provisions are somewhat similar in the three studied panchayats, the participation of the members of the scheduled castes and women in the panchayat (Marshaghai) headed by a scheduled caste sarpanch is relatively higher in terms of attendance in meetings, raising of issues in meetings, etc. To go by the share in development measures, the scheduled castes are in a better position in this panchayat than that of the other two panchayats, however small it may be. Therefore, Marshaghai panchayat has witnessed stronger reactions from the dominant sections, particularly from upper caste male members. Moreover, in this panchayat the *naib*-sarpanch also is a member of scheduled caste and, moreover, a woman. True, the panchayat (Dashipur) headed by a woman sarpanch is dominated by the sarpanch's husband, but the women members in this panchayat made attempts to voice their concerns and they attended the panchayat meetings although with male members of their families. It is interesting to note that the sarpanch presided over almost all the panchayat meetings and for the first three years of her tenure she was managing the routine affairs of the panchayat independently, and only from the time of super-cyclone relief distribution work, her husband took all decisions and she signed only the papers. It may be safe to conclude that a slow a process of social change is gradually setting in rural areas following the 73rd Constitutional Amendment. Baviskar (2009: 38) rightly observed, '[...] the process of empowerment is not one quantum jump. You do not jump from a zero power situation to an all power situation. Empowerment is a long journey and there are several stages on it path'. In this sense, the deprived sections of women and scheduled castes have a long way to go to share power in a way that transforms their lives and their relations with dominant and privileged sections of the rural society.

REFERENCES

Baboo, B. 1992. *Economic Exchanges in Rural Orissa*. New Delhi: Manak Publications.

Bailey, F.G. 1963. 'Politics and Society in Contemporary Orissa', in C.H. Philips (ed.), *Politics and Society in India*. London: George Allen and Unwin Ltd.

Baviskar, B.S. 2009. 'Including the Excluded: Empowering the Powerless through Panchayati Raj in Maharashtra', in B.S. Baviskar and G. Mathew (eds), *Inclusion and Exclusion in Local Governance: Field Studies from Rural India*. New Delhi: SAGE Publications.

Baviskar, B.S. and G. Mathew. 2009. 'Introduction', in B.S. Baviskar and G. Mathew (eds), *Inclusion and Exclusion in Local Governance: Field Studies from Rural India*. New Delhi: SAGE Publications.

Berreman, G.D. 1972. *Hindus of the Himalayas*. Berkeley: University of California Press.

Beteille, A. 1971. *Caste, Class and Power*. Berkeley: University of California Press.

Byres, T.J. 1981. 'The New Technology, Class Formation and Class Action in the Indian Countryside', *Journal of Peasant Studies*, 8(4): 405–54.

Carter, T.A. 1974. *Elite Politics in Rural India Political Stratification and Political Alliances in Western Maharashtra*. New Delhi: Vikas Publishing House Pvt. Ltd.

Dasgupta, B. 1977. 'India's Green Revolution'. *Economic and Political Weekly*, 12(6–8): 241–60.

Frankel, F. 1971. *India's Green Revolution: Economic Gains and Political Cost*. Princeton: Princeton University.

Harriss, J. 1999. 'Comparing Political Regimes Across Indian States. A Preliminary Essay'. *Economic and Political Weekly*, 34(48): 3367–77.

Jena, B.B. 1966. *Feudal Grip*. Seminar, November: 26–32.

Laxminarayana, H.D. 1970. 'Dominant Caste and Power Structure'. *Behavioural Science and Community Development*, 4(2): 146–60.

Lieten, G.K. 1996. *Development, Devolution and Democracy Village Discourse in West Bengal*. New Delhi: SAGE Publications.

Lieten, G.K. and R. Srivastav. 1999. *Unequal Partners, Power Relation and Development in Uttar Pradesh*. New Delhi: SAGE Publications.

Manor, J. 2000. 'Small-time Political Fixers in Indian States: "Towel Over Armpit"'. *Asian Survey*, 51(5): 816–35.

Mathew, G. and R. Nayak. 1996. 'Panchayats at Work, What It Means For The Oppressed?' *Economic and Political Weekly*, 31(27): 1765–71.

Mayer, A.C. 1958. 'The Dominant Caste in a Region of Central India'. *Southwestern Journal of Anthropology*, 14: 407–27.

Mohanty, B.B. 2000. 'Agricultural Modernisation in Rural Orissa: Land Transfer and Ownership Pattern'. *Sociological Bulletin*, 49(1): 63–90.

———. 2001. 'Land Distribution Among Scheduled Casters and Tribes'. *Economic and Political Weekly*, 36(40): 3857–68.

———. 2009. 'Power to the Excluded Groups and Panchayati Raj in Coastal Orissa', in B.S. Baviskar and George Mathew (eds), *Inclusion and Exclusion in Local Governance: Field Studies from Rural India*. New Delhi: SAGE Publications.

Mohanty, M. 1990. 'Class, Caste and Dominance in a Backward State: Orissa', in F.R. Frankel and M.S.A. Rao (eds), *Dominance and State Power in Modern India. Vol. II*. New Delhi: Oxford University Press.

Mohanty, M. and B.K. Bahidar. 1993. *Odisha Daridra Kahinki* (Oriya). Cuttack: Binod Bihari.

Moore, B. 1967. *Social Origins of Dictatorship and Democracy, Lord and Peasant in the Making of Modern Word*. Middlesex: Penguin Books Ltd.

Oommen, T.K. 1970. 'Rural Community Power Structure in India'. *Social Forces*, 49(2): 226–39.

Pai, S. 2000. 'New Social and Political Movements of Dalits: A Study of Meerut District'. *Contributions to Indian Sociology*, 34(2): 191–218.

Pathy, J. 1981. 'Class Structure in Rural Orissa', *Sociological Bulletin*, 30(2): 163–83.

Sahu, B.P. 1998. 'The Orissan Society: Past Trends and Present Manifestations', in K.L. Sharma (ed.), *Caste and Class in India*. New Delhi: Rawat Publications.

Sengupta, J. 2001. 'State, Market, and Democracy in the 1990s: Liberalisation and the Politics of Oriya Identity', in N.G. Jayal and S. Pai (eds), *Democratic Governance in India Challenges of Poverty, Development, and Identity*. New Delhi: SAGE Publications.

Srinivas, M.N. 1959. 'The Dominant Caste in Rampura', *American Anthropologist*, 61(1): 1–16.

Chapter 8

Between Order and Chaos

Jaffna's Local Images of Governance during Conflict

EVA GERHARZ

In May 2009, the Sri Lankan Army defeated the secessionist Liberation Tigers of Tamil Eelam (LTTE) and ended one of Asia's bloodiest civil wars. The efforts which were made to achieve this goal were massive and so were the civilian casualties. The last five months of Sri Lanka's 30-year-old civil war in particular were extremely bloody and claimed a large number of human lives.[1] With the fighting ceasing by the middle of May, hundreds of thousands of civilians crossed the frontline into government-held territory. They were interned in emergency camps run by the security forces and screened in order to identify those who were suspected of being LTTE activists. The cadres who had survived the last days and who could be singled out from the masses of internally displaced persons (IDPs) were put into detention camps.

The last stages of the war remained largely concealed from the eyes of international and national media. In September 2008, the Sri Lankan government restricted humanitarian operations in the war zone and ordered UN and international aid organizations to leave. The food and medical supplies organized by the government, however, were not sufficient for the large number of IDPs. Humanitarian operations attempting to ease the desperate situation of the trapped civilians came under attack (International Crisis Group, 2010: 10). Apart from international actors

[1] The numbers of civilian casualties have remained a matter of speculation and the estimates have varied from 7,000 to over 20,000 (International Crisis Group, 2010: 5).

pointing out the terror of war and civilian atrocities, only few critical voices could be heard within Sri Lanka. Mahinda Rajapakse, who was elected as the president in 2005, set up a regime that utilized the 'war on terror' against the LTTE to establish repressive ways of governance. Dissenting media remained under threat and were silenced by rank brutality (Wickramasinghe, 2009b: 65). The attempts of international organizations and members of the donor community to put pressure on the Sri Lankan government were not effective; instead, they led to the government becoming increasingly inward-orientated and alienated from the international community. Those few civil society groups that raised human rights issues had accusing fingers pointed at them and were suspected of having sympathized with the much-abhorred international community (Wickramasinghe, 2009a: 1047). In a similar vein, the Sri Lankan government heavily opposed the UN Secretary General's move to install a 'Panel of Experts on Accountability in Sri Lanka', obstructed the experts' fact-finding mission and rejected the report, published in April 2011, as being unacceptable.[2]

The end of the war and of the LTTE also ushered in an era marked by the Sri Lankan government's uncontested power over the national territory. Since the LTTE was founded in the mid-1970s, initially as a guerrilla group, it had continuously worked towards gaining enough strength, not only to control the Tamil-inhabited areas in Sri Lanka's north and east in military ways, but also to establish a system of governance regulating various spheres of civilian life. The organization had established its own police force, a banking system, humanitarian organizations, schools, orphanages, a television station and a judicial system including its own penal code in the areas under its control (see Stokke, 2006; Cheran, 2009). This system was running parallel to the local institutions representing the Sri Lankan state and produced a peculiar situation: the coexistence of two competing governance systems during the war, with which Tamil civilians had become accustomed to living.

Ensuring uncontested state control over the entire national territory had been the vision of Mahinda Rajapakse's regime, and to achieve this

---

[2] Retrieved from http://articles.cnn.com/2011-04-26/world/united.nations. sri.lanka_1_tamil-tiger-rebels-war-crimes-government-troops?_s=PM:WORLD (accessed on 15 July 2012); the report is available at: http://www.un.org/News/dh/ infocus/Sri_Lanka/POE_Report_Full.pdf (accessed on 15 July 2012).

goal a large part of the Sinhalese population living in Sri Lanka's south was mobilized to back the Sri Lankan Army's campaign against the LTTE. This method of bringing about the end of the ethnic conflict had not always been the dominant one. 'Softer' forms of conflict resolution, based on mediation and negotiation in order to find a peaceful solution satisfying all parties, had dominated Sri Lanka's war theatre only a few years before. In 2002, Rajapakse's predecessor's government had signed a ceasefire agreement with the LTTE which was already the fifth such attempt, and the one which showed the most promise to lay the grounds for sustainable peace. The agreement officially accepted the borders between the territories held by the government and the LTTE at the time.

During the ceasefire of 2002, optimistic voices also talked about a 'post-conflict situation', but one marked by attempts to find ways to accommodate the parties' differing interests through comprehensive reforms of the system of governance. The approach favoured by more progressive Sinhalese and Tamil politicians and civil society representatives, along with large sections of the Tamil population, was to create a federal state with far-reaching devolution of power (Bigdon, 2003; Uyangoda, 2003). This would also have implied considerable concessions to the LTTE, which utilized the ceasefire to consolidate its governance institutions. But, like earlier attempts (see for example Tiruchelvam, 1999, 2000), this option was heavily disputed by the conservative sections of the Sinhalese establishment and the resultant political polarization paved the way for Rajapakse's electoral victory. Having ended a military impasse, however, the ceasefire of 2002 was seen as a turning point by many, especially by the international community, which agreed to allocate large sums of money for reconstruction and development. The temporal stabilization of the peace process encouraged the war-weary population in the Tamil-dominated areas to develop visions of reconstruction and development[3] in a context where two competing governance systems of the Sri Lankan state and the LTTE coexisted.

It is exactly this situation of dual governance which shaped people's everyday lives in the northern Jaffna peninsula during the ceasefire of

---

[3] Showing how reconstruction and development is negotiated and tracing the visions of development in northern Sri Lanka was at the core of my research interest, pursued at the University of Bielefeld (Gerharz, 2014).

2002, and which is at the centre of interest here. During the ethnographic fieldwork that I conducted in Jaffna and other parts of Sri Lanka between 2002 and 2004, I observed that although Jaffna was under government control, the LTTE exerted enormous influence in different ways. And while the official rhetoric has condemned the LTTE as oppressing the local population (which, therefore, needs to be liberated by the Army), I found that the perspectives are more varied and the relationship between the LTTE and the population of Jaffna is indeed much more complex. The aim of this article is, thus, to reveal the local perspectives on the LTTE or the Government of Sri Lanka and their systems of governance, and how their respective modes of exerting power impinged on people's everyday lives. First, the concept of locality (Appadurai, 1995; Pfaff-Czarnecka, 2005) will be explained in order to gain a clearer understanding of why the focus on local space can be a fruitful entry point, and how it serves as an analytical tool to grasp the complexity of the relationship between the local society and the state.[4] Later, the local images of governance in Jaffna after 2002 will be analysed with a focus on different societal realms. Based on my empirical data I will firstly show how people viewed and negotiated the governance protagonists' ability to ensure law and order. The second part deals with how Jaffna Tamils regarded the civilian administration, the military and the LTTE as being actors in local development. The final part of this chapter looks at the situation today and asks questions about the visions of governance in a post-LTTE world.

JAFFNA—A TAMIL LOCALITY

Jaffna peninsula, the northernmost part of Sri Lanka, is almost exclusively inhabited by Tamils[5] and claimed to be the cultural centre of

---

[4] Debates on the reconstitution of the ethnographic field (for example Gupta and Ferguson, 1997) have highlighted the necessity to think beyond local boundaries. In the case of the research presented in this article, however, it makes sense to take a somewhat deeper look into the qualities of the local in relation to the nation-state.

[5] Tamils are a numerical minority in Sri Lanka's population. According to the 1981 census, Tamils constituted 18.1 per cent of the total population. Since the war started, the northern and eastern districts have been excluded from the national census and no reliable numbers on the composition of the population are available.

Tamil Eelam.[6] It is the place where the LTTE was established by its leader V. Prabakharan in the mid-1970s and where, according to the most common version of history, the war began in 1983 (Tambiah, 1986; Somasundaram, 1998). Jaffna has been regarded as centrally important to the conflict for both parties throughout the war, which has in turn been the result of continuous construction of the peninsula as an important locality. Being a peninsula, Jaffna has certainly clearly demarcated natural territorial boundaries. But what else makes a locality special? In order to answer this question, Appadurai's (1995: 204) theoretical concept of locality seems to be useful:

> I view locality as primarily relational and contextual rather than as scalar or spatial. I see it as a complex phenomenological quality constituted by a series of links between the sense of social immediacy, the technologies of interactivity, the relativity of contexts. This phenomenological quality which expresses itself in certain kinds of agency, sociality, and reproducibility, is the main predicate of locality as a category (or subject) that I seek to explore.

As such, locality is a phenomenological property of social life, a structure of feeling produced by several forms of intentional activity, whereas the relational aspect of it is directly connected to the actual settings in and through which social life is produced. Pfaff-Czarnecka (2005) has taken Appadurai's theoretical insights and comes to the conclusion that a locality is characterized by four dimensions of interaction. These dimensions have helped me to structure the complex locality constructions in the case of Jaffna, too.

The first dimension is the conceptualization of locality as an administrative unit with specific characteristics (Pfaff-Czarnecka, 2005: 495). Second, locality is a space of contracted interpersonal relationships, wherein face-to-face interactions take place under conditions of reciprocity. The locality constitutes a dense social field with aggregated social interactions (Pfaff-Czarnecka, 2005: 495). In Jaffna, the density of social relations intensified from the late 1990s until the ceasefire agreement, because it was in a state of isolation and almost completely detached from

---

[6] Tamil Eelam is the emic concept of the Tamil homeland promoted in nationalist discourses and was used to refer to the territory claimed by the LTTE.

the mainland.[7] Consequently, economic and social relations were highly inwardly-oriented (van Horen, 2002). The ceasefire temporarily ended the isolation. Third, a locality can be understood as a space for identity construction (Pfaff-Czarnecka, 2005: 495). In Jaffna, identities have been constructed through a complex process with dimensions of both time and space. The label 'Jaffna Tamil' entails an equation incorporating ethnic and local identities. At the same time, it gains particular meaning in relation to other Sri Lankan Tamils. One demarcation line has been constructed between 'Jaffna Tamils' and 'Batticaloa Tamils'. Basically, Tamils from Jaffna are regarded as predominantly high caste and as generally hegemonic in the dynamics of the ethnic struggle.[8] As the people constituting the population of the 'heart of Tamil culture', they are constructed and construct themselves as collectively representing the culturally purest and most authentic Tamils. 'Tamilness' as a regionally based local identity implies belonging to these smaller local categories, which are encapsulated within the larger locality construction. At a more general level, locality constructions in Jaffna entail aspects of caste, positioning within the national economy and politics,[9] including Tamil resistance, since the LTTE as well as most other separatist groups originate from Jaffna. A fourth dimension refers to the significance of the locality as representation, which takes

---

[7] The peninsula, which is connected to the mainland only through a small strip of land called Elephant Pass, was cut off for military strategic and security reasons. Moreover, the only connecting road had been blocked because of fighting in the Vanni and LTTE control. Since August 2006, Jaffna has been cut off again due to the deteriorating political and military situation in Sri Lanka.

[8] The construction of different Tamil identities in Sri Lanka is much more complex and does not only rely on a differentiation between Jaffna and Batticaloa Tamils. Rather, various dynamics of counter-identity construction take place between 'Sri Lankan' and 'Indian' Tamils, the latter working in the tea plantations in the up-country. Moreover, Wilson (1994) and Hellmann-Rajanayagam (2004), as well as many other authors, refer to the significance of the 'Colombo Tamils' as a distinct identity group. Another aspect is the doubtful attempt to incorporate the Eastern Muslim population made by the LTTE and lately Karuna's organization. Particularly in the east, these attempts are complicated by reciprocal demarcation and ethnic stereotyping (McGilvray, 2001). The various demarcation processes are deeply embedded into political struggles, and economic and cultural differences; the caste-aspect often referred to is just a very limited aspect within these processes.

[9] Almost all Tamil politicians who have appeared as strong representatives originated from Jaffna.

place in reciprocal perspectives about the self and the other. This aspect is closely related to the aspect of identity construction but highlights the ways in which identity markers are strategically used for representation.

Historically, Jaffna as a space for identity construction contributed to the emergence of Tamil armed resistance in the late 1970s. A large section of the younger generation of relatively educated Tamils in Jaffna appeared as a politicized segment in society, producing a whole range of groups, political parties and associations. The militancy of the LTTE along with a couple of other groups was a reaction to the inability of the Sri Lankan state to address the political demands of the minority Tamils. At the same time, it also provided an alternative to the upper-class political establishment of Jaffna origin that had failed to make Tamil voices heard in Sri Lankan politics (Cheran, 2009: xxxiii). The LTTE was able to consolidate its position as the main group in a multiplex, fractured setting (Hellmann-Rajanayagam, 1986). Although it developed a strategy of incorporating other localities and extending the locality of reference for Tamil identity (Tamil Eelam), stressing that all Tamils are equal, Jaffna remained a major place of reference apart from the Vanni, where the LTTE had established its stronghold after 1995. Whether the LTTE was able to represent all Tamil-speaking people in Sri Lanka in such a way as its leadership claimed, remained highly disputed inside and outside the organization. More critical voices highlighted the fact that most high-ranking cadres were from Jaffna.

COMPETING SYSTEMS OF GOVERNANCE

During the mid-1980s, the LTTE had systematically pushed aside other groups and established a hegemonic position in representing Tamil nationalism and resistance to the chauvinistic oppression of the Sinhala-dominated state.[10] During this time, the Jaffna peninsula came under full control of the LTTE, which attempted to regulate all aspects of civilian life there:

> The LTTE tried its hand at social welfare projects, initiating primary health units, running co-op hospitals, opening reading rooms, libraries

[10] Cheran (2009) provides an excellent analysis of the LTTE's evolution and its political programme.

and children's playgrounds. Cultural activities were also organized. They introduced a tax system and made mutually beneficial arrangements with merchants and businessmen. Rural courts under the LTTE functioned creditably when compared with the bureaucratic delays and costs of the official courts. A crusade was launched against trafficking *kasippu* (illicitly brewed liquor), narcotics and *ganja*. LTTE put up a daily bulletin at all road junctions and requested feedback suggestions from the public through the 'yellow mail boxes'. Much of their propaganda work was carried out through their television network (*Nidershanam*), the local press which they controlled, posters, village-level organizations, meetings and 'loud-speaker vehicles'. The LTTE quietly infiltrated almost all organizations, administrative bodies, public committees, hospitals, schools, and so on. They claimed that there was a 'Tiger supporter' in every home. (Somasundaram, 1998: 66)

The peninsula, which was cut off from the mainland both for security reasons and as a result of battles, was the first locality to come under LTTE administration. It remained in the hands of the LTTE without much interference by the central government, except that salaries to government officials were still paid by the central government. As I was told by several interviewees and as descriptions from literature substantiate, the administration run by the LTTE functioned effectively. But its repressive attitude towards those who criticized the absence of democracy and human rights has placed their lives under severe threat. In October 1995, LTTE rule was ended by the troops of the Sri Lankan government. The LTTE ordered the population to move to the areas further east and to the Vanni located to the south of Jaffna in 'the great exodus', as local people called this human tragedy. While almost the entire Jaffna peninsula came under the control of the Sri Lankan Army, the LTTE consolidated its power in the Vanni area, with Kilinochchi as the base.

During the ceasefire of 2002, the LTTE consolidated its state-like structures and institutions in the territory which was assigned to it in the ceasefire agreement. The LTTE constructed a huge administrative complex in Kilinochchi, hosting the main branches of its governing body. The complex also comprised a kind of welcome centre, where representatives from foreign countries, donors and peace negotiators were hosted. Much like the situation in Jaffna before 1995, the LTTE controlled public life in its territory in all respects. Tamil Eelam Courts were established, and the Tamil Eelam Police Force enforced law and order. The Bank of Tamil Eelam monopolized the banking sector and diverse welfare and development organizations established their offices in the town of Kilinochchi. The public space was dominated by LTTE symbols such as posters, flags and monuments, and so was the service sector: guesthouses and restaurants serving predominantly international visitors were in the pocket of the LTTE.

In Jaffna, on the other hand, administration was performed by the bodies representing the central government. This was strongly influenced by the Sri Lankan Army and security personnel that showed a massive presence all over the peninsula. Jaffna's rural hinterland was marked by a large number of army camps and considerable parts of Jaffna town were also occupied by their camps. The military-controlled High Security Zones (HSZ) remained inaccessible to civilians. At the same time, the ceasefire agreement made it possible for the LTTE to re-establish offices for political work. At the time this research was conducted, in 2003 and 2004; I could see that LTTE political offices were established in many villages in Jaffna. Not permitted to carry weapons or wear the camouflage uniforms common to LTTE cadres elsewhere, however, they remained largely invisible to an outsider. According to local people, the Sri Lankan Monitoring Mission (SLMM),[11] and the International Red Cross members, LTTE cadres were omnipresent beneath the surface.

The presence of military rule and a civilian administration, representing the central government of Sri Lanka on the one hand, and the LTTE on the other, created a peculiar situation. Jaffna was officially a part of the Sri Lankan state, which was represented by its institutions at all administrative levels. Apart from the government agent and his office, divisional secretaries were paid by the central government to work on their behalf. While they depended on the payroll of the central government, the LTTE controlled their work. Furthermore, the government officials were under critical observation by the local population, who remained suspicious about their dedication to the needs of the people. Moreover, military rule led to a subordination of civil administration (Shanmugaratnam and Stokke, 2008: 108).

After its capture by the Sri Lankan Army, Jaffna was, thus, characterized by two parallel systems of governance. The state governed the peninsula

---

[11] The SLMM is a mission consisting of several Nordic countries. It is responsible for observing the compliance of the ceasefire agreement.

officially, the LTTE unofficially. Both systems were in strong competition with each other and both state(-like) actors were present in people's everyday lives and perceptions. This situation had terrible consequences for the civilians during the war: Somasundaram (2010) shows how the population was trapped between the two sides, both of whom terrorized them in the course of the so-called counter-insurgency operations. The ceasefire of 2002 relieved the tight control on the local population and eased their daily life. Curfews, controls and searches at check posts, arbitrary arrests and revenge killings became less common; although cases of disappearance, torture and intimidation continued to be reported, they were lesser in number. In terms of governance, the Government of Sri Lanka acted as the state, exerting full power over the territory. The LTTE, which had established a state-like system in the Vanni, made use of the more open situation after the signing of the ceasefire and enhanced its influence and power over certain domains in Jaffna—from the economic sector to political opinion formation—in a more open way than before. The contested status of the locality itself raises the question of how the local population viewed the opposing rulers' legitimacy.

WHO CAN ENSURE LAW AND ORDER?

During my fieldwork a great deal of public discourse was centred on the so-called 'moral degradation'. One Sunday morning a dead body was found right opposite our house. At first, nobody knew where it came from, but I was later told that it was a man who did not behave in a morally upright manner. He was known as a 'bad person' who had allegedly committed robberies, sexual harassment and a number of smaller crimes. One informant blamed a 'group to protect from cultural degradation' which had been formed by activists at the beginning of 2004 as a 'watchdog'. Their aim was the maintenance of 'traditional culture' in the locality and to avenge negative behaviour. The emergence of this group was supposedly related to the number of cases of sexual harassment and other forms of 'moral degradation' that, as local people claimed, increased during the period of research between 2002 and 2004. Women, including visitors from Western countries, were subject to sexual harassment and were physically attacked by male youths while walking or cycling on the street. These incidents happened during the day as well as in the evening.

When discussing these events, most local people expressed regret that these incidents had happened. Some argued that they indicated a lack of respect, especially towards Western women, arising as a result of stereotypes. Others claimed that these kinds of attacks happened to local women as well and that they were a general problem in today's Jaffna. Some men said that women in general should not go out after seven o'clock in the evening. Others regretted that it was unsafe for women to go out at night; they felt that men should respect women, enabling them to feel safe. Several conversation partners claimed that in the LTTE-controlled Vanni, women could go out at any time and be completely safe. One idea regarding possible action initiatives to charge this kind of 'small crime' was to make a complaint at the police station. This was rejected immediately, because 'they would not do anything'. The same was said of the military. Instead, several interviewees claimed that the best option would be to go to the political office of the LTTE and make a complaint there, since this would be the only effective way to prevent such incidents in the future. The LTTE was also suspected of having been responsible for the killing.

Jaffna had become a locality under government control, with the law enforced by the Sri Lankan security forces, the law and order situation had changed negatively in people's perception. In the images of many inhabitants of Jaffna, the security situation was often contrasted with law and order conditions under LTTE rule. This was also related to the observation that, although the peninsula was not under LTTE rule, the organization was seen as a more forceful and effective institution than the military in enforcing law and order.

Many locals perceived the state of military control in Jaffna as a de facto foreign occupation. For the last 20 years, the military forces had represented the Sri Lankan government as a party to the conflict, and as opposition to the claims put forward by Tamil nationalists. One should be careful, of course, not to equate the LTTE with the opposing conflict party and with the Tamil people in general. But still, many interviewees expressed the view that the peninsula was in a state of being 'occupied', rather than 'liberated', as the peninsula's state was officially labelled by the Sri Lankan government. Interviewees claimed that as long as there was military presence, normalcy could not be restored in the peninsula. In their view, the army presence meant the absence of the necessary conditions for sustainable peace. Moreover, fighting had affected civilian lives in often terrible ways and caused several civilian casualties. Experiences of violence initiated by members of the Sri Lankan Army led to a considerable lack of trust among the local population. Although some people stated during interviews that the relationship between army personnel and the people had become more relaxed during the ceasefire, cases of harassment perpetrated by the omnipresent security personnel were still reported. Outbreaks and incidents of violence against civilians in Jaffna also indicated that the improvement was a temporary phenomenon and as such not to be trusted.

In addition to a general sense of mistrust, it was argued by some local interviewees that the army and the police force were not interested in maintaining law and order on behalf of the Tamil civilians. The almost exclusively Sinhalese security personnel, without proficiency in Tamil language or any sensitivity for Tamil customs and cultural specifics, would not show any interest in setting the conditions for peaceful coexistence. Nor would they attempt to reinforce decency in public. Elderly Tamils in particular explained this to be an important aspect of Tamil culture, which the younger generation would not adopt without it being enforced. Regarding the cases of sexual harassment one interviewee stated:

> This is the young crowd, nobody controls them. It also affects Tamil girls. The police are not doing a proper job of controlling them. In the LTTE-controlled areas it is very different, they are showing the young people how to respect women. In general, our culture is very good. The Sinhalese army people are not worried about our discipline, they don't care about our culture. They don't want to control the young crowd.

The relationship between the security forces and the local population appeared to be characterized by a sense of mutual distrust and alienation, which was, to a large extent, an expression of ethnic polarization based on a strong reference to local culture. Jaffna was represented as a locality in which 'Tamil culture' was regarded in a very static way as self-disciplined, strict and morally pure (Tambiah, 1986: 105). These qualities were not valued by the Sinhalese soldiers because of their being culturally, but also ethnically different: because the soldiers did not belong to the same ethnic group, they did not have the ability to understand and appreciate the qualities inherent in Tamil culture.

Another explanation for the rise of sexual harassment is related to the perception that the Sinhalese soldiers represented immoral behaviour, since they were known and feared as perpetrators of sexual harassment. Like many other conflict situations, the war perpetuated practices of prostitution and sex trade in the north and east (de Alwis and Hyndman, 2002: 36). In Jaffna itself, a trend for increased prostitution began with the takeover by the military in 1995 (Somitharan, 2005). In situations where law and order was not ensured, people tended to contrast the present situation with that under LTTE rule. Jaffna's past as an LTTE-controlled locality was used as a model. Interviewees and conversation partners referred to effective law enforcement under LTTE rule, which implied that incidents of immoral behaviour were addressed immediately. One interviewee said: 'When the Tigers were here, things like that never happened. A boy did not even dare to look at a girl because he knew that he would be punished. Under them, women were absolutely safe in Jaffna.'

The LTTE-controlled Vanni also served as a contrasting model. In Kilinochchi, the LTTE attempted to establish a de facto state, exercising full control over the district's territories, as well as maintenance of its border control and its structures entailing three basic functions: security, welfare and representation (Stokke, 2006). The security function was implemented particularly effectively and was based on the Tamil Eelam judicial system, consisting of Tamil Eelam Courts and the Tamil Eelam Police Forces. Stokke highlights that the political background for the judicial system was

> the subversion of the rule of law by the Prevention of Terrorism Act and protracted warfare. This created the need for a functioning judicial system, both to maintain law and order and to reinstate legitimacy for the rule of law itself. (Stokke, 2006: 1027)

Hence, it was the answer to the war's erosive effect on law and order. At the same time, it reflects the LTTE's aim to tailor a judicial system based on 'Tamilness', as opposed to the Sinhala-dominated rule of law of the state.[12]

---

[12] See the interview with the Head of the Judicial Division of the LTTE: http://www.tamilnet.com/art.html?catid=79&artid=10277 (accessed on 16 July 2011).

Stokke (2006: 1028) points out that the judicial system run by the LTTE carried a certain degree of legitimacy. Several informants in the field supported his assertion that it worked well and that the majority respected the courts' decisions. Law enforcement was based on oppressive force, and quite often it was rather draconian (see Cheran, 2009: xlv). Its effectiveness, however, was valued by many. The same applied for the Tamil Eelam police, even though this was due to authoritarian rule rather than community policing. I observed strict obedience to LTTE rule whenever I travelled from Jaffna to the Vanni. The drivers used to speed up in the government-controlled peninsula, despite speed limits. But immediately after crossing the checkpoints and entering the LTTE-controlled area, they started to strictly adhere to the speed limit. This turned out to be well reasoned: behind the trees next to the road Tamil Eelam police forces could be seen with radar, ready to collect a large fine for exceeding the speed limit. Most people, even the visitors from the south who had travelled to Jaffna, valued the high fines positively, because they were regarded as an effective measure for maintaining law and order. The general security situation in the Vanni was also welcomed in contrast to Jaffna: 'When you go to Vanni, even as a woman you can walk on the street even at twelve o'clock in the night. Nothing will happen to you'. Indeed, when I visited Kilinochchi with a German and a Jaffna Tamil friend, we three women had dinner at a restaurant quite late in the evening. The Tamil woman stressed quite excitedly that we could walk back to the guesthouse safely. She expressed the view that she enjoyed the freedom of movement in contrast to the everyday situation in Jaffna. The LTTE's ability to maintain law and order and to prevent small crime was valued highly by civilians in Jaffna, despite the LTTE's undemocratic and authoritarian mode of maintaining law and order and its bad human rights record.

AMBIVALENT LEGITIMACY

The situation of parallel governance in Jaffna was further complicated by the equivalence of civilian and military administration, both representing the state. The civilian administration—comprising the government agents' office at the district level, divisional secretaries and the *grama sevakas*—was appointed by the central government. A parallel structure, based on the provincial council system, included *pradeshiya sabha*s and municipal councils at the lower level, parallel to the divisional secretariats (Bigdon, 2003: 16). Although these latter institutions represented local governance, the members were, in contrast to the other areas of Sri Lanka, usually not elected in a democratic manner (Bigdon, 2003: 21). The civilian administration was additionally weakened due to the military presence, because civil administration was subordinate to the state's military command under the Prevention of Terrorism Act. Among most local people, the local governance institutions were not regarded as legitimate institutions representing local interests. Moreover, the government agent and the divisional secretaries were seen as being powerless, because their room to manoeuvre depended on the central government. A study conducted by Mayer (2002: 220) revealed that only a few youths in Jaffna attributed problem-solving capacities to local officials, in contrast to politicians and members of parliament. Mayer came to the conclusion that there was general frustration with the political system and that the youth were becoming increasingly marginalized within society (Mayer, 2002: 241). Hence, the relationship between the governmental system and the population was characterized by a lack of trust, whereas the military seemed to be a much stronger representative of the central state.

At the same time, the LTTE made use of the ceasefire and offered the people the opportunity to make complaints with regard to conflicts in the local public and private spheres, through its political offices and its women's wing representative. The legitimacy of governance institutions at the local level was thus contested by the LTTE. Along with the general lack of trust in the security forces, perceptions of the weak performance of local institutions in southern Sri Lanka contributed to a lack of trust in the state system. In Jaffna several interviewees drew the logical conclusion and argued that if the system does not work in the south, it would not work in the north, where the state and its representatives (the military) do not even feel a sense of responsibility since they had no personal and ethnic affiliation to the locality.

In contrast to the security forces, the LTTE evoked a feeling of attachment to the local community based on family bondage and ethnic identity. Many cadres originated from Jaffna. Quite often, local interviewees reported that cadres were their sons, daughters, cousins, brothers, sisters or former schoolmates. This kind of attachment gave the LTTE certain legitimacy. At the same time, the LTTE not only posed a threat to dissidents, but also changed societal dynamics at a more general level. It was stressed by women I interviewed that the parent–child relationship changed in a negative way. In cases of unwanted marriages and other claims made by parents against their children, it had become common among the youngsters to threaten to join the LTTE if the parents would not respect their wishes. None of the parents I got to know were happy about such statements.[13] One female interviewee stated that many women admire the female Tigers for being progressive with regard to gender roles. But at the same time, the female Tigers would avoid contact with civilians, so that the 'Tigress' as a role model had no impact on gender relations in society. Instead, they were considered to be too different from the rest of the community due to their attire. A civilian boy would never marry an LTTE girl, another interviewee stressed.

The relationship between Jaffna's civilians and the LTTE was, thus, highly ambivalent. Many people had suffered from attacks by the LTTE, for being suspected as opponents to the political position of the movement. At the same time, the 'boys', as the LTTE cadres were usually called by the civilians, were accepted in a leap of faith. However, having been exposed to the ruthless and brutal method of governance of the LTTE in Jaffna, the expression used by one interviewee might indicate the quality of the relationship: he described the connection between people in Jaffna and the LTTE as a 'love–hate relationship'.

To make sense of this highly ambiguous situation many people tried not to be partial, but maintained a certain distance from both systems of governance in what appeared to be an apolitical manner. Both the LTTE and the government were subject to critique. The central government, despite all its deficits, was accepted with a kind of resignation for the sake of peace. Meanwhile, the LTTE was criticized for child abductions, authoritarianism and ruthlessness, but at the same time admired for its strength, good organization and ability to maintain control. Moreover, for the sake of the recognition of their rights as equal citizens belonging to an

[13] Cases of forced abductions were never mentioned at least in my interviews in Jaffna, but it remains a serious issue in the LTTE-controlled areas in the north and east.

ethnic minority, it seemed that quite a lot of people would rather opt for the LTTE than for the central government, if they had the option to do so.

LOCAL GOVERNANCE REFORMS AND ECONOMIC DEVELOPMENT

The international donor community was highly committed to the Sri Lankan peace process after 2002. At the Donor Conference in Tokyo in 2003, it was agreed that $4.5 billion would be allocated for reconstruction and development. Moreover, both conflict parties and the donor community agreed on certain mechanisms to implement reconstruction measures in the northeast.[14] In concert with the Sri Lankan government, a pragmatic approach to peace was adopted which suggested that an immediate economic dividend needed to be created in order to lay a sustainable, broad-based foundation for a more complicated long-term political solution, given the many failed attempts to establish peace in the past. This strategy did not remain unchallenged. As Sriskandarajah has stated in a rather ironic way, the 'development cart' was put 'before the political horse' (Sriskandarajah, 2003).

Although economic development was regarded as first priority, donor agencies also acknowledged the need for reforms of the political system. Shortly after the signing of the ceasefire agreement, two Strategic Conflict Assessments (SCAs) were conducted in Sri Lanka and have become the major joint policy documents prepared by Sri Lanka's donor community. Both SCAs broach the issue of the crisis of the state as a framing characteristic of the conflict, stemming from a failure of governance. Accordingly, they state that the problem of governance should be at the centre of the donor's attention in the course of conflict management (Pirani and Kadirgamar, 2006: 1790). Among the basic problems of the Sri Lankan state is its highly centralized nature, which leaves only a little space for local institutions. Moreover, corruption, clientelist networks and, most

---

[14] The main institution created in the course of this process was the Subcommittee on Immediate Humanitarian Relief and Rehabilitation (SIHRN). It was allocated authority over activities financed with a Northeast Reconstruction Fund under the World Bank's supervision (see Kelegama, 2005: 3). In its initial phase, the SIHRN initiative failed.

importantly, the ethnicization of the whole state apparatus contribute to the weaknesses of the Sri Lankan state. The first SCA thus recommends that donors should support 'initiatives that help build a strong, legitimate and responsive state' (Goodhand, 2001: 17). It is widely felt that the main remedy for Sri Lanka's weak state, and thus the way to create sustainable peace, is devolution of power, or the establishment of a federal state. As a concept the latter has a history in Sri Lanka due to the continued negotiation on the issue in the national political space.[15] It has also been taken up by the international community as a goal to be achieved with the involvement of the parties on both sides of the conflict. The devolution of power to local government institutions was regarded as an important step in the improvement of governance, and thus a necessary precondition for consolidating the peace process and laying the foundation for development. In line with globally promoted ideas of conflict resolution as being dependent on the performance of the state, it has become the 'means for attaining a certain stage of development' (Wickramasinghe, 2001: 60).

Local perspectives on the devolution debate, however, have been more critical. A couple of interviewees expressed the opinion that the entire administrative set-up should be reformed and that this would not be in line with the interests of the central government. During the ceasefire, local government institutions were acting under the control of the central government, rather than under an institution governing the northeast. Although a provincial council system had been already set up in the late 1980s, the North East Provincial Council could not serve as a democratically legitimized tool for decentralization (Tiruchelvam, 2000: 203). There has been a widely held view that the a tension between the effort to devolve power to the provincial level and the unitary character of the state prevails, and that while devolution is not agreed upon at the central government level, the provincial council system cannot work towards ethnic reconciliation.[16] Interviewees in Jaffna argued that their local government bodies, being dependent on the central government, basically duplicated the

---

[15] The devolution debate in Sri Lanka is an old one, which goes back to the 1980s and the Indo-Lanka Peace Accord and has been continuously taken up as a possible solution to the conflict. See, for example, Uyangoda (1996) and Tiruchelvam (1999).

[16] For a discussion on the fallacies of the provincial council system, see Shastri (1994).

political practices and the political culture prevalent all over Sri Lanka. Because these practices were considered as ineffective, corrupt, and 'weak', the local institutions in Jaffna would not be able to perform any better than the central government that indirectly controlled them.

A different line of argument related to the state of development, according to many local people, was that the south was much better off in terms of development than the war-affected north. The Sinhala-dominated state was criticized for its inability to create conditions necessary for development. On the contrary, according to many local interviewees, the state itself was an obstacle to development. A dominant view in Jaffna was that the peninsula had done better in terms of development before the war (Sarvananthan, 2003). The production of agricultural goods and a couple of factories had supported Jaffna's economy. The large factories were destroyed during the war and due to the uncertain political situation investors were reluctant to move into Jaffna. Large parts of the agricultural land were mined. Several entrepreneurs I interviewed expressed their anger towards the government. One interviewee said:

> Before the ceasefire, four ships carrying goods from Jaffna got lost, two were bombed. The government has not paid compensation until now. What do they give now? Nothing. They should give us our money back. If something like this happens in other parts of Sri Lanka, even where minorities live, the government pays compensation immediately. In Jaffna bombing has stopped. That's all. If peace comes, we can develop easily. We do not want interference from the government. We want freedom, then we can develop easily.... If there is no interference, then everything will be okay. We will develop ourselves. The main problem of the people here is that they don't have freedom.

This quotation shows that there is a tendency to blame the state not only for not initiating development, but even for destroying the status quo that existed in Jaffna before the war. Although some local people tended to romanticize the 'good old days' before the war, the grievances of certain sections of the local population were also directly related to the performance of the government. However, it was not only the government that was blamed for obstructing development; the LTTE were also blamed, because they imposed taxes on salaries, earnings, imports, and remittances. During the ceasefire, people had to pay a certain amount for the import of a variety of goods such as electronics and motorized vehicles. Entrepreneurs in particular were subject to forced tax collections that bothered many people and prevented substantial economic investments (Sarvananthan, 2009). The LTTE also benefited from the increase in diaspora circulation after 2002. Tamils living outside Sri Lanka used the opportunity presented by the ceasefire agreement to return to Jaffna for short visits. These visitors and their relatives were subject to forced tax collection, as Human Rights Watch (2006)[17] has pointed out. These practices prevented diaspora Tamils from making investments that might have contributed to development and economic recovery in the north and east.

The military as the major representative of the state came into the picture when people complained about the so-called HSZ that remained largely inaccessible for the civilian population. The occupation of large areas of land in Jaffna presented a barrier to relocation and rehabilitation for the large numbers of IDPs who possessed land in the HSZ. A university professor referred to the collective desire to return to one's village of origin located in a HSZ: 'The resettlement issue is important for us. It is about access to our ancestral villages and it has a lot to do with our dignity. Before we die, will they allow us to see our village?' This statement reveals that people's grievances were quite often forgotten in the highly politicized debates. The LTTE, in turn, capitalized on the HSZ issue. Pretending to represent the people's needs and desires, it used the issue for propaganda purposes and for winning over the Jaffna Tamils' sympathy. In 2003 and 2004, the LTTE got the local non-governmental organizations (NGOs) together and organized public rallies, as well prominently presenting facts and figures on the HSZ on its website, gathering the support of the Tamil diaspora. The economic importance of the HSZ issue was highlighted: HSZ occupation meant that large areas of agricultural land could not be made use of. The fishing sector was affected as well, because Tamil fishermen were prevented from entering into their fishing grounds while large vessels from the Sri Lankan south harvested maritime resources further offshore. For many Jaffna inhabitants, the big question was how civilian

---

[17] See the report 'Funding the Final War: LTTE Intimidation and Extortion in the Tamil Diaspora' (Human Rights Watch, 2006). The report is available online: http://www.hrw.org/reports/2006/ltte0306/index.htm (accessed on 16 July 2006).

institutions could promote development in Jaffna, when the military was the actual ruling force in the peninsula.

Although the ceasefire agreement opened an array of economic opportunities, these were not perceived as contributing to sustainable development. Local entrepreneurs and development experts complained in concert that the opportunities were only in trade, not in any productive sector. Some people were also unhappy with the performance of foreign assistance agencies. In the Vanni, in contrast, economic development was much more dynamic, as one interviewee explained:

> Jaffna is a dead city. People are frustrated because no development is going on here. The organizations reduce their work here and go to the Vanni. Nine major organizations are working there. They are doing good work, not like in Jaffna. Here you are not getting a picture of what they are doing, you have to go to Kilinochchi. This is because the LTTE is not responsible for Jaffna, the government is here and the LTTE cannot do anything. Nobody is interested in development in Jaffna.

This interviewee opined in an extraordinarily clear way that Jaffna did not receive any development assistance because it was under the control of the government. His view is based on the assumption that the government is not interested in fostering development activities in Tamil-inhabited areas. This view is not just the result of the conflict, but originates in the pre-conflict era: before 1983, the per capita expenditure in Jaffna was less than half the national average, and between 1977 and 1982 the utilization of foreign aid in Jaffna was zero (Committee for Rational Development, 1984: 15, cited in Herring, 2001: 148). The interviewee's conclusion that hardly any development assistance reached Jaffna is not entirely correct, as there were a number of initiatives from bilateral and multilateral agencies. He assumed that the LTTE had influenced the donors to provide more support for the areas under its control. This assumption was based on the belief that the LTTE was more concerned with development in Tamil-inhabited areas than the government. It was true that more humanitarian agencies were present in the Vanni, but this was not down solely to the LTTE. Many development experts argued that the Vanni was considered to be in greater need than Jaffna. The latter had already received assistance before the ceasefire, and its population received much more benefit from diaspora remittances. It was rather an unintended effect that this kind of visibility worked for the LTTE's local credibility.

DIASPORA, NGOs AND DEVELOPMENT

The large number of Tamils who had emigrated from Sri Lanka became an important factor influencing governance after the ceasefire agreement. More than 800,000 Tamils were estimated to be living outside the country, of which at least 700,000 resided in Western countries (Sriskandarajah, 2002. 293). Many of them originated from Jaffna[18] and a large number of them regularly remitted money throughout the war and helped sustain the lives of their relatives (Cheran, 2001; Gerharz 2010; Van Hear, 2002). This considerably enhanced the chances of survival among Jaffna residents, compared to other regions in the northeast. Remittances continued to sustain many private households in Jaffna and were an important financial contribution to the reconstruction of damaged private property.

Apart from the financial contributions to individual families, a second kind of diaspora support for a variety of local organizations was also on the rise during the ceasefire. Home village organizations, Hindu temples, Christian development organizations and many alumni networks of Jaffna's schools could initiate reconstruction work thanks to remittances from abroad. These organizations received financial support from diaspora members who wished to make a contribution to the social institutions located in their place or village of origin. A third category was profession-based: health and medical organizations supported by diaspora Tamils had an especially visible presence in the northeast. The Medical Institute of Tamils and the Tamils Health Organization collected donations from Tamils living in Europe, North America and Australia and sent volunteers to work as experts to support ill-equipped local health care institutions. Fourthly, local NGOs also received support from the diaspora. The representatives of a variety of Jaffna-based NGOs told me in interviews that they were seeking financial contributions from Tamil friends, relatives,

---

[18] Gunaratna (1998: 301) states that about 90 per cent originated from Jaffna peninsula.

and associations abroad, and a few of them hosted volunteers who supported them in their daily work.

The development NGO sector was dominated by the Tamil Rehabilitation Organization (TRO) which had been registered as an independent non-profit organization, but was nevertheless regarded as being the developmental wing of the LTTE. The TRO was a true transnational organization: it was originally founded in Tamil Nadu, India in 1985 to serve the refugees from northern Sri Lanka. Later, it established offices in a range of countries where Tamils reside, which consolidated its presence there as well. After the LTTE was expelled from Jaffna in 1995, the TRO's headquarters were located in Kilinochchi next to the premises of the LTTE administrative complex. It served as the major humanitarian relief provider in the LTTE-controlled areas during the war and turned more towards developmental activities during the ceasefire. In 2003, its operating costs were Sri Lankan rupees (SLRs) 617.5 million; 73 per cent of the total funds received were from the diaspora.[19] The TRO was flanked by several other organizations operating in LTTE-controlled areas which benefited from the transnational linkages set up by the LTTE and TRO. At the same time, diaspora Tamils themselves initiated developmental activities in the LTTE-controlled Vanni: for example, Tamil IT specialists from the United States established Vanni Tech, a training academy for information technology, in Kilinochchi to enhance the Tamil youth's chances of obtaining higher education in Tamil-inhabited areas.

The above initiatives clearly dominated the field of diaspora-engagement during the ceasefire. They were much larger and far more visible than the activities of local actors in Jaffna and created the impression that developmental activities in the LTTE-controlled areas were more comprehensive and more dynamic. Although most actors operating in the LTTE-controlled areas claimed that these were in greater need than Jaffna, the LTTE was certainly involved and besides, it benefited from the developmental successes of these organizations. With the TRO and other organizations gaining a good reputation for delivering services to the people and enhancing their development, the LTTE-controlled areas were regarded as the 'hotspots' of post-conflict reconstruction and

---

[19] Retrieved from http://www.sangam.org/articles/view/?id=340 (accessed on 25 July 2011).

development after the signing of the ceasefire agreement. This image became even stronger in the aftermath of the tsunami in December 2004. Whereas the Sri Lankan state's centralized structures showed relative incapacity,[20] non-governmental institutions were quick in delivering aid to the affected population. The LTTE benefited from the TRO's capacity and the experience it had gained with 20 years of working experience as a humanitarian organization, which could be well combined with the LTTE's military precision and administrative efficiency (Uyangoda, 2005: 349).

By demonstrating its efficiency and progress in developmental and humanitarian work, the LTTE addressed not only the international community, but the local and diaspora Tamil population as well. Along with its disciplined way of ruling the areas under its control, the help of Tamil diaspora members with a Western education and work experience enhanced the local legitimacy of the LTTE as a competent development actor. This instigated a contrasting image between the localities of Kilinochchi and Jaffna, the latter left behind in terms of developmental progress.

(UN)CERTAIN FUTURE?

On the one hand, the ceasefire of 2002 bringing an end to war confirmed Jaffna's government-controlled status. On the other hand, it created an opportunity for the LTTE to get hold of the local population once more. The ways in which Jaffna Tamils negotiated the situation of dual governance and how they constructed legitimacy for both of the actors who sought to rule the peninsula, show how multilayered the construction of locality is. From the empirical material presented in this chapter, it can be seen that these negotiations deal with the different dimensions of governance in this particular locality, in contrast to Sri Lanka's south and the LTTE-controlled areas. There have been differing levels of trust and confidence in the capabilities of the Sri Lankan state and the LTTE. The latter could play the 'ethnic card', after all, and certainly managed to win over more conservative people's respect by maintaining discipline and order, and thereby providing a sense of security in the face of uncertainties

---

[20] Uyangoda (2005: 348) argues that the inability of the central state to devolve power to the regional and local institutions was mainly responsible for its inability to deliver humanitarian assistance.

that accompanied the conflict. People used to refer to situations of LTTE control in Jaffna's past, as well as in the Vanni, in order to point to the inability and unwillingness of the central government to maintain law and order, and subsequently, to enhance the chances of development. By developing images of law and order or of development in Jaffna in contrast to others, the boundaries of the locality have been reaffirmed.

The belief in the LTTE's ability to ensure law and order had to do with the fact that the movement and particularly its leadership were mystified by large sections of the Tamil population inside and outside Sri Lanka. Military success, a large transnational network, and a self-assured way of representing itself as being capable of running an independent state, Tamil Eelam, created the image of the LTTE as an unchallengeable movement. I finally realized how much Jaffna's Tamil population believed in the immortality of the LTTE in a conversation I had with a friend from Jaffna during the final stage of the war. On Monday, 18 May 2009, I emailed him, saying that I heard about the death of the LTTE's leader. He replied:

> Yes, the news say he and his guards were killed. You ask if the Tamils' situation will improve! If it is to improve it is a God's gift, but we doubt it might be worse than before. Now half the population is in prison in the name of refuge. Our point of view: If the government says that he is killed only the victory is there, we doubt that he has been killed, he might have escaped well in advance with the other seniors.

However, this does not mean that the LTTE enjoyed local people's undisputed loyalty. Although the authoritarian behaviour of the movement was tolerated for the sake of effectiveness, the movement was criticized for its deficiencies in democracy and human rights, and its suppression of opponents. Hardly any interviewee agreed with the LTTE's recruitment practices and was ready to sacrifice his or her child to the movement. On the contrary, there was a desperate desire to put an end to the armed conflict and get rid of the militarization of everyday life that was imposed on the local population from both sides.

From such a perspective the developments after the defeat of the LTTE appear to be quite dismal. More than two years after the LTTE's defeat, foreigners were still not allowed to visit the north without permission of the Ministry of Defence, which makes it difficult to do research on how development and reconstruction is progressing. The government claims that it seeks to develop the former war zones and apparently does so mainly through military rule. Sarvananthan (2011) points out that the military dominates the restaurants and food stalls along the A9 road connecting Jaffna with the south and that it has monopolized the domestic air transport system. He also highlights that the defence budget remains excessively high and that representatives of the military increasingly fill important posts in the administration in the north and east. Moreover, the military still seems to be omnipresent in the north, accompanied by flourishing illegal activities. In Sarvananthan's words: 'Security forces are directly and indirectly involved in breaking the law, abusing public property and undermining democratic governance at the local level' (Sarvananthan, 2011: 208). The enduring military presence at the local level is in line with the overall militarization of the government and the erosion of democratic procedures and human rights. DeVotta notes:

> The government has already set up numerous police stations and army camps in the areas the LTTE controlled, and the goal appears to be to blanket the military throughout the northeast and thereby ensure that there will never again be a minority insurrection even as conditions are created for Sinhalese colonizers to lord over their newly bestowed lands. (2010: 341)

It remains to be seen whether the fact that the Tamil National Alliance, which allegedly tended to tolerate the LTTE, won the vast majority of seats in the local government elections in July 2011 will bring about any change. These voting patterns indicate that, even while the security barriers that separated the north and east from the rest of the country until recently have become much less prominent, the political divide persists with little or no change. This is likely to have significant implications for development in the north and east.

REFERENCES

Appadurai, A. 1995. 'The Production of Locality', in R. Fardon (ed.), *Counterworks. Managing the Diversity of Knowledge.* London/New York: Routledge, pp. 204–25.

Bigdon, C. 2003. Decentralization, Federalism and Ethnic Conflict in Sri Lanka: An Assessment of Federal Proposals, Devolution Policy and the Realities of Recognition of Minorities at the Local Level. Heidelberg Papers in South

Asian and Comparative Politics, Working Paper No. 14. Heidelberg: South Asia Institute Department of Political Science, University of Heidelberg.

Cheran, R. 2001. *The Sixth Genre: Memory, History and the Tamil Diaspora Imagination.* Colombo: Marga Institute.

———. 2009, 'Pathways of Dissent: An Introduction to Tamil Nationalism in Sri Lanka', in R. Cheran (ed.), *Pathways of Dissent. Tamil Nationalism in Sri Lanka.* London: SAGE Publications, pp. xiii–xvii.

de Alwis, M. and J. Hyndman. 2002. *Capacity Building in Conflict Zones. A Feminist Analysis of Humanitarian Assistance in Sri Lanka.* Colombo: International Centre for Ethnic Studies.

DeVotta, N. 2010. 'From Civil War to Soft Authoritarianism: Sri Lanka in a Comparative Perspective'. *Global Change, Peace and Security*, 22(3): 331–43.

Gerharz, E. 2010. 'When Migrants Travel Back Home: Changing Identities in Northern Sri Lanka After the Ceasefire of 2002'. *Mobilities*, 5(1): 147–65.

———. 2014. *The Politics of Reconstruction and Development in Sri Lanka.* London: Routledge.

Goodhand, J. 2001. *Aid, Conflict and Peace Building in Sri Lanka.* London: The Conflict, Security and Development Group.

Gunaratna, R. 1998. 'Impact of the Mobilized Tamil Diaspora on the Protracted Conflict in Sri Lanka', in K. Rupesinghe (ed.), *Negotiating Peace in Sri Lanka. Efforts, Failures and Lessons.* London: International Alert, pp. 301–28.

Gupta, A. and J. Ferguson. 1997. 'Discipline and Practice: The "Field" as Site, Method and Location in Anthropology', in A. Gypta and J. Ferguson (eds), *Anthropological Locations. Boundaries and Grounds of a Field Science.* Berkeley/Los Angeles, CA: University of California Press, pp. 1–46.

Hellmann-Rajanayagam, D. 1986. 'The Tamil "Tigers" in Northern Sri Lanka: Origins, Factions, Programmes'. *Internationales Asienforum*, 17(1/2): 63–85.

———. 2004. 'From Differences to Ethnic Solidarity Among the Tamils', in S.H. Hasbullah and B.M. Morrison (eds), *Sri Lankan Society in an Era of Globalization: Struggling to Create a New Social Order.* Colombo: Vijitha Yapa Publications, pp. 102–18.

Herring, R.J. 2001. 'Making Ethnic Conflict: The Civil War in Sri Lanka', in M.J. Esman and R.J. Herring (eds), *Carrots, Sticks and Ethnic Conflict: Rethinking Development Assistance.* Michigan: University of Michigan Press, pp. 140–74.

Human Rights Watch. 2006. *Funding the "Final War": LTTE Intimidation and Extortion in the Tamil Diaspora.* New York: Human Rights Watch.

International Crisis Group. 2010. War Crimes in Sri Lanka. Bussels: ICG, Asia Report No. 191.

Kelegama, S. 2005. *Transforming Conflict with an Economic Dividend: The Sri Lankan Experience.* Helsinki: UNU-WIDER.

Mayer, M. 2002. 'Violent Youth Conflicts in Sri Lanka: Comparative Results from Jaffna and Hambantota', in S.T. Hettige and M. Mayer (eds), *Sri Lankan Youth: Challenges and Responses.* Colombo: Friedrich-Ebert-Foundation, pp. 204–46.

McGilvray, D. 2001. *Tamil and Muslim Identities in the East*. Colombo: Marga Institute.

Pfaff-Czarnecka, J. 2005. 'Das Lokale als Ressource im entgrenzten Wettbewerb: Das Verhandeln kollektiver Repäsentationen in Nepal-Himalaya'. *Zeitschrift für Soziologie*, Special Issue 'Weltgesellschaft': 479–99.

Pirani, C. and A. Kadirgamar. 2006. 'Internationalisation of Sri Lanka's Peace Process and Governance. A review of Strategic Conflict Assessments'. *Economic and Political Weekly*, May 6: 1789–95.

Sarvanathan, M. 2003. *Economic Imperative for Peace in Sri Lanka*. Colombo: International Centre for Ethnic Studies.

————. 2009. Economic Freedom: The Path to Economic and Political Emancipation of the Conflict-Affected Region, Working Paper No. 12. Point Pedro: Point Pedro Institute of Development.

————. 2011. 'Sri Lanka: Putting Entrepreneurship at the Heart of Economic Revival in the North, East and Beyond'. *Contemporary South Asia*, 19(2): 205–13.

Shanmugaratnam, N. and K. Stokke. 2008. 'Development as a Precursor to Conflict Resolution: A Critical Review of the Fifth Peace Process in Sri Lanka', in N. Shanmugalingam (ed.), *Between War and Peace in Sudan and Sri Lanka: Deprivation and Livelihood Revival*. Oxford: James Currey, pp. 93–115.

Shastri, A. 1994. 'The Provincial Council System in Sri Lanka: A Solution to the Ethnic Problem?', in S. Bastian (ed.), *Devolution and Development in Sri Lanka*. Delhi: Konark Publishers, pp. 198–227.

Somasundaram, D. 1998. *Scarred Minds. The Psychological Impact of War on Sri Lankan Tamils*. New Delhi/Thousand Oaks/London: SAGE Publications.

————. 2010. 'Parallel Governments: Living Between Terror and Counter Terror in Northern Lanka (1982–2009)'. *Journal of Asian and African Studies*, 45(5): 568–83.

Somitharan, S. 2005. 'Society: Lack of Guidance Leads Jaffna Youths to Stray', *Northeastern Herald Monthly*, August 2005. Retrieved from http://www.tamilcanadian.com/pageview.php?ID=3428&SID=520 (accessed on 15 July 2011).

Sriskandarajah, D. 2002. 'The Migration-Development Nexus: Sri Lanka Case Study', *International Migration*, 40(5): 283–305.

————. 2003. *The Returns of Peace in Sri Lanka: The Development Cart Before the Political Horse?* Colombo: International Centre for Ethnic Studies.

Stokke, K. 2006. 'Building the Tamil Eelam State: Emerging State Institutions and Forms of Governance in LTTE-controlled Areas in Sri Lanka'. *Third World Quarterly*, 27(6): 1021–40.

Tambiah, S.J. 1986. *Sri Lanka. Ethnic Fratricide and the Dismantling of Democracy*. Chicago, IL: University of Chicago Press.

Tiruchelvam, N. 1999. 'Devolution and the Elusive Quest for Peace', in R.I. Rotberg (ed.), *Creating Peace in Sri Lanka: Civil War and Reconcilition*. Washington, D.C.: Brookings Institution Press, pp. 189–201.

Tiruchelvam, N. 2000. 'The politics of Federalism and Diversity in Sri Lanka', in Y. Ghai (ed.), *Autonomy and Ethnicity: Negotiating Competing Claims in Multi-Ethnic States*. Cambridge: Cambridge University Press, pp. 197–218.

Uyangoda, J. 1996. 'Militarization, Violent State, Violent Society: Sri Lanka', in K. Rupesinghe and K. Mumtiaz (eds), *Internal Conflicts in South Asia*. London/ Thousand Oaks/New Delhi: SAGE Publications, pp. 118–31.

———. 2003. 'Constitutionalizing Federalism', in J. Uyangoda and P. Morina (eds), *Sri Lanka's Peace Process 2002: Critical Perspectives*. Colombo: Social Scientist's Association, pp. 74–7.

———. 2005. 'Ethnic Conflict, the State and the Tsunami Disaster in Sri Lanka'. *Inter-Asian Cultural Studies*, 6(3): 341–52.

Van Hear, N. 2002. 'Sustaining Societies Under Strain. Remittances as a Form of Transnational Exchange in Sri Lanka and Ghana', in N. Al-Ali and K. Koser (eds), *New Approaches to Migration? Transnational Communities and the Transformation of Home*. London/New York: Routledge, pp. 202–23.

van Horen, B. 2002. 'Planning for Institutional Capacity Building in War-Torn Areas: The Case of Jaffna, Sri Lanka'. *Habitat International*, 26(1): 113–28.

Wickramasinghe, N. 2001. *Civil Society in Sri Lanka: New Circles of Power*. New Delhi/Thousand Oaks/London: SAGE Publications.

———. 2009a. 'After the War: A New Patriotism in Sri Lanka?'. *The Journal of Asian Studies*, 68(4): 1045–54.

———. 2009b. 'Sri Lanka in 2008. Waging War for Peace'. *Asian Survey*, 49(1): 59–65.

Wilson, J.A. 1994. 'The Colombo Man, the Jaffna Man, and the Batticaloa Man: Regional Identities and the Rise of the Federal Party', in C. Manogaran and B. Pfaffenberger (eds), *The Sri Lankan Tamils: Ethnicity and Identity*. Boulder/ San Francisco/Oxford: Westview Press, pp. 126–42.

PART IV
IDEAS AND INTERESTS
IN GOVERNANCE AND DEVELOPMENT
IN CONFLICT-RIDDEN SOCIETIES

Chapter 9

Economic Growth to Conflict Mitigation

Changing Aid Strategies of Nepal's Donors

LAXMAN ACHARYA

FOREIGN AID IN NEPAL

Nepal's Foreign Aid Policy

A drastic change has occurred in modern Nepal's foreign aid policy (FAP): a conversion from an isolating policy to total dependence on foreign countries. The late King Prithvi Narayan Shah, the founder of modern Nepal, was popular for his policy of maintaining balanced relations with India and China and isolating the country from foreigners, especially the Europeans. The following very popular sayings of King Prithvi Narayan Shah provide examples of this:

> 'Nepal is a yam between two boulders'
>
> 'Do not allow foreign businessmen to come any closer than Parsha-Gadhi [a border town with India]. If foreign merchants come into the country, they will leave the people destitute'

Nepal practised this policy of isolation by restricting the movement of Europeans inside the country (Khadka, 1997). However, the Rana regime in Nepal, which ruled the nation for 104 years, had a good relationship with British India. Interestingly, soon after the downfall of the Rana regime in 1951, Nepal started to engage with foreign countries in order to modernize the country, and in less than half a century's time, Nepal had become so dependent on foreign countries that it demanded their help even when settling small internal disputes.

Ever since the 1950s, successive governments in Nepal have tried to become more open towards the foreign world. The late King Mahendra (1956–72) made every effort to expand both diplomatic and economic relations with as many countries as possible, mostly to reduce Nepal's dependence on India (Khadka, 1997). His successor, King Birendra, continued with the same policy. Meanwhile, Western countries also tried to establish relations with Nepal because of its strategic geopolitical location. The major tool which they used to develop these relationships was foreign aid. As a result, the number of donors as well as the amount of foreign aid pouring into Nepal increased sharply over successive decades. Being neutral towards superpowers and attracting as much foreign aid as possible being the major implicit aid policies, Nepal accepted all and any form of aid, as and when provided. As a result, a wide range of donors— from capitalist and communist countries, to bilateral and multilateral sources, to missionary organizations and international non-governmental organizations (INGOs)—began providing aid to Nepal.

Nepal only formulated and made public its first official FAP in 2002, after it had been receiving foreign aid for more than half a decade. The long-term objective of the policy was to achieve economic self-reliance by enhancing domestic resource mobilization, whereas the short-term objective was to increase the quality of aid. However, these objectives have yet to be fulfilled. Donor countries, and Nepal as a recipient, are both currently not happy with the effectiveness of aid in Nepal. Donor communities are worried about the lack of ownership, lack of leadership and poor institutions in Nepal which are the major factors for aid ineffectiveness, while Nepal's concern is that foreign aid projects are still supply driven (MOF, 2009).

> Each donor agency may have its own policies, perceptions and priorities of Nepal's development needs which at times are not only divergent but also contradictory to each other. As a result, foreign aid does not always flow into the sectors where it is most needed, leading to significant resource gaps in some sectors and acute overlapping and duplication to each other. (MOF, 2009: 7)

Nepal's political change, from a constitutional monarchy to a federal democratic republic, has made its mark on its new FAP. Inclusion and equity issues have become cross-cutting aspects of the policy.

Foreign aid policy will be directed towards attaining the over-arching national goal of lasting peace and all-out socio-economic transformation of Nepali society. This will involve fostering broad-based, sustainable and inclusive high economic growth by enhancing the productive capacity of the economy as well as building social capital of the country. (MOF, 2009: 11)

The Entry of Donors into the Country and Their Motives

American assistance under the Point IV programme in 1951 was the first systematic entry of foreign aid into Nepal (Mihaly, 2003 [1965]). However, Nepal used to receive a certain amount of money annually from Tibet, as agreed in the Nepal–Tibet War agreement, as well as cash grants from the British Government as compensation for services provided by Gurkha soldiers (Baidya, 1984). Soon after the initiation of American aid, India also began its aid programme after the Indian premier Nehru's visit to Kathmandu (Baidya, 1984). China and the USSR followed suit not much later. During the 1960s, several Western countries started their aid programmes in Nepal, one after another. Japanese aid began to flow two years after the establishment of Nepali-Japanese diplomatic relations in 1965. Germany also started giving aid in the same year. Canada started a regular assistance programme in 1970. The Netherlands and other small European countries including Denmark, Norway and Finland also joined the foreign aid bandwagon with small contributions made during the 1970s and 1980s, respectively. These countries became vital donors to Nepal after the restoration of democracy in 1990. Besides these countries, France, Sweden, Australia and the Korean Republic have also been providing bilateral assistance to Nepal on a smaller scale. The expansion of Nepal's international relations, the Cold War and the introduction of periodic development plans were three major reasons for the sharp increase in the amount of assistance received after the mid-1950s (Baidya, 1984).

Several UN agencies also began assisting Nepal in the 1950s, and today over a dozen do so. Likewise, multilateral banks—namely, the

Asian Development Bank (ADB) and the World Bank (WB)—started their aid programmes in the early 1970s, providing technical assistance and concessional loans to Nepal. Similarly, the European Commission started assistance in 1977 after two years of diplomatic relations. Besides the aforementioned multilateral donors, Nepal receives aid from other non-Development Assistance Committee (non-DAC) multilateral donors such as the Organization of Petroleum Exporting Countries and the International Fund for Agriculture Development. In 1976, the WB, the US, the UK, France, Germany, the Netherlands, Switzerland, Finland, Austria, Canada, Australia, Japan and the United Nations Development Programme (UNDP) formed the Nepal Aid group in order to provide development assistance to Nepal in a more systematic and coordinated manner. Besides the aforementioned bilateral and multilateral donors, the number of INGOs working in Nepal increased sharply after 1990. By 2010, the number of INGOs and non-governmental organizations (NGOs) registered with the government of Nepal had reached more than 200.

Donors to Nepal have entered the country with different initial motives, but the moral and ethical grounds for providing help to Nepal and its people are agreed upon by all donors and stated very frankly. In addition to this, commercial, political and strategic interests are also pervasive motives, although the donors do not admit to this easily. There is no historical evidence to suggest that donor nations assist others over longer periods of time without expecting some corresponding benefits (for example, political, economic, or military benefits) (Todaro, 1985). Donors' motives can also change depending on the time period and the recipient.

The major and influential donor countries such as the US, the USSR, India and China started their aid programmes in Nepal with political and strategic motives. The main objective behind the US's entry into Nepal was to prevent communist incursion, encouraging political and economic stability by helping vulnerable people in the periphery of the communist world (Mihaly, 2003 [1965]). The motive of what was then the USSR was to counter the American strategy and to spread its own political ideology while it was at it. Similarly, India and China started their aid programme in Nepal because of their rivalry and their strategic interest in Nepal due to its location. Despite the fact that both countries were themselves recipients of foreign aid and also possessed economic conditions not much better than that of Nepal, they parted with their resources to aid Nepal. This is a concrete example of the strategic interest behind their provision of aid to Nepal.

India's foreign policy has three major and yet interrelated objectives, strategic, political and economic. Strategic interest i.e. to meet any threat coming from China via Nepal.... The political objective constituted mainly of maintaining a 'special relationship' under the 1950 treaty, countering the China and other powers, containment of communism, supporting a regime with a pro-Indian orientation, and looking after the interest of Nepalese of Indian origin and people of India living in Nepal. Its economic objective has been guided by to main considerations, to exert influence on harmonizing economic policies between the two countries, and sharing of water resources for 'mutual benefits'. (Khadka, 1997: 231)

Similarly, Chinese aid to Nepal is impelled primarily by the following foreign policy goals: to establish Chinese presence in Nepal and earn political goodwill, and to reduce or at least undermine India's dominant position in this region (Baidya, 1984). We still find that these two nations compete in the giving of aid to Nepal. For example, India assisted Nepal in laying an optical fibre cable under the East–West Highway (which runs through their border), and China did the same for the Araniko Highway—a road linking Kathmandu with the border of China.

Aid is sometimes driven by idealism, generosity and international solidarity, but often also by political expediency, ideological confrontation and commercial self-interest (UNDP, 1994). The desirability of keeping Nepali people, who are considered hardy soldiers, in the British Army was the basis of the beginning and continuation of the UK's aid programmes in Nepal (Mihaly, 2003 [1965]). The Swiss people apparently responded to the concept of an aid programme to Nepal because of feelings of affinity due to the topographical similarity between the two nations (Mihaly, 2003 [1965]). The purpose of German aid, globally, has two facets: to prove its technological and economic capability as an economically powerful nation, and its own economic self-interest (Khadka, 1991). Furthermore, Japanese aid to Nepal might be motivated by the cultural similarities between the two countries, such as the monarchical system and Nepal being the birth place of Lord Buddha.

Donors' major commercial interests behind provision of aid to poor countries include capturing the market in those countries and making conditions more favourable for their own trade. One can see many examples of conditionality in bilateral donor programmes, such as requirements for Nepal to purchase machines and vehicles, or appoint advisors from donor countries. Small European donors such as Denmark, Norway, Finland and the Netherlands seem to be providing aid more on humanist grounds, aiming to transfer their own development experiences to Nepal.

Volume, Sources, Types and Priority Sectors of Foreign Aid

Different donors provide various types of foreign aid in different ways. However, no proper record of the total inflow of foreign aid into the country exists in a consolidated form. Generally, the Economic Survey, an annual publication by the Ministry of Finance (MOF) in Nepal, only provides a record of the foreign aid that the country receives as budgetary support. The Economic Survey's record accounts for loans and grants shown in government budgets; it excludes technical assistance, contributions from INGOs and other bilateral/multilateral assistance disbursed outside of central government channels. Budgetary aid accounts for less than half of the total inflow of development assistance. 'Even the MOF does not have access to full information on actual foreign assistance received and its use. The amount of foreign assistance included in the budget is almost equal to the amount of foreign assistance that is not included in the budget' (Acharya, 2004: 35). In addition to this, some missionary organizations and INGOs provide assistance without a formal record. It is therefore difficult to acquire exact information about the inflow of foreign aid into Nepal.

During the 1950s and 1960s there were a limited number of donors: most aid came from India, China and the US. These countries contributed to more than 90 per cent of the total inflow of aid. OECD statistics show that Nepal had received, in humanitarian and development assistance (military aid not included), a total of $133 million in the 1960s and $525 million in the 1970s. As several bilateral donors, as well as multilateral donors such as the WB and ADB, gradually started their aid programmes in Nepal the inflow of foreign aid increased tremendously during the 1970s and reached $2.71 billion in 1980s. In this decade, Japan was the largest donor, and it continued to be so in the 1990s. From the late 1980s, the

Netherlands, Norway, Finland and Denmark also increased their development assistance. The trend of increasing foreign aid continued in the 1990s and from 2000 onwards. In addition to this, after the restoration of democracy in 1990, several INGOs increased their assistance to the country. As a result, the total inflow of foreign aid in the 1990s and 2000s reached $4.08 billion and $5.12 billion, respectively. But these aid statistics do not include the assistance provided by countries like India and China which are not in the DAC.

Since the year 2000, multilateral agencies such as the WB and the ADB have drastically decreased their assistance, mostly due to the stalling of some of their major approved programmes. But most bilateral donors (except Japan) have increased their assistance. The UK and the US have been rapidly increasing their assistance in each successive year, while India and China have been regularly providing certain fixed amounts of aid to Nepal.

Bilateral aid, multilateral aid and contributions from INGOs are Nepal's major sources of aid; and the main components of this aid are grants, concessional loans and technical assistance. Bilateral donors and multilateral agencies—such as UN agencies and the European Community—mainly provide grants and technical assistance, whereas the WB and ADB provide some negligible technical assistance along with large chunks of concessional loans. Likewise, INGOs provide both grants and technical assistance. Before 1990, INGOs' share of the contribution was negligible. Technical assistance received was not recorded in the government budget, while most loans and grants were spent through central government channels. After the 1990s, however, disbursement of bilateral assistance—in the case of certain donors who did not require repayment—was carried out outside of government channels (mainly through NGOs and INGOs). This is now a continuing trend. However, the concessional loans provided by the WB and the ADB are still spent almost entirely through government channels.

Loans and grants are the two main components of budgetary aid. In the 1950s, development aid consisted of grant components only. From the mid-1960s, some bilateral donors started to provide loans as well, but loans made up a very small proportion of the total aid received. However, from the 1970s, as the WB and ADB gradually increased their support, the proportion of the total aid made up of loans increased accordingly and reached its peak during the 1990s (Table 9.1). But after that, the

Table 9.1
Proportion of Loans/Grants and Bilateral/Multilateral Aid (in Percentages)

Aid components	1950s	1960s	1970s	1980s	1990s	2000–09
Grant	100.0	95.9	66.5	35.3	31.1	60.0
Bilateral	100.0	95.9	57.2	29.5	24.9	34.3
Multilateral	0.0	0.0	9.4	5.4	6.3	25.8
Loan	0.0	4.1	33.5	64.7	59.1	40.0
Bilateral	0.0	4.1	8.9	10.7	8.4	5.3
Multilateral	0.0	0.0	25.2	54.3	60.4	34.7
Total	100.0	100.0	100.0	100.0	100.0	100.0

Source: Economic Surveys (various issues), Ministry of Finance, Government of Nepal.

Note: Aid data consist only of loans and grants (budgetary support) and excludes other types of aid.

proportion of loans decreased again as a result of a reduction in the WB and ADB's disbursements.

Up until the 1960s, the flow of foreign aid was entirely from bilateral sources. From the 1970s, Nepal started receiving multilateral aid as well. In the 1970s, aid was two-thirds bilateral and one-third multilateral. The proportion of multilateral aid then increased gradually during the 1980s, and by the 1990s, the proportions of bilateral and multilateral aid making up the total were the opposite of those during the 1970s. The total proportion of aid provided by multilateral institutions increased rapidly after Nepal initiated the launch of huge, capital-intensive projects financed by international loans. However, the proportion of bilateral aid has begun to increase again since the beginning of the new millennium.

Right from the beginning, the infrastructure sectors—areas such as transport, power and communication—have received first priority as recipients of foreign aid, and this is still the case. The prioritization of different sectors in Nepal is mainly determined by international development paradigms. Examples of this include the fact that priority was given to the agriculture sector in the 1980s, that the proportion of aid given to the social sector increased from the 1990s and that lower priority was given to the industrial sector during this time. Spending on social services

Table 9.2
Trends in Sectoral Distribution of Foreign Aid (Percentage in Total)

Sectors	Late 1970s	1980s	1990s	2000–09
Agriculture, irrigation and forestry	19.3	28.1	23.7	15.0
Transport, power and communication	58.7	45.3	47.2	36.5
Industry and commerce	7.8	8.3	4.8	1.0
Social services	13.7	17.5	24.3	45.5
Others	0.5	0.9	0.4	2.0
Total	100.0	100.0	100.0	100.0

Source: Economic Surveys (various issues), MOF/Nepal Government.

Note: These statistics include only the loan and grant components of foreign aid (that is, budgetary support).

has sharply increased since 2000. Table 9.2 shows the trends in sectoral distribution of foreign aid.

THE CHANGING STRATEGIES BEHIND AID IN NEPAL

The main goals associated with foreign aid in all developing countries are to achieve overall development and to improve the living standards of the population, by bridging existing financial and technological gaps. Although these development goals have always been the same, the strategies used to achieve them are constantly changing globally.

After the end of the Second World War, foreign aid and development theories grew interdependently. Foreign aid has always been used to create the foundation for development in developing countries, using techniques propounded by development theories of the time.

In the post-colonial period, three major shifts occurred in the global development paradigm, broadly speaking. In the 1950s, soon after development had begun to be initiated in the third world, development was defined in terms of economic development and higher economic growth. But from the late 1960s onwards, it was realized that mere economic growth was not sufficient to raise the living standard of the masses.

The fulfilment of basic needs and the reduction of inequalities then became additional development agendas.

But with the global democratic movement, especially after 1990, came development issues such as democracy, human rights and good governance. These became additional agendas. From 2000 onwards, especially in the case of Nepal, conflict mitigation also became one of the major concerns related to development. The subsequent paragraphs discuss the aid strategies of Nepal's major donors, along with the global development paradigm and Nepal's development strategies.

1950–70: A Purely Economic Agenda

Soon after the Second World War, economists and development practitioners found that a very low level of gross national product (GNP) existed in the former colonies. Maximizing growth was thus considered an important goal of development. Hence, large investments in physical capital and infrastructure became the priority, as they were considered the primary means of development. The most important donors—such as the WB, the US, the UK and France—developed their aid strategies within a very simple framework: the provision of experts and financial assistance for the improvement and implementation of projects involving modern technology. There was a particular focus on the development of physical infrastructure, such as roads, ports, telecommunications, electricity and other forms of energy (Martinussen and Poul, 2005). The practice of this concept was also influenced by the success of the Marshall Plan in Western Europe and several contemporary growth theories of that period.

Nepal implemented three periodic plans between 1950 and 1970. These plans had the overall development goal of raising the standard of living by increasing economic growth. Nepal's investment priorities were the creation of economic infrastructure (by improving areas such as transportation, communication and irrigation), raising the productivity of the economy and building government institutions (NPC, 1956, 1962, 1965).

In the early 1950s, the US and India were Nepal's main donors. American aid was guided by the principles of the US Government's Point IV programme—to improve the quality of people's lives in developing countries, something that was considered to be necessary for political stability and hence to stop the influence of communist ideologies. On the other hand, Indian and Chinese aid began with development of infrastructure that was strategically important to them. Kathmandu Airport and the Tribhuvan Rajpath—a road joining India and Kathmandu—were the pilot programmes under Indian aid. To counter India, China also started to build the Araniko Rajpath, a road joining China and Kathmandu. Chinese aid to Nepal was primarily impelled by two foreign policy goals: to establish Chinese presence and earn political goodwill in the Kingdom of Nepal, and to reduce or at least undermine India's dominant position in this region (Baidya, 1984). The first Chinese grant was worth $12.8 million, which Nepal used to lower the exchange rate of the Indian rupee (Mihaly, 2003 [1965]).

In addition to these hidden political and strategic interests, the donors' aid strategy in Nepal was to be guided by a global development paradigm—the acceleration of economic growth. The economic infrastructure—areas such as transport, communication and power development—received first priority from most of the donors. Chinese and Russian aid was more focused on the transport, industry and power sectors. Meanwhile, Indian aid focused additionally on the communication sector. In addition to physical infrastructure, American support was also directed to institution-building exercises. The priority of UNDP's assistance was to carry out several feasibility studies to encourage more donors to invest in physical infrastructure. As a result, almost three-quarters of all foreign aid were spent in the transport, communication, power and industry sectors during the 1960s.

1970–90: Addressing Social Issues As Well

The experience of the 1960s showed that despite the increasing GNP of several developing countries, mass poverty still remained a pressing issue. Inequality increased further. Thus, from the 1970s, income distribution and equity became additional objectives of development and of enhancing the capabilities of the poor became the strategy for poverty alleviation. This broadened the definition of development from a merely economic concept to an all-encompassing socio-economic phenomenon. But different aid agencies adopted different strategies to achieve their goals. One school of ideas, represented by the WB, still focused on 'growth' (Martinussen and Poul, 2005: 26) but suggested approaches such as raising the level of domestic savings, reallocation of investments in favour of poor groups, introduction of fiscal measures to distribute benefits and the transfer of existing assets. However, UN agencies such as the International Labour Organization and Food and Agriculture Organization suggested some more pragmatic approaches to this goal: for example, the adoption of labour-intensive methods of production, people's participation and distribution of assets in favour of the poor sections of society (Khadka, 1991). As a result, programmes centred on basic needs and rural development became the priority for many donor agencies until the mid-1980s.

But by the 1980s, the welfare approach adopted by developing countries in the past was held back by heavy debt problems, unfavourable balance of payment, inflation and state deficits. The situation further deteriorated with the oil crisis in the 1980s. The global economy stagnated and ultimately became more and more dependent on external resources. At the same time, the governments of three large donor countries—the US, the UK and West Germany—revived the neoclassical approach to development theory of market-led growth strategies, which was a great departure from the global aid paradigm. The adoption of liberal economic policies such as privatizaton, state disengagement from economic activities, price de-regulation and trade liberalism became the conditions for getting aid from multilateral as well as some bilateral aid agencies. Most of the developing countries pursued and adopted these policies in order to get aid under the WB's Structural Adjustment Programme (SAP) and Enhanced Structural Adjustment Facilities as well as the International Monetary Fund's (IMF) Poverty Reduction Growth Facilities.

Nepal's fourth, fifth and sixth periodic plans (1970–90) were formulated using a global development paradigm which gave additional importance to people-oriented development initiatives, such as the fulfilment of basic needs and rurally integrated and labour-intensive programmes (NPC, 1970, 1975, 1980). Priority was given to the agriculture sector, regional balance and the creation of more equal societies. But from the mid-1980s, Nepal also entered into the liberal development model, as a prerequisite for accessing multilateral donor support (NPC, 1985).

When global development paradigms shifted to 'growth with distribution' in the mid-1970s, the focus of some donors in Nepal also shifted—from large-scale capital investments to livelihood and social sector programmes. Integrated rural development programmes and investments in agriculture, health and education programmes became new focus areas for development assistance, addressing rural and poor people directly. Several pilot studies were conducted in the health, education, agriculture and rural development sectors with US aid. Manpower development training, integrated health services, integrated cereal crops projects and several educational projects were major projects run under the US aid during this period. Social service sectors, such as health, education and drinking water, became additional priority sectors for UK aid. But still, infrastructure development remained the first priority for many donors, such as the ADB, the WB, India and China. However, hospital construction and scholarship programmes were new focus areas for Indian aid programmes. During this period, the ADB approved some lending programmes for the vocational education sector and the Integrated Rural Development Project (IRDP). As a result, the aggregated share of foreign aid expenditure in two sectors—social services, and agriculture, irrigation and forestry—increased in the 1980s compared to the late 1970s. This aid strategy was followed until the 1980s.

From the second half of the 1980s, in the lead-up to the push for democracy, three trends seemed to emerge in the donors' aid strategies: the continuation of physical infrastructure development, social development and poverty reduction, and enhancement of the liberal development model. Donor countries such as India, China and Japan were still prioritizing physical infrastructure development. However, Japanese assistance also provided wide coverage in the social and livelihood sectors.

Unlike the aforementioned donors, Canada and some European donors were more focused on social development and poverty reduction. A multi-sector, multi-year British aid agreement was signed in 1984, delivering immediate socio-economic benefits to the people including several projects in the forestry sector, road projects and health and population projects (Khadka, 1991). The IRDPs were implemented with Canadian support and German aid.

On the other hand, with the introduction of the SAP, the WB started advocacy work with the Nepali government for policy reform from the mid-1980s onwards. The US started advocating macroeconomic reforms, such as private sector involvement in the development process, decentralization, minimization of the role of government in economic activities and price policy through market mechanism.

Meanwhile, the UNDP's aid objectives were to increase mobilization of domestic resources, to improve the government's capacity to manage development programmes and to attain balanced rural and regional development. It also took up inter-sectoral development strategies, such as increased community participation, provision of basic needs, private sector expansion and integration of population policies within development programmes.

1990s: Emphasizing Political Elements

During the 1990s, poverty reduction became the explicit development goal globally, while political elements such as human rights, democracy and good governance became cross-cutting issues.

In this decade, led by the WB, donor communities continuously advocated for a liberal development model. Furthermore, in the late 1990s, the WB and the IMF prescribed the use of Poverty Reduction Strategy Papers (PRSPs)—a new anti-poverty framework. This was to be a national strategy, drawn up by governments of low-income countries, encouraging government expenditure on poverty-reducing measures (PANOS, 2002). Most of the developing countries of the world pursued PRSPs as if they were a condition to get support from the WB and IMF, and also to be legitimized for other bilateral support.

On the other hand, several UN agencies along with some bilateral donor agencies—such as those in the US and Canada—continued to use the 1970s approach to aid and focus more on the issue of poverty. Despite general favour for the WB's liberal development model, these donors distributed foreign aid with regard for poverty, but still within the framework of structural adjustment and thus within the logic of global capitalism (Martinussen and Poul, 2005). As a result, poverty reduction through social and economic development of the poor became the overall goal of foreign aid in the 1990s. In addition to this, after the end of the Cold War, some bilateral donors also added political agendas, such as promoting democratization, respect for human rights and the adoption of good governance, as criteria for development assistance. The rationale behind this was that these practices were essential to promote economic development and poverty reduction.

In the same line, Nepal's seventh, eighth and ninth periodic plans adopted the liberal economic framework, giving priority to poverty reduction and human development; whereas the 10th plan (2002–07) was developed based on the country's PRSP. Poverty reduction got higher priority and became the single development goal from late 1990s, coinciding with Nepal's governance reforms and the introduction of parliamentary democracy.

Like the multidimensional and vague nature of poverty, the strategies of different donors to achieve the goal of poverty reduction were also found to be very diverse. Some donors such as the WB, the ADB and the United States Agency for International Development (USAID) gave more emphasis to the economic aspects of poverty through macroeconomic policy reform, including strengthening of the private sector. The WB fixed its flexible lending level based on the speed of such reform processes as structural and governance reform, improved public resource management, civil service reform, and privatization and financial sector reform. Similarly, basic social service development, environmental protection and private sector development were major strategic objectives of the ADB. USAID's support was directed towards making market-friendly government policy (USAID, 2001). The UK adopted the strategic objectives of infrastructure development and more effective management of natural resources to attain broad-based economic growth.

Some donors put more emphasis on basic social aspects of poverty such as health, education, drinking water and other basic needs; others gave more importance to the political dimensions of development, such as democracy, human rights, peoples' participation and empowerment. Human rights, democracy and governance formed the strategic approach of Danish aid, which was aimed at achieving sustainable, democratic and equitable social development in Nepal. The main goal behind the EU's cooperation was to support sustainable economic development and improve the living standards of the poorest strata, with regard to cross-cutting issues of human rights, democratization, gender and environment. The main objective behind Finnish aid was sustainable poverty reduction, which they aimed to achieve through promotion of economic and social development, including democracy and good governance. Similarly, the main approach of the Swiss Development Cooperation (SDC) was to support sustainability of democratization, improved subsistence agriculture and sustainable forest management. Likewise, the strategic objectives of UNDP were to promote social mobilization, and to support decentralized governance and peoples' participation in the development process. Japanese donors aimed to provide support under Nepal's own periodic plans framework (JICA, 2003). Likewise, the Norwegian aid strategy in Nepal was to support Nepal's own endeavours towards sustainable economic, social and political development, with particular emphasis on the needs of the poorest segments of the population.[1]

Some donors such as Canada and *Stichting Nederlands Vrijwilligers*—Netherlands Development Organization—put more emphasis on a bottom-up approach: enhancing the demand side of development, in particular capacity building for grassroots institutions and individuals (UNDP, 2000).

But in the case of some donors, such as India and China, little change can be found in their aid strategies. Assistance from these countries is usually extended based on the criterion of urgency. In addition to certain fixed amounts of assistance provided regularly, these countries also agree to provide funding for certain development projects planned by the Nepalese government if they agree with the projects' aims. However, the 1990s saw one vital shift in Indian economic cooperation—it began to support grassroots projects which were high in number, but each of which received relatively small amounts of funding. Larger projects were also continued, but only on-and-off.

In addition to the aforementioned donors' aid strategies, the 1990s saw a great departure in donors' aid behaviour in terms of their aid transparency. Mainly after the mid-1990s, many donors started to publicize strategy papers about the objectives, strategies and priorities of their assistance.

After 2000: Trying to Address the Political Situation

The heightening of the Maoist insurgency and the King's political coup were two major political events that occurred during the first few years of

---

[1] The Memorandum of Understanding between the Government of the Kingdom of Norway and His Majesty's Government of Nepal on Development Cooperation, 22 November 1996.

the new millennium. These events influenced the country's development agenda as well as donors' aid strategies in Nepal. In the first few years of the Maoist insurgency, the effects were limited to remote areas and were small scale. However, because of the massacre of the royal family and a number of successively unstable governments, the intensity of the conflict started to escalate sharply after 2001—at which point a new political conflict emerged between the parliamentarian political parties and the monarch. This new context narrowed down the scope for development, compelling Nepal and its donors to rethink their development strategy. As a result, in addition to the two-pronged strategy of economic growth and social development implemented from the late 1990s, addressing the root cause of the Maoist conflict became a new development strategy. The 10th periodic plan (2002–07) identified social exclusion, inequality and lack of good governance as Nepal's main problems, relevant both to the Maoist conflict and to poverty and it was, thus, designed to address these issues. Inclusion became the commonly agreed-upon development agenda. Furthermore, the three-year interim plan (2008–11), formulated after the Maoist party entered mainstream politics, envisioned an inclusive development process in order to build a prosperous, modern and just Nepal. In addition to this, the Millennium Development Goals also have an influence over Nepal's present development paradigm.

Donor agencies also responded to these political events through their development assistance. To show their displeasure with the King's coup, many donor agencies either withdrew or stalled their support. It was mainly the Scandinavian donors who announced that they would cease to work on new programmes with the government until political democracy was re-established. Many other donors adopted a 'wait and see' strategy.

Similarly, most of the donor agencies changed their aid strategies to address the changed context. Identifying and addressing the root cause of the Maoist conflict was the common agenda. In addition to their general strategy of working towards sustainable higher economic growth, the WB, the ADB, USAID and the Department for International Development (DFID) placed additional importance on good governance, along with special attention to poor and socially excluded people. 'Better governance for equitable growth' became the USAID aid strategy (USAID, 2001: 3); the WB recognized that poor governance was the main factor responsible for insufficient delivery of development benefits to rural and poor people, and it designed its strategy accordingly; the ADB aimed to generate productive employment and rural income opportunities through faster, broad-based economic growth, equitable improvements in basic social services and good governance (ADB, 2009); DFID made a commitment to address social exclusion, social justice and the conflict present in the country (DFID, 2004).

In the changed context, most of the European donors prioritized human rights, democracy, social inclusion and conflict mitigation. For example, governance reform and a peaceful and sustainable solution to the conflict became the additional focus of Danish assistance;[2] supporting conflict mitigation and consolidating democracy became the EU's major strategies (EU, 2002); democracy, human rights, good governance and conflict resolution became the additional focus of Finland's programmes; Norwegian aid focused on human rights and governance, and on conflict mitigation.[3] Meanwhile, the SDC adopted the following principles: 'work around the conflict, work in the conflict and work on the conflict' (SDC, 2005).

The year 2006 became a milestone in Nepali politics. After the peace agreement, the Maoist party entered mainstream politics and the country converted from a constitutional monarchy to a republic. Despite these drastic political changes, few distinct differences in donors' aid strategies can be seen before and after the peace agreement. Many donor agencies continued to prioritize the same sectors, and there was no sharp increase or decline in the amount of aid provided.

However, many donors' strategies formulated after 2006 were focused on tackling the fluid situation in Nepal. Since then, an inclusive development process and a conflict-sensitive approach to formulating development programmes have been the common strategy of all donors. In addition to this, institutionalization of the democratic system and encouraging good governance are commonly found in many donor agencies' strategy plans. The interim strategy of the WB, and the ADB's Country Strategy Paper (2010–12), place an emphasis on aligning their priorities with the development priorities of Nepal. The UK's support to Nepal

---

[2] http://www.un.org.np/uploads/agencyprofiles/danida/danida.php?agencyID=14 (accessed on 2 July 2006).

[3] http://www.norway.org.np/Devcoop/norwaynepal/DevCoop.htm (accessed on 2 July 2006).

aims to strengthen efforts to reduce political instability. The US has a vision for measurable progress in expanding and deepening democracy. Scandinavian donors have a similar strategy to that of the new Nepal: protecting freedom, democracy and human rights; enhancing the peace process; helping democracy take root in society and building an inclusive new Nepal based on democratic principles, human rights, and social and economic equity.[4] The strategy behind Swiss cooperation is to support inclusive, democratic state-building and to promote human security and socio-economic development.

In addition to the aforementioned changes, some other major changes have occurred in Nepal's aid modality in the new millennium. These include changing donor–recipient relationships into development partnerships; more emphasis being placed on poverty, social inequality and social inclusion; transparency, accountability, decentralization, human rights, democracy and good governance as new cross-cutting issues; putting emphasis on the participatory approach; strengthening of local capacity and ownership through user groups and Community-Based Organizations, from planning to implementation of development programmes; the concept of conflict-sensitive programming and combined efforts from donors in certain sector-wide programmes.

CONCLUSION

This chapter comes to five main conclusions. First, Nepal has been receiving foreign aid regularly for the last 55 years, with an increase in the number of donors as well as the amount of foreign aid in each successive decade. But the Nepalese government does not have an integrated and proper record of the inflow of foreign aid into the country. Taken alongside the trend for the spending of foreign aid through central government channels, this indicates that the government has faced problems with making the aid process sufficiently transparent. After receiving aid for more than half a century, Nepal formulated its first FAP in 2002. This policy made several provisions for the effective use of foreign aid in the country, but

[4] http://www.finland.org.np/public/default.aspx?nodeid=35080&contentla n=2&culture=en-US and http://www.norway.org.np/Embassy/Development-cooperation/DevCoop/ (both accessed on 2 July 2006).

has yet to be achieved. With the lack of a proper aid management system and the presence of a large crowd of donors, foreign aid administration has essentially been chaotic.

Second, during the initial decades of foreign aid, Nepal's major rationale behind expanding the number of donors as well as the amount of aid was to bridge domestic resource gaps and to reduce dependence on India. In theory, foreign aid should have helped to bridge resource gaps in short term, so that in the long term Nepal would be able to mobilize its own resources for sustainable development. But in reality, Nepal was never able to mobilize its internal resources to meet the financial requirements of its development activities. Nepal has historically been dependent on foreign aid from an economic perspective, and this dependence now has social and political aspects as well. Despite the creation of some socio-economic infrastructure and awareness-raising among the population, development activities without foreign aid have now become totally unimaginable. Foreign aid has failed to achieve all of its set goals. For example, when foreign aid began in the 1950s it had the objective, first and foremost, of economic and political stability. But despite a regular inflow of millions of dollars for more than half a century, the Maoist insurgency took hold and Nepal has now become the most unstable it has ever been, politically as well as economically.

Third, Nepal's donors are continuously changing their aid strategies and modalities, and their sectoral priorities, in order to achieve sustainable development and poverty reduction in line with the global trend. In earlier decades, foreign aid was used as an important tool to intervene in the economic aspects of the development process. This trend then shifted to social aspects in the 1970s. Ultimately, aid began to be used to intervene in political aspects starting from the 1990s; but even then, with a fledgling democratic government struggling to govern the country, donors largely focused on the global trend of poverty alleviation. Political intervention through aid became more tangible in Nepal through the response of many donors to the royal coup in 2005. Despite claims from the WB, the ADB and the UN that they are politically neutral, their current emphasis on governance and decentralization are fundamentally political interventions. However, all of these shifts in the donors' aid strategies have occurred in accordance with global shifts in development paradigms. Furthermore, donors have not been able to fully achieve their desired goals. Rather than identifying Nepal's specific needs and developing programmes accordingly, donors are trying to make their prevailing global strategy fit with Nepal.

Fourth, donors' aid strategies have been focused on addressing Nepal's specific issues since 2000, which is a good start. Most development agencies, including the government, seem to understand the Maoist conflict in a similar light. The reasons for the escalation of the conflict are understood to be poverty, inequality and failure of past governments to address the socio-economic conditions affecting the people. However, they have undermined the Maoist leadership's ability to raise awareness amongst the poor and disadvantaged populations of their exploitation by the political and socio-economic system that has been in place for several decades. Most of the development agencies have a common strategy of addressing what they perceive to be the root cause of the Maoist conflict, and so their plans centre on social inclusion and good governance, and give special consideration to poor and marginalized people. Conflict-sensitive programming has been the priority in these donors' aid models. The donors' strategies seek to involve certain targeted groups of people in the development process. However, it remains to be seen how these strategies will be implemented in reality.

Last but not least, there is a danger that donors and the government will lose what progress has been achieved in recent years after the Maoist party becomes grounded in mainstream politics. There is a danger that donors will understand Nepal as a post-conflict country and shift their engagement towards implementing the current (and deeply flawed) post-conflict reconstruction paradigm. Nepal would be better served if donors were to redouble their efforts to address the extant conflict issues across the country.

BIBLIOGRAPHY

Acharya, L. 2004. *A Review of Foreign Aid in Nepal, 2003*. Kathmandu: Citizens' Poverty Watch Forum and Action Aid Nepal.

Asian Development Bank (ADB). 1999. *Nepal Country Operation Strategy 1999*. Kathmandu: ADB.

————. 2004. *Nepal Country Strategy and Program, 2005–09*. Kathmandu: ADB.

Baidya, B.P.R. 1984. *Foreign Aid and Economic Development: Nepal's Experience with Chinese Aid.* New Delhi: Konark Publishing House.

EU/Nepal. 2002. *Country Strategy for Nepal, 2002–06.* Kathmandu: European Union/Nepal.

Department for International Development/Nepal. 2004. *Nepal Country Assistance Plan 2004–2008.* Kathmandu: DFID Nepal.

Japan International Cooperation Agency (JICA). 2003. *Country Program for Nepal (Draft).* Kathmandu: JICA.

Khadka, N. 1991. *Foreign Aid, Poverty and Stagnation in Nepal.* New Delhi: Vikas Publishing House.

————. 1997. *Foreign Aid and Foreign Policy: Major Powers and Nepal.* New Delhi: Vikash Publishing House.

Martinussen, J.D. and E.P. Poul. 2005. *AID: Understanding International Development Cooperation* (2nd edition). London/New York: Zed Books Limited.

Mihaly, E.B. 2003 [1965]. *Foreign Aid and Politics in Nepal.* Kathmandu: Himal Books.

Ministry of Finance (MOF). 1990. *Economic Survey, Fiscal Year 1989/90.* Kathmandu: MOF/HMG.

————. 1996. *Memorandum of Understanding Between the Government of the Kingdom of Norway and His Majesty's Government of Nepal on Development Cooperation.* Kathmandu: MOF.

————. 2001. *Economic Survey, Fiscal Year 2000/01.* Kathmandu: MOF/HMG.

————. 2009. *Foreign Aid Policy 2009 (A Draft for Discussion at the Nepal Development Forum Stakeholders' Consultation Meeting, May 12–14, 2009).* Kathmandu: MOF.

————. 2010. *Economic Survey, Fiscal Year 2009/10.* Kathmandu: MOF/GoN.

National Planning Commission. (NPC). 1956. *Draft Five Year Plan: A Synopsis.* Kathmandu: NPC/GoN. Retrieved from http://www.npc.gov.np (accessed on 12 October 2010).

————. 1962. *The Second Plan.* Kathmandu: NPC/GoN. Retrieved from http://www.npc.gov.np (accessed on 12 October 2010).

————. 1965. *The Third Plan 1965–70.* Kathmandu: NPC/GoN. Retrieved from http://www.npc.gov.np (accessed on 12 October 2010).

————. 1970. *Fourth Plan 1970–1975.* Kathmandu: NPC/GoN. Retrieved from http://www.npc.gov.np (accessed on 12 October 2010).

————. 1975. *The Fifth Plan 1975–1980.* Kathmandu: NPC/GoN. Retrieved from http://www.npc.gov.np (accessed on 12 October 2010).

————. 1980. *The Sixth Plan 1980–1985, A Summary.* Kathmandu: NPC/GoN. Retrieved from http://www.npc.gov.np (accessed on 12 October 2010).

————. 1985. *The Seventh Plan 1985–1990.* Kathmandu: NPC/GoN. Retrieved from http://www.npc.gov.np (accessed on 12 October 2010).

————. 1992. *The Eighth Plan 1992–1997,* Kathmandu: NPC/GoN. Retrieved from http://www.npc.gov.np (accessed on 12 October 2010).

National Planning Commission. (NPC). 1997. *Ninth Plan 1997–2002*. Kathmandu: NPC/GoN. Retreived from http://www.npc.gov.np (accessed on 12 October 2010).

———. 2002. *Tenth Plan 2002–2007*. Kathmandu: NPC/GoN. Retrieved from http://www.npc.gov.np (accessed on 12 October 2010).

———. 2007. *Three Year Interim Plan 2007–2010*. Kathmandu: NPC/GoN. Retrieved from http://www.npc.gov.np (accessed on 12 October 2010).

PANOS. 2002. *Reducing Poverty: Is the World Bank Strategy Working?* London: The PANOS Institute.

Swiss Development Cooperation (SDC). 2005. *Swiss Cooperation Strategy for Nepal (SCSN) 2005–08*. Kathmandu: SDC.

Swiss Development Cooperation (SDC). 2009. *Swiss Cooperation Strategy for Nepal 2009–12*. Kathmandu: SDC.

Todaro, M.P. 1985. *Development in the Third World* (3rd edition). London: Orient Longman.

UNDP. 1994. *Human Development Report*. New York: Oxford University Press.

UNDP. 2000. *Nepal's Development Partners*. Kathmandu: His Majesty's Government of Nepal/United Nations Development Programme/Nepal.

USAID. 2000. *Country Strategy Paper, 2001–05*. Kathmandu: USAID Nepal.

———. 2001. *Half a Century of Development: The History of US Assistance to Nepal 1951–2001*. Kathmandu: Multi Graphic Press.

———. 2009. *Nepal Country Assistance Strategy, 2009–2013*. Kathmandu: US Mission.

World Bank. 2003. *Nepal Country Assistance Progress Report, 2003*. Kathmandu: WB.

———. 2004. *Nepal Country Assistance Strategy, 2004–07*. Kathmandu: WB.

———. 2009. *Interim Strategy Note for Nepal, July 2009–June 2011*. Kathmandu: WB.

Chapter 10

Good Governance and Development in a Shrinking Local Policy Space

GATS and Service Sector Reforms

DILEEPA WITHARANA

A core element of good governance and good development practice is ensuring the maximum participation of people in decision-making and policy formulation. Examples of less formal forums of decision-making are civil society organizations and trade unions, while parliaments, legislative bodies at the national or provincial level, and local- and village-level councils are all formal structures consisting of elected representatives. These representatives are responsible for decision-making and, more importantly, policy formulation. There are also forums for cooperation in decision-making and policy formulation at a regional level (for example, the South Asian Association for Regional Cooperation [SAARC]). It is the availability of the spaces provided by such forums/structures that allows people with diverse cultures, histories and worldviews to implement their own development models and to achieve their own development targets.

The current world order, however, offers contradictory proposals to world citizens. On the one hand, best practices in good governance, human development and sustainable development are widely discussed in governmental, civil society and private sector forums and are considered essential for human progress. On the other hand, the spaces available for participation in policy-making at the regional and village level, which are important for achieving a meaningful level of development, are shrinking rapidly. As a result the vast majority of the world's population is left out of decision-making processes, while a few powerful international financial and trade organizations (whose operational processes have little resemblance to the guidelines of good governance or the best practices of development) increasingly occupy the policy-making space.

This chapter identifies the importance of the availability of 'local policy space' for diverse communities in the world to achieve development based on what they believe and value, and discusses ways by which international trade and financial institutions and multilateral agreements shrink this local space for decision-making. Using the concept of policy space, this chapter attempts to demonstrate the contradictions within those global initiatives that promote good governance and development while simultaneously promoting multilateral free trade arrangements and market-led reforms.

This chapter will present two case studies which demonstrate the shrinking of local policy space, as a result of which the concepts of good governance and development are rendered meaningless.

A DISCUSSION ON POLICY SPACE

Local policy space within the context of this chapter is identified as the space for free selection of development policies based on the needs of people at regional to village levels, and hence, the space for best governance practices. The shrinking of policy space restricts the range of development policies available to a community and makes a mockery of the rhetoric of development and good governance.

How Local Policy Space Is Shrinking

Local policy space, a dynamic space that comes under the influence of complex power relations, may shrink as a result of many factors. These factors can be grouped into two broad categories: internal and external. Which category the main cause of shrinking policy space is, remains an issue for debate. All direct and indirect influences (for example, structures, frameworks, conditions, threats, bribes, hegemonic discourses, provision of one-sided information, ignorance and lack of communication between upper and lower levels of society and between different generations) restrict policy formulation by not taking into account the development interests of the people. Authoritarian leadership of governments, corruption in the state sector and disempowerment of civil society and the public all result in the erosion of local policy space. People's lack of belief in their own resources and wisdom, especially as a result of the colonization of most of the developing world, is another internal factor that results in the shrinking of local policy space—or rather, it results in local policy space being unused. By accepting the more obvious view that local policy space is an important dimension of good governance and development, and that shrinking of policy space is a serious challenge and a reality, this chapter confines its scope to investigating the external influences that shrink local policy space. This exercise can be interpreted as one which explores the theoretically available policy space for people living within a local territory to practise good governance and to meaningfully achieve the development of their choice.

An analysis of the operations of the World Trade Organization (WTO) and International Financial Institutions (IFIs) leads us to identify at least three main ways through which this freedom of choice is restricted.

Firstly, the freedom to address a wide range of local needs is restricted as a result of commitments undertaken by countries under international and trade agreements. Although these commitments look voluntary on the surface, they are actually undertaken under enormous pressure (Actionaid, 2004; Jawara and Kwa, 2004). The pressure on developing and least-developed countries is generated by several means: direct and indirect threats forcing developing countries to reach 'consensus'; developing countries' lack of expertise making it difficult for them to assess the wide-ranging implications of intensive trade negotiations within strict timeframes; ambiguity of the wording of international legal and trade agreements, leaving room for differing interpretations and allowing power to play a role in the final acceptance of an interpretation; forums such as 'green rooms'[1] excluding powerless developing countries from decision-making processes; and demands for local policy to change through judiciary mechanisms if any local policy contradicts free trade guidelines.

---

[1] After being introduced during the Uruguay Round, 'green room' meetings have become an integral and important part of WTO Doha Round negotiations. These are informal meetings at which a selected group of members meet unofficially to discuss and reach agreement on contested issues. No records are maintained or minutes kept of these meetings (Jawara and Kwa, 2004).

Secondly, aid and loan conditionalities divert the attention of a country from addressing country-specific problems and hence limit the freedom of choice for policy. Channelling funds for certain issues, themes and projects that the funding agency considers important, thereby influencing the direction of development interventions, also limits the policy choices people have.

Thirdly, technical assistance is provided by international institutions so that recipient countries will be compliant with international economic and trade agreements, and will reform country operations in line with 'one-size-fits-all' models promoted by the IFIs.

The following two case studies, 'General Agreement on Trade in Services (GATS)' and 'Electricity and Water Reforms in Sri Lanka' illustrate the range of ways in which local policy space can be restricted as a result of external influences.

CASE STUDY 1: GENERAL AGREEMENT ON TRADE IN SERVICES (GATS)

An Introduction to GATS

The WTO was established in 1995. Its roots, however, go back to the 1947 General Agreement on Tariff and Trade (GATT), which was the first major international agreement aimed at reducing trade restrictions and barriers and promoting multilateral trade between countries. The WTO replaced GATT and came into force in 1995. The WTO is an outcome of almost eight years of negotiations by GATT member countries, which started in September 1986 at Punta del Este, Uruguay and were concluded with the signing of the Marrakesh Agreement in April 1994 in Morocco (Singh, 2000). The WTO marks an expansion of GATT's coverage of issues as well as the power it exercises. While the coverage of GATT was basically limited to goods, WTO expanded its scope to cover many more areas such as services, intellectual property, dispute settlement, trade policy reviews, competition policy, electronic commerce and environment in addition to its continuing goods coverage. Corporate lobbies in the developed world played a decisive role in the expansion in scope represented by the WTO and in the formulation of the rules of WTO agreements. While the multilateral trade rules on agriculture come under the Agreement on Agriculture, rules on market access for non-agricultural products come under the agreement on Non-Agricultural Market Access. The rules in relation to trade of intellectual property rights come under the agreement on Trade Related Intellectual Property Rights, investment measures related to multilateral trade are covered by Trade Related Investment Measures and the set of rules on trade in services come under the GATS. In this chapter, the shrinking of local policy space will only be discussed in relation to GATS.

Corporate lobby groups were instrumental in introducing services to GATT/WTO multilateral trade negotiations, leading to the development of GATS. According to the European Commission, 'GATS is not just something that exists between governments. It is first and foremost an instrument for the benefit of business' (Wesselius, 2002: 3). As far back as 1981, the executive officers of American International Group, American Express and Citicorp identified the need for a business coalition to push for a services agreement in the GATT agenda. The US Coalition of Services Industries (USCSI), which is considered a major driving force behind GATS, was officially formed in 1982. The close coordination of work between USCSI and trade representatives of the US and its Department of Commerce saw the formation of a Group on Negotiation of Services at the start of the GATT Ministerial Conference in Uruguay in 1986. USCSI remained a major force throughout the Uruguay Round discussion on services that lasted from 1986 to 1994 (Wesselius, 2002: 6). The role of corporate lobby groups was well acknowledged by the then director of the services division of the WTO, Davis Hartridge, in his famous statement made in 1997: 'Without the enormous pressure generated by the American financial service sector, particularly companies like American Express and Citicorp, there would have been no services agreement and therefore perhaps no Uruguay Round and no WTO' (Juhasz, 2002). By learning from the successful influence exerted by USCSI on the services agreement, the European Services Network was launched in January 1999 to play a similar role in defending the business interests of the European service sector. This was renamed the European Services Forum in October 1999. The Japan Services Network, the Global Services Network, the Liberalisation of Trade in Services (LOTIS) Committee and the Hong Kong Coalition of Service Industries are a few examples of major corporate lobby groups that played a significant role in GATS negotiations (Wesselius, 2002: 11). It took almost five years after the initiation of GATS for it to receive public scrutiny and become a topic for dialogue and debate. Sinclair and Grieshaber-Otto (2002) provide an interesting account of this initial stage of the debate. The main proponents of GATS in this debate at the global level were officials from the WTO, the Organization for Economic Cooperation and Development (OECD) and trade ministries (mainly those of the United States, the European Union, Japan and Canada). They received the full backing of corporate lobby groups in the service sector. Non-governmental organizations, in both developed and developing countries, took leadership in representing possible public concerns about GATS. 'GATS: Fact and Fiction' and 'Open Services Market Matter', published by the WTO Services Secretariat and the Trade Policy Committee of the OECD, respectively, are two famous documents that challenged the arguments which emerged in the public debate (Sinclair and Grieshaber-Otto, 2002: iii). Some of the responses from non-governmental organizations, which are important documents in the early history of the public debate on GATS, include: 'Separating WTO Fact and Fiction' by the Council of Canadians (Gould, 2001), Technical Comments on the WTO's 'GATS: Facts and Fiction' by Friends of the Earth International (Friends of the Earth International, 2001), a summary response to the same document by the World Development Movement (World Development Movement, 2001), 'GATS—Facts and Fiction: At Best a Partial Truth' by Third World Network (Ragavan, 2001) and 'GATS—What Is Fact and What Is Fiction' by a coalition of civil society organizations (Coalition of Civil Society Organizations, 2001). The challenges posed by GATS to government services attracted serious attention (Sinclair and Grieshaber-Otto, 2002: 17–25). The ways in which GATS shrinks local policy space are discussed in detail later in this chapter.

GATS: Some Technical Details

GATS covers trade in a wide variety of services under four modes. Mode 1 covers services crossing the borders of countries (for example, telecommunications and postal services). Under Mode 2 come services consumed abroad by non-residents (for example, hotels, restaurants or medical services provided for non-residents). If the supplier of a service is a locally established affiliate, subsidiary, or representative office of a non-resident service supplier, such services come under Mode 3 (for example, this applies to offices of multinational service companies). Mode 3 is the most familiar and the most important mode with respect to the implications of GATS on developing country interests. Movement of natural persons is covered under Mode 4. This covers persons travelling from their own country to supply services in another (for example, software engineers, musical groups or health workers) (International Trade Centre, 2002). Developing countries which have a highly skilled labour force are interested in negotiations in this mode as it offers opportunities for expanding the labour market.

GATS works on a 'request-offer' basis. WTO member countries are expected to offer (that is, open up) service sectors under GATS and also to request other member countries to open up. It is through negotiations between member countries that the final decision is made on which service sectors are offered and to what extent. These negotiations can happen on a bilateral basis between two countries, or on a pluri-lateral basis, where a group of countries request the opening up of services sectors from another member country or countries. Opening up a sector means the removal of various kinds of barriers to free trade that exist for that sector within a country. However, GATS allows member countries to have their own reservations when they open up sectors in their country schedules (a 'country schedule' is the document that describes how a country is committed to opening up sectors and with which limitations) (WTO, 2006).

GATS, being based on the above principles, is a document of members' rights and obligations. There are two sets of obligations: general obligations and conditional obligations. When a country gains membership of the WTO, the general obligations apply with immediate effect. Conditional obligations—or specific commitments to opening up markets and providing equal treatment for both domestic and foreign services, which therefore have far more implications for local policy space—apply only when a country commits itself to a service sector under GATS (International Trade Centre, 2002; WTO, 1995a).

Defensive and Offensive Interests in GATS Negotiations

The history of GATS negotiations can be seen as a battle between developed and developing countries. While the developed countries, along with a few fast growing economies in the developing world, were trying to rush the full implementation of GATS and other agreements, the developing countries organized themselves into blocs (Group 20, Group 33 and Group 90) and tried their best to slow down negotiations and protect their defensive interests (Shah, 2005).

How GATS Shrinks Local Policy Space

This chapter will look at the GATS legal text (WTO, 1995a), the fundamental framework used in services sector negotiations and dispute settlements, and examine the notion of shrinking local policy space. The legal text has been selected for discussion for two reasons. Firstly, although they would have provided an ideal way of investigating challenges to local policy space, there are not many examples of GATS disputes since some countries have yet to commit themselves comprehensively under GATS. Secondly, in comparison with the various short- and medium-term measures taken at the General Council and the Ministerial levels of the WTO, the legal texts provide an insight into the long-term vision of GATS.

GATS challenges local policy spaces in many ways. The GATS rules selected for discussion are of special interest to developing countries and are discussed under the following headings: GATS' extensive coverage; enforcement procedures (with punitive mechanisms); limitations on favouring certain countries (in trade-related matters); limitations on favouring domestic services (and service providers); restrictions on market control (in the service sector); irreversibility of commitments (even if the commitments prove to be disastrous); challenges even when no specific rule is violated and the precedence given to free trade policies. This chapter also focuses its attention on exemptions and other flexibilities offered by GATS, and assesses their actual impact on the local policy space.

GATS' Extensive Coverage

GATS' extensive coverage shows the extent to which it invades local policy space. All measures, taken by all levels of governance, that affect trade in services come under GATS coverage and hence under the influence of GATS' free trade rules. The legal text of GATS defines 'measures taken by members' (WTO, 1995a: Article I[3][a]), and hence measures under GATS coverage, to be measures taken by 'central, regional or local authorities and non-governmental bodies in the exercise of powers delegated by central, regional or local governments or authorities' (WTO, 1995a: Article I[3][a]). The legal text goes on to define 'measures' taken by members to include 'any measure by a member, whether in the form of a law, regulation, rule, procedure, decision, administrative action, or any other form' (WTO, 1995a: Article XXVIII). In other words, GATS' challenge to policy space is not just an issue for a central government. GATS' authority is felt even at the level of the village or local authority, if the authority is involved with a measure affecting trade in services. As well as this, GATS is not only limited to measures taken by the state structure, but also encompasses those taken by non-governmental bodies if these bodies are authorized by the state.

The GATS legal text identifies services covered under GATS to be 'any service in any sector except services supplied in the exercise of government authority' (WTO, 1995a: Article I[3][b]). The legal text continues to define a 'service supplied in the exercise of government authority' as 'any service which is supplied neither on a commercial basis, nor in competition with one or more service suppliers' (WTO, 1995a: Article I[3][c]). This clarification could possibly mean that many modern day services under government authority could be potentially included under GATS. Whether the Sri Lankan public school and university system comes under GATS rules or not, for instance, will depend ultimately on the way the Dispute Settlement Body (DSB) defines the word 'competition' within the above rule in a future trade dispute. In addition, the traffic rights of the air transport sector are exempted from the scope of GATS (WTO, 1995a: Annex on Air Transport Services).

When discussing the implications of the extent of GATS coverage in shrinking local policy space, it is important to understand the flexibility offered by the Services Agreement. The question of flexibility can be understood in relation to Article XIX of the GATS legal text. GATS is considered a flexible agreement. Member countries have the freedom to decide whether or not they want to liberalize the service sector under GATS and also to decide the extent to which they want to liberalize the relevant sectors (Sauve, 2005). The flexibility is considered particularly applicable to developing countries. This is highlighted in Article XIX(2) of the GATS legal text, 'Progressive Liberalization'. It says,

> There shall be *appropriate flexibility* for individual developing country members for opening fewer sectors, liberalizing fewer types of transactions, progressively extending market access in line with their development situation and, when making access to their markets available to foreign service suppliers, attaching to such access conditions aimed at achieving the objectives referred to in Article IV. (WTO, 1995a: Article XIX[2])

This is the paragraph developing countries use in their defence when they are pressured through various means to aggressively liberalize the service sector.

However, paragraph 4 of the same Article XIX challenges the above space for flexibility. It says, 'the process of progressive liberalization shall be advanced in each such [negotiation] round through bilateral, pluri-lateral or multilateral negotiations directed towards increasing the general level of specific commitments undertaken by members under this agreement'. (WTO, 1995a: Article XIX[4]). In previous negotiations, this section has been used to put pressure on countries to open their services sector faster. The highly stressful Geneva services negotiations, leading to the WTO Ministerial Conference held in Hong Kong in 2005, can be seen, in principle, as a battle between paragraphs 2 and 4 of Article XIX[2] (Das, 2005; WTO-Watch, 2006).

When addressing the issue of flexibility it is important to discuss the flexibility offered to the least developed countries (LDCs). LDCs are given special concessions in the current round of negotiations. The Declaration

---

[2] By the end of September 2005, several developed countries such as the EU member states, Japan, Switzerland and Korea forwarded proposals that required member countries to aggressively liberalize services. However, they had been opposed strongly by a number of developing countries.

of the Ministerial Conference held in Hong Kong in 2005 'recognise[s] the particular economic situation of LDCs, including the difficulties they face, and acknowledge[s] that they are not expected to undertake new commitments' (WTO, 2005: paragraph 26). The concessions, however, are provided while maintaining the need for LDCs to stay within the multilateral free trade framework. The Declaration continues, 'We reaffirm our commitment to effectively and meaningfully integrate LDCs into the multilateral trading system' (WTO, 2005: paragraph 47).

Enforcement Procedures: The DSB of the WTO

With the exception of the North American Free Trade Agreement, the WTO contains the most powerful enforcement procedures of any international agreement now in force. In comparison to the multilateral agreements of the past, which were 'conventions' through which signatories agree to substantive rules which are only enforceable by each signatory, the WTO system, including GATS, contains a mechanism for dispute resolution which is binding on its members.[3] The WTO is equipped with a powerful enforcement system that can issue recommendations and rulings backed by the threat of trade sanctions for non-compliance (WTO, 1995b). Unlike the GATT resolution system, which relied more on diplomatic negotiation over disputes and which required consensus by all countries for rulings to be adopted, the WTO panel rulings are automatically binding and only the unanimous consent of all members can halt the adoption of panel rulings. That means any country wanting to block a ruling has to persuade all other WTO members, including the country that brought the case against it in the first place, to vote in consensus to have the ruling overturned.

Disputes under GATS occur when a member country is deemed to have violated a GATS rule or nullified the benefits a foreign service provider could expect within the opened sectors, even if a specific GATS rule is not violated. The aim of the dispute settlement mechanism is to secure a positive solution to a dispute. A positive solution to a dispute ideally means a

---

[3] http://www.wto.org/english/thewto_e/whatis_e/tif_e/disp1_e.htm (accessed on 16 July 2006).

solution that is mutually acceptable to the parties involved and consistent with the covered agreements. In the absence of a mutually agreed solution, the first objective is to secure a withdrawal of the 'offensive' trade measures. The provision of compensation will be resorted to only if the immediate withdrawal of the measure is impracticable. The last resort offered by this understanding is the possibility of trade sanctions (Wallach and Woodall, 2004; WTO, 1995b). The GATS dispute settlement mechanism makes it extremely difficult for a member country to ignore a ruling made against a domestic measure even if the measure is of great local policy value.

Limitations on Favouring Certain Countries: The Most Favoured Nation Rule

The Most Favoured Nation (MFN) rule shrinks local policy space in several ways. Unless exemptions are obtained, the MFN rule does not allow a member country to favour one or a group of other member countries for measures coming under GATS. This rule is in application from the day the country becomes a member of WTO (see WTO, 1995a: Article II[1]).

Exemptions are allowed within the GATS context, but they are of a temporary nature. The approach by the WTO on MFN exemptions is made clear in the following clause: 'In principle, such exemptions should not exceed a period of 10 years' (WTO, 1995a: Annex on Article II Exemptions [6]). In addition, the Council for Trade at the WTO is empowered by the Agreement to conduct reviews on MFN exemptions for a period of not more than five years.

Unless exemptions are obtained, the benefits of liberalization of a service sector under GATS by a member country (as a result of bilateral or pluri-lateral negotiations held with a country or a group of countries) can automatically be enjoyed by all the other member countries as a result of the MFN rule. MFN also requires the payment of compensation to the entire membership of the WTO if a country violates certain GATS rules, such as allowing monopolies or exclusive service suppliers in sectors already opened under GATS (Article VIII) or modifications to the original schedules (Article XXI).

There are two rules that are of importance in a discussion on the impact of MFN on the policy spaces of regional country blocs. The first rule defines the context in which a country is allowed to favour its neigh-bouring countries in services trade, and the second defines the conditions on which other trade (liberalization) agreements in services (other than GATS) are allowed. The second rule requires other agreements for liber-alizing trade in services to have substantial sector coverage (number of sectors opened, volume of trade affected and all four modes of supply); it also requires the elimination of (all) existing discriminatory measures and the prohibition of further discriminatory measures (WTO, 1995a: Article V[1]). Though flexibility is provided for developing countries (paragraphs 2 and 3 of Article V), the bias of flexibility is towards freer trade. That is, bilateral and regional trade agreements are allowed only when the level of liberalization among the trading partners goes beyond the liberalization commitments undertaken at the WTO.

Limitations on Favouring Domestic Services: The National Treatment Rule

National Treatment is one of the main rules in application when a country opens up a sector under GATS and is also one of the main rules respon-sible for shrinking the policy space for a country to protect its services sector from strong competition from foreign services suppliers. After being offered or opened up, the member country is obliged to provide services and service providers from any other member country with the same treatment received by its own services and service providers. This is the case unless exemptions are obtained. Any measure considered to directly or indirectly favour a local services sector is a violation of the National Treatment rule if exemptions are not obtained (see WTO, 1995a: Article XVII[i]).

If the health service, for example, is offered without reservations, then the Sri Lankan free healthcare policy could be challenged by foreign health service providers before the DSB. The interpretation given by the DSB on the competitive nature of the Sri Lankan public health sector determines whether the free healthcare policy can survive. Although a country is free, in principle, to identify whatever exemptions it chooses, the final list of exemptions is decided through a process of negotiation among the countries. In addition, there are continuous references in the WTO literature for the need for countries to make 'quality' offers, that is, offers which keep exemptions to a minimum (for example, WTO, 2005: paragraph 2). GATS' extensive coverage of all measures affecting supply of services requires comprehensive studies to be conducted before offering a sector if a member country wants certain measures to be identified for exemption. Whether developing countries have the resources or the expertise to conduct such detailed studies in order to assess the impact of offering sectors is questionable. This raises the issue of the extent to which countries are aware of the implications when they 'voluntarily' open up sectors.

Restrictions on Market Control: The Market Access Rule

The Market Access rule is about the limitations a country, a province, or any other regional subdivision of a country can impose on services and service providers of foreign member countries operating within the country under any one of the four modes of GATS. Market Access is also a conditional obligation such as the National Treatment rule and is only applicated after a specific services sector is opened up under GATS. When committing services, countries are expected to identify reservations they would like to keep for themselves and are expected to list these in their country schedules. As in the case of National Treatment, the final list of limitations is decided through negotiations with the countries requesting services sectors to be opened and offering them. If limitations are not secured in their schedules through negotiations, member countries are not allowed to introduce measures to set limitations on the total number of service suppliers, on the values of service transactions or assets, on service options or on natural persons that may be employed in a particular service; they are also not allowed to restrict legal entities or joint ventures; they may not limit the participation of foreign capital by specifying a maximum percentage (WTO, 1995a: Article XVI[2]).

Market Access further shrinks local policy space by restricting the ability of a forum of governance to manage the market in the best interests of the country or the province. For example, in the initial offers made in September 2003, Sri Lanka expressed commitments to open Mode 3 of hotel and lodging services with no limitation on market access (WTO, 2003). This limits policy options in any of the above forms to protect interests of the local hotel industry and also limits policy choices to safeguard other interests such as coastal conservation, integrated development of regions with high tourism, protection of the environment and respect for cultural values.

Irreversibility of Commitments: Loss of Local Policy Space for Future Generations

It is widely believed that GATS commitments are not reversible even if the liberalization of a country's services sector under GATS proves to be disastrous (Thomas and Hall, 2006). In fact, modifications to a country's schedule of commitments require the compensation of the entire membership of the WTO under the MFN rule; for a developing country, this can safely be assumed to be difficult if not impossible (see WTO, 1995a: Article XXI(2)[a]). It requires compensatory adjustments to be made with regard to the MFN rule (WTO, 1995a: XXI[2][b]).

Furthermore, GATS sets barriers for member countries to grant monopoly rights or exclusive service provision rights in a services sector after the sector is opened up under GATS. If monopoly rights or exclusive service provision rights (created by substantially preventing competition) are granted, the member country is bound to make compensatory adjustments not just to the foreign service provider that gets affected by the newly introduced monopoly rights, but to all member countries under the MFN rule. If no compensatory adjustment is made, the affected member country is allowed to 'modify or withdraw substantially equivalent benefits' (WTO, 1995a: Article VIII(4), Article XXI(2–4); WTO, 1995b: Article 22) through the Council for Trade in Services, which is equivalent to imposing sanctions. If the Sri Lankan transport sector is offered, for example, the formation of one public transport agency by combining the existing, state-owned bus companies could be successfully challenged, leading to Sri Lanka having to compensate all member countries.

Challenges Even When No Specific Rule Is Violated: The Rules of Nullification and Impairment

GATS includes provisions for member countries to challenge measures taken by another member country in sectors opened under GATS, even if these measures do not violate the rules. Here the challenge is made for nullifying or impairing benefits a foreign service-provider could have expected from the relevant measure taken. If the challenge is judged to be valid, the country in question should either modify or withdraw the measure or compensate for the lost benefits by the other country; otherwise, they could face suspension of concessions (WTO, 1995a: Article XXIII(3); WTO, 1995b: Article 22).

Free Trade Policies Get Precedence

GATS is not just about trade in services, but about all measures *affecting* trade in services. The scope of GATS is applicable 'to [all] measures by Members affecting trade in services' (WTO, 1995a: Article I[1]). For example, the measures introduced by member countries (including the measures introduced by provincial and local authorities) to safeguard other development interests such as strengthening the domestic economy, protection of the environment, safeguarding of cultural diversity, safety of human health or food security could come under the purview of GATS if these measures affect trade in services. The countries are bound to modify or withdraw these measures if they are declared to be in violation of GATS rules.

GATS legal text, however, provides general exceptions to measures taken by member countries 'to protect public morals or to maintain public order' and 'to protect human, animal or plant life or health' (WTO, 1995a: Article XIV[a and b]). However, it limits the use of these exceptions by introducing additional conditions under which the exceptions are allowed. A member country is permitted the above exceptions only if the measure in consideration is 'not applied in a manner which would constitute a means of arbitrary or unjustifiable discrimination between countries where like conditions prevail or a disguised restriction on trade in services' (WTO, 1995a: Article XIV). If the measure is a law or a regulation, for which exceptions are allowed, there is the additional constraint of requiring it not to be 'inconsistent with the provisions of the Agreement' (WTO, 1995a: Article XIV[c]). It can be argued that the constraints engendered by this need to maintain consistency with other GATS rules make it impossible for the law or regulation to be exempted on the basis of maintaining public order, or protecting human health or the environment (Wallach and Woodall, 2004: 130). General exceptions are also allowed for measures on the basis of 'essential security interests' (WTO, 1995a: Article XIV *bis* [1][b]). Compared to the general exception for health, public morals and environment, the exceptions given on the basis of security are clearly worded with no constraints attached (see WTO, 1995a: Article XIV *to* [1][b]). The actual policy space left for a member country as a result of the exceptions is an interesting area for investigation, something that can only be done after a long-term and thorough analysis of the rulings of the DSB. Since GATS is still at the initial implementation stage and most of the countries are yet to make significant commitments under it, there are a very few reference case studies available. However, when the record of WTO cases is scrutinized by topic (without limiting the search to cases on GATS), nearly every health, food safety or environmental law (except for two) challenged at the WTO up to 2004 has been declared a barrier to trade (Wallach and Woodall, 2004: 242).

The US's challenge of the EU's policy of setting aside a specific small portion of its market for bananas exported by the Caribbean countries (as a concession offered to its former colonies), and Antigua's and Barbuda's challenge of the US's policy of preventing gambling and betting on a cross-border basis, are two examples of successful GATS challenges that resulted in shrinking local policy spaces (Thomas and Hall, 2006; Wallach and Woodall, 2004).

CASE STUDY 2: ELECTRICITY AND WATER SECTOR REFORMS IN SRI LANKA

An Introduction to Electricity and Water Sector Reforms

It is important to place these reform exercises in the electricity and water sectors within the broader context of electricity and water issues in Sri Lanka. The Sri Lankan electricity and water sectors can both be considered to be in a state of crisis. The inability of the authorities in the electricity sector to design a proper electricity generation plan, one that takes into consideration the diverse and valid national, economic, environmental and social interests represented by various stakeholder groups (such as large- and small-scale consumers in industrial, commercial and domestic sectors; people in isolated villages who do not have access to electricity yet; trade unions; environmentalists; people who become displaced by electricity generation projects; conventional energy producers as well as renewable energy producers; etc.) can be identified as the root cause of the current electricity crisis. The 'least financial cost' approach (used as the only planning guideline), the unrealistic assumptions made by the electricity planners and the limitations of the Wien Automatic System Planning software used for the long-term electricity generation planning are main factors contributing to this inability to design a proper plan (Energy Forum, 2006). Unnecessary political interference in the implementation process, the serious financial crisis of the Ceylon Electricity Board (CEB), campaigns against the proposed coal power plants by environmentalists and the high cost of electricity are all symptoms of the root cause mentioned above. The theft of electricity, continuingly high transmission losses and corruption in the state-owned utility make the crisis even more complicated. Electricity reforms that have already been introduced—through the Electricity Reform Act and the Public Utility Commission Act—but which have yet to be fully implemented, and which aim to establish several electricity companies and to transfer their ownership gradually from the state to the private sector, have also become part of the problem rather than offering any solution (Witharana, 2007).

The water issue for Sri Lanka is of a different nature. Sri Lanka is generally considered a country of abundant water resources, with an annual per capita water supply of 2,400 cm. Sri Lanka's challenges in water, however, are the seasonal shortages of water for irrigation, domestic use and hydropower generation as well as the degradation of the quality of surface water through domestic and industrial effluents and agricultural runoff. Water use for agriculture development and improvements in socio-economic and industrial development over the last two decades, coupled with rapid urbanization, have increased demand (Nanayakkara, 2003; Ariyabandu and Aheeyar, 2004). The development of a national water policy and the implementation of policy measures to address the question of current seasonal shortages of water, as well as the future concerns related to water scarcity can be considered to be the challenges of the day. As in the case of electricity, market-driven water reforms have not contributed to solving the Sri Lankan water crisis, but instead have aggravated it by generating public resistance.

The Spectrum of Policy Options

The Sri Lankan expert dialogues and public debates over the past few years at various seminars and conferences,[4] and also in the newspapers, radio and television, on the electricity and water crisis informs us of a wide spectrum of policy solutions that are available for the country. At a more general level, there are two diametrically opposite approaches to the treatment of both electricity and water. That is, either to treat them as *services to the public* and as a non-profit-earning investment in infrastructure that aims to achieve the overall development goals of the country or to treat them as *economic goods* that have to be brought under market mechanisms so that they are managed cost-effectively.

The debate on electricity reforms also provides different interpretations of the crisis: as a crisis of the state monopoly ownership of the CEB, or as a crisis of governance of the electricity utility. While some argue that by changing the ownership of the utility a solution could be found, others are of the opinion that it is governance that matters and not ownership.[5]

---

[4] Presentations made at a training programme on 'Water Policy' organized by the Post Graduate Institute of Agriculture of the University of Peradeniya on 12 May 2005; a conference on 'Electricity Reform: Global Experience' organized by Practical Action and held in Colombo on the 10 March 2006; a seminar on 'Water and its Use' organized by the Institution of Engineers, Sri Lanka on 25 April 2006 and a seminar on 'Public Comments on the National Water Resources (Draft)' organized by the National Water Policy Study Team and held in Colombo on 30 October 2006 are used as special references.

[5] A conclusion of the conference on 'Electricity Reform: Global Experience' organized by Practical Action and held in Colombo on 10 March 2006 (Practical Action, 2006).

There are at least three major lines of thinking adopted by powerful lobby groups that explain the reasons for the crisis and hence propose distinct policy choices to solve the problem.

The first main explanation for the crisis, given by right-wing lobbies and supported by the IFIs, is that there is corruption and mismanagement within the state-owned electricity monopoly. The formation of several companies by unbundling the integrated utility, along with a gradual shift in ownership to the private sector, is seen as the way out. This line of thinking is mainly backed by a powerful group of energy sector officials, as well as by some of the politicians from the two main political parties that have been in power in Sri Lanka and who took and continue to take policy decisions in the energy sector.

The non-implementation, for over a decade at least, of the 'least cost' generation expansion plan prepared by the Electricity Generation Planning Branch of the CEB (as a result of public protests and the interference of politicians) is a widely accepted second explanation of the crisis. This forced the CEB to go for an expensive emergency private power option, while maintaining the selling price of a unit at level below unit generation costs, causing heavy financial losses to the utility and higher prices for consumers (Prelis, 2005). Here, the immediate implementation of the 'least cost' Electricity Generation Expansion Plan is seen as the main step in solving the crisis. This is generally the view taken by almost all trade unions of the CEB, who resist the unbundling and privatization of the CEB, the solution proposed by the group referred to above. This line of thinking promotes the addition of coal power plants to the national grid—plants that have been identified as the cheapest generation options.

The narrow framework on which the generation expansion plan is based, without taking into consideration the country's wider interests (such as energy independence, energy security, energy equity, job creation and protection of the environment and human health) is the third explanation for the crisis, given mainly by those who are more concerned about the environment and the broader development interests of Sri Lanka.[6] This argument assumes that public protests and political interference could be minimized if the externalities of the electricity sector were to

---

[6] A study concluded by the Energy Forum of Sri Lanka was based on this interpretation of the electricity crisis (Energy Forum, 2006).

be internalized in future expansion planning. Environmental organizations, organizations working on renewable energy, political parties with a 'green' agenda, private sector renewable energy producers, organizations preferring a broader definition of development over mere economic development and academics promoting sustainable energy options belong to this somewhat powerful lobby.

Within the Sri Lankan context there is a general consensus that water is a limited natural resource. There is also consensus on the need to improve the accessibility of water to all Sri Lankans and on the need for a national water policy that considers water from a holistic point of view (Ministry of Agriculture, Livestock, Land and Irrigation, 2004, 2005; Water Resources Secretariat, 2000, 2001, 2004). There is, however, a divergence of views within this general consensus: people are divided on whether water should be treated as a scarce resource and also on the extent to which developing policy should be holistic. The point of divergence stems from a difference in approaches, mainly between the modern approaches to water management and the historical, indigenous approaches. The concept of reuse plays a significant role in indigenous water management, and it is based on the logic that some consider water not to be scarce, even though as a resource water is limited. While the set of draft national water policies introduced by consecutive governments highlighted the need for treating water holistically by taking the entire water cycle (rain, surface and ground water) into consideration, there is also the view among certain experts and sections of the public that water should be treated not in isolation but as a part of the entire ecosystem. According to the latter view, water policy is part of a wider ecosystem policy and hence is linked directly to national policies on environment, pollution control, forestation, soil conservation, agriculture, etc. (Ministry of Agriculture, Livestock, Land and Irrigation, 2004, 2005).

An investigation of the wide spectrum of policy options offered by the current Sri Lankan debate on water management reveals that there are proposals for water management based on four distinct principles. The first principle is to consider water as a basic human right, as well as something that belongs to all living beings. According to this principle, the state is just a trustee which safeguards the right to water of all living beings. Hence, water should not be sold. Regulation through state policy is considered the best option for water management. The second principle considers water to belong to all, which means that nobody should make money from it. People are, however, expected to pay for the service that supplies it. The third principle treats water fundamentally as a social good (based on the principle of considering water to be a basic human right), but in cases such as uncontrolled bulk water extraction, as an economic good. The thinking behind the fourth principle is that water is an economic good, and the market is the best mechanism to manage it efficiently.

At the public level there is very strong resistance to the concept of water as an economic good and a commodity to be sold. Policies that are based on modern 'Integrated Water Resources Management' principles, within which water is treated as an economic good, are popularly identified as policies to 'sell water'. Left-wing political movements, civil society organizations, trade unions and the media provide leadership for the general public's resistance to 'selling water'.

Reform Models

Although reform in theory means the reformation of a sector according to the specific evolving needs of the country or the region concerned, the 'reforms' introduced worldwide as a trend since the 1980s propose 'one-size-fits-all' models in many sectors, including the electricity and water sectors. The word 'reform' is used in this chapter to refer to these 'one-size-fits-all' models being promoted all over the world by the IFIs. Reforms in the electricity sector try, in general, to address the financial crisis of the state-owned integrated electricity utilities in countries worldwide and to introduce efficient management of the electricity systems; in the water sector, reforms attempt to address this century's predicted global water scarcity. The fundamental guideline of current reforms, in order to achieve the above objectives in the electricity and water sectors, is to move away from the state as the service provider towards multiple private service providers.

There are three major elements in electricity reforms: unbundling the integrated electricity utility and the formation of several companies for electricity generation, transmission and distribution; changing the ownership of the utility gradually from the state to the private sector, firstly by commercializing the sector, then by introducing private generation and ultimately privatizing the entire industry; and introducing independent regulation without political interference. Reforms also mark a shift away from treating electricity as a service to society and the country, towards considering it as a profit-making resource. Cost recovery and removal of cross-subsidies are important measures taken at the commercialization stage (Karekezi and Sihag, 2004).

The basis of water reform is to consider water as an economic good. Integrated water management, introduction to transferable water rights, full cost recovery and private sector participation or public-private partnerships are the main characteristics of water reforms (Asian Development Bank [ADB], 2003).

The Role of Reforms Led by IFIs in a Shrinking Local Policy Space

Though the reform exercise in Sri Lanka started a long time ago, the country has yet to see the full implementation of both electricity and water sector reforms.

The Sri Lankan electricity reform process started in the early 1990s. A preliminary study followed by a more detailed one, considering various options for electricity sector restructuring, was conducted in 1993 and 1997. Power sector policy directions and guidelines were set in 1998 and 2002, respectively (Ministry of Irrigation and Power, 1998; Ministry of Power and Energy, 2002). The Electricity Reform Act, along with the Public Utility Commission Act, was passed in Parliament in 2002 (Government of Sri Lanka, 2002a, 2002b). The Gazette notification, introducing the 'Scheme for Reorganization of the Electricity Industry', was published in 2004 (Government of Sri Lanka, 2004). Public and trade union resistance to the privatization of the sector has now brought the restructuring process of the utility to a standstill. The change of government in April 2004 strengthened this position against privatization. A committee was formed in 2005 to examine the crisis of the sector and propose solutions. The report submitted by this committee identified reforms as one of the three steps to be taken and received cabinet approval (Piyatilake, 2007). However, no progress has been made so far in this direction. Resistance to privatization by trade unions and the public at large still plays a major role in the reluctance of the government to take firm steps in implementing reforms.

In the water sector, there are up to 20 drafts of the water policy and over eight drafts of the Water Resources Bill, each presented and then taken back as a result of public protest (Ariyabandu, 2005). The Water Resources Bill presented to parliament in 2003, which aimed to privatize pipe borne water supplies in both rural and urban areas, was successfully challenged in the Supreme Court as being unconstitutional. The latest draft of the water policy was presented to the cabinet of ministers in February 2006 (Kulatunga, 2007). This draft was published for public comments on 9 October 2006 and the public resistance it generated has brought the reform process to a standstill once again.

Protests from various sections of the Sri Lankan society, and the resulting failure of the implementation of electricity and water reforms so far, are a result of the fact that market-based 'one-size-fits-all' reform models have failed to address the root causes of the crisis and the wide-ranging issues in electricity and water sectors, and hence, gain the consensus of interested parties and the public at large. Rather than being a forum to discuss a wide spectrum of policy choices, as discussed above, the reform process shrank the space for policy dialogue by demanding consensus on the 'one-size-fits-all' model introduced elsewhere. The overemphasis on market-led reforms has diverted attention away from the need to attend to the deep-rooted crisis in both sectors by addressing multiple issues as a whole.

The IFIs played a strong role in both electricity and water reforms by shrinking the policy space left in which to constructively address the actual crisis in the electricity sector and the actual issues in the water sector. Their role covers the entire spectrum of policy space and seriously limits policy choices in a number of ways: by attaching reforms as conditions to lending, by providing policy advice on reforms through documents produced by the institutions, by offering technical assistance for sector reforms through consultants to design and implement sector reforms, by funding public projects that advance sector reforms and by supporting private projects. Within the context of this chapter the roles placed by the World Bank (WB) and the ADB are discussed.

Attaching Conditions to Lending and Finance

The improvement of cost recovery in the irrigation, urban water, and electricity sectors and the restructuring of loss-making public enterprises have been the conditions for financing by the WB since the latter part of the 1990s. Any increase or reduction in lending has been linked to the progress made in reforms. In the 2003 Country Assistance Strategy, the WB offered to lend a greater amount under the condition that it would cut the amount by half if there was 'a lagging behind of structural reforms and a failure to maintain satisfactory macroeconomic performance as evaluated by IMF' (WB, 2003a: 24).

The ADB introduced performance-based allocations in the early 2000s: structural reforms, improvement of financial viability of the CEB and water sector reforms were important criteria for assessing performance (ADB, 2002a, 2004, 2005). The ADB also provided direct financial assistance for water and power sector reforms. The loan of US$60 million, agreed by the ADB in October 2002, was to be released in two instalments under certain conditions. These included the enactment of the Public Utilities Commission Bill and the Electricity Reform Bill in parliament, the establishment of the Public Utilities Commission, the appointment of members and the unbundling of CEB's generation, transmission and distribution functions. The loan of US$19.7 million agreed to in August 2000 included as conditions the granting of cabinet approval for the National Water Resources Act and the formal establishment of the National Water Resources Authority as a part of reforms (Noble, 2006).

Providing Policy Advice

The WB publishes various policy documents, providing advice and recommending necessary policy changes. 'Private Sector Assessment' (WB, 1995), 'Non-Plantation Crop Sector Policy Alternatives' (WB, 1996), 'Recent Economic Developments and Prospects' (WB, 1998b), 'Recapturing Missed Opportunities' (WB, 2000), 'Promoting Agricultural and Rural Non-Farm Sector Growth' (WB, 2003b), 'Improving the Rural and Urban Investment Climate' (WB, 2005b) and 'Sri Lanka Development Forum: The Economy, the Tsunami and Poverty Reduction' (WB, 2005a), all carry various pieces of policy advice related to the commercialization of irrigation systems and the electricity sector, the restructuring of the CEB, the encouragement of private sector participation in the electricity and water sectors, and the introduction of reforms acts to parliament.

Offering Technical Assistance

The WB has provided regular funding for consultancies to design, manage and implement functions related to electricity and water sector reforms. Contracts have been issued to individuals as well as to international consultancy firms such as Halcrow and PricewaterhouseCoopers. Consultancy assignments have included providing advice on power and water sector reforms in general, and on special issues such as bringing the private sector into the provision of water services, reviewing privatization of infrastructure enterprises, defining functions and developing an operation manual for the Public Utility Commission of Sri Lanka (Alexander, 2005). As a supplement to the reform process, the WB funded top-level advisory services, such as special economic and political advisors to the prime minister, in 2003 (Noble, 2006).

There are many examples of ADB funded consultancies in electricity and water reforms: the preparation of a strategic framework and an action plan for water reforms; the development of a national Water Sector Policy and the National Water Act; the drafting of the Act and setting guidelines for the implementation of various provisions; the preparation of operational procedures for water rights and the introduction of the concept of water rights and allocation in river basins; the preparation of the Power Sector Restructuring Loan, which had the aim of assisting the detailed planning and implementation of power sector reforms and the Energy Sector Master Plan, which was described as a strategy formulated in accordance with market-oriented policy requirements (Noble, 2006).

Funding Public Projects That Use the Principles of Sector Reforms

Both the WB and the ADB finance the expansion of the piped water and irrigation systems. The WB and ADB expect these systems, implemented generally on a pilot basis, to be based on principles that have yet to be adopted in a National Water Policy. Examples of such principles are the 'full cost recovery' and systems of bulk water entitlements to users (ADB, 2000; Ariyabandu and Aheeyar, 2004; WB, 1998a). The ADB provided loans for the creation of the National Water Resources Authority, intended to play a main role in water reforms[7] and provided a sector loan to unbundle the CEB (ADB, 2002b).

Supporting Private Projects

The International Finance Corporation (IFC) and the Multilateral Investment Guarantee Agency (MIGA) are separate arms of the WB which support private sector projects. IFC provides loans exclusively to private companies for investment and especially for the private provision of infrastructure services such as electricity and water. MIGA offers political risk insurance to private companies. IFC has mainly been active in the Sri Lankan power sector, while MIGA has also issued guarantees to private power plants. Through its projects such as the Private Sector Infrastructure Development Project, the Energy Services Delivery Project and the Renewable Energy for Rural Economic Development Project, the WB has also provided funds for power generation and distribution by the private sector (Noble, 2006).

CONCLUSION

In the modern world, people are struggling to find a balance between the benefits of accepting ever-increasing international rules and commitments, and the constraints posed by the accompanying loss of policy space. The central themes in dialogues on good governance and development in this situation are the availability of forums, which allows people to get involved with decision-making at all levels of society, and people's freedom to choose development policies. The existing equation is unfair in relation to the developing world. This is reflected in the increasing

[7] http://www.adb.org/Documents/Profiles/LOAN/31288013.ASP (accessed on 1 July 2006).

demand by developing countries for a space to meaningfully decide their own policy in the face of international rules and commitments, in civil society dialogues as well as in inter-governmental forums.

As shown by the two case studies on GATS and on the role of the IFIs in Sri Lankan electricity and water reforms, meaningful local policy space has shrunk in multiple ways. The issue is not just one of shrinking policy space at central government level. As GATS shows, the influence of international rules are now extending as far as the local authority level. GATS poses a major challenge to the ability of local policy space to defend and develop the local services sector, resulting in limited policy options for the maintenance of public services and the strengthening of the local economy. By preferring free trade values over any others, GATS also limits policy options for protection of the environment, achievement of food security and maintenance of cultural diversity, for example. Due to the fact that, especially for a developing country, it is virtually impossible to reverse a commitment once made, GATS also shrinks the policy space for the future. The strong role played by the WB and the ADB in the Sri Lankan electricity and water sectors also shows how the wide range of policy options available for Sri Lankans to address their development needs in these sectors are being limited. The reform models advocated by the IFIs leave little room for Sri Lankans to design reforms based on the way that they approach electricity and water services, in keeping with heterogeneous community needs, social values, indigenous knowledge and cultural meanings, but instead requires the acceptance of privatization as the only solution.

Much of the flexibility offered by international rules and commitments, as shown by GATS, is either of a temporary nature or not easy to obtain as a result of the way it is worded in the legal text. The flexibility allowed as part of the right to have reservations also generates a paradox for developing countries. To safeguard the space for local policy, countries are on the one hand expected to declare their reservations at the time they begin to liberalize their services under GATS. However, on the other hand, the implications of GATS on that country's various interests can be far-reaching, so that it is almost impossible for a country to foresee them and include them in the list of reservations at the time.

This chapter reveals two major challenges faced by the initiatives to establish good governance and achieve development. While evolving understanding of good governance and development remains at the academic level advanced and sophisticated, addressing all the major concerns of the world's diverse populations, the concepts' practical meaning remains narrow when it comes to implementation. Good governance, in practice, refers exclusively to getting rid of corruption and mismanagement, especially in the state sector. The use of the terms 'developed' and 'developing' is still based on the indicators of macro-level economic development. The implementation of the best practices of good governance and development is demanded from small players at the micro level, while powerful actors at the global macro levels, such as the WTO and IFIs, are allowed to violate them. Achieving good governance and development in a shrinking local policy space is an extremely difficult task.

REFERENCES

Actionaid. 2004. 'Divide and Rule: The EU and US Response to Developing Country Alliances at the WTO'. Available at http://www.actionaid.org.uk/doc_lib/30_1_divide_rule.pdf (accessed on 17 April 2013).

Alexander, N. 2005. 'The Role of the IMF, the World Bank, and the WTO in Liberalization and Privatization of the Water Services Sector. Citizen's network on essential services'. Available at http://www.geocities.ws/monlarslk/publications/Water/Role_of_IFIs_in_Water_Privatization.pdf (accessed on 17 April 2013).

Ariyabandu, R. 2005. 'National Water Resources Policy—Why Can't We Achieve Consensus?'. *Daily News*, 11 February 2005.

Ariyabandu, R. and M. Aheeyar. 2004. *Secure Water Through Demand Responsive Approaches: The Sri Lankan Experience*. London: Overseas Development Institute.

Asian Development Bank (ADB). 2000. *Project Completion Report on the Second Water Supply and Sanitation Project (Loan 1235—SRI {SF}) in Sri Lanka. PCR SRI 23209*. Manila: Asian Development Bank.

———. 2002a. *Country Strategy and Program Update (2003-5) Sri Lanka (July 2002)*. Manila: Asian Development Bank.

———. 2002b. *Report and Recommendation of the President to the Board of Director on Proposed Loans to the Democratic Socialist Republic of Sri Lanka for the Power Sector Development Program: RRP: SRI 30207*. Manila: Asian Development Bank.

———. 2003. *Water for All: The Water Policy of the Asian Development Bank. Our Framework: Policies and Strategies*. Manila: Asian Development Bank.

Asian Development Bank (ADB). 2004. *Country Strategy and Program Update 2005–6 Sri Lanka. CSP: SRI 2004–14.* Manila: Asian Development Bank.
———. 2005. *Country Strategy and Program Update 2006–8 Sri Lanka. CSP: SRI 2005.* Manila: Asian Development Bank.

Coalition of Civil Society Organizations. 2001. 'GATS—What is Fact and what is Fiction?' Available at http://www.gatswatch.org/docs/rebuttal.html (accessed on 17 April 2013).

Das, B. 2005. 'Rocking the WTO boat once again', Third World Network. Available at http://www.twnside.org.sg/title2/twninfo277.htm (accessed on 17 April 2013).

Energy Forum. 2006. *Incorporating Social and Environmental Concerns in Long Term Electricity Generation Expansion Planning in Sri Lanka: Draft. Report for Public Comments.* Colombo: Energy Forum.

Friends of the Earth International. 2001. *Technical Comments on the WTO's 'GATS—Fact and Fiction'.* Amsterdam: Vice, Y.

Gould, E. 2001. *Separating WTO Fact and Fiction.* Ottawa: Council of Canadians.

Government of Sri Lanka. 2002a. *Electricity Reform Act, No. 28 of 2002.* Colombo: Parliament of the Democratic Socialist Republic of Sri Lanka.
———. 2002b. *Public Utilities Commission of Sri Lanka Act, No. 35 of 2002.* Colombo: Parliament of the Democratic Socialist Republic of Sri Lanka.
———. 2004. *Scheme for the Reorganization of the Electricity Industry in Sri Lanka under Chapter VI of the Electricity Reform Act, No. 28 of 2002.* The Gazette of the Democratic Socialist Republic of Sri Lanka: Extraordinary, No. 1321/21, 2 January 2004. Colombo: Department of Government Printing.

International Trade Centre. 2002. *Business Guide to the General Agreement on Trade in Services* rev. ed. Geneva: International Trade Centre.

Jawara, F. and A. Kwa. 2004. *Behind the Scenes at the WTO: The Real World of Negotiations—The Lessons from Cancun.* Updated Edition. London/New York: Zed Books.

Juhasz, A. 2002. 'Servicing Citi's Interests: GATS and the Bid to Remove Barriers to Financial Firm Globalization'. Available at http://www.thirdworldtraveler.com/Banks/Citis_Interests.html (accessed on 17 April 2013).

Karekezi, S. and A. Sihag (eds). 2004. *Energy Access Theme Results.* Roskilde: 'Energy Access' Working Group, Global Network on Energy for Sustainable Development.

Kulatunga, G. 2007. 'Implications of Recently Proposed Water Policies on the Marginalised in Water Reforms and the Poor'. Liberalizsation of Services and Reforms. *Discussion Papers 1.* Colombo: Practical Action (ITDG) South Asia.

Ministry of Agriculture, Livestock, Land and Irrigation. 2004. *National Water Resources Use, Conservation, and Development Policy (a Draft).* Colombo: Ministry of Agriculture, Livestock, Land and Irrigation.
———. 2005. *National Water Resources Use, Conservation, and Development Policy (Final Draft).* Colombo: Ministry of Agriculture, Livestock, Land and Irrigation.

Ministry of Irrigation and Power. 1998. *Power Sector Policy Directives.* Colombo: Ministry of Irrigation and Power.

Ministry of Power and Energy. 2002. *Proposed Power Sector Policy Guidelines.* Colombo: Ministry of Power and Energy.

Nanayakkara, V. 2003. *Sri Lanka's Efforts in Introducing Water-sector Policies and Initiating Related Institutional Development.* Project Final Report, V, Appendix III. Colombo: International Water Management Institute, pp. 68–86.

Noble, K. 2006. *International Influences on Water and Power Sector Reforms in Sri Lanka* (Unpublished Report). Colombo: Movement for Lanka and Agricultural Reform and Practical Action.

Piyatilake, A. 2007. 'Implications of the General Agreement on Trade in Services (GATS) on the Sri Lankan Electricity Sector', Liberalization of Services and Reforms. *Discussion Papers, 3.* Colombo: Practical Action (ITDG) South Asia.

Practical Action. 2006. 'Report of the Conference on Electricity Reforms: Global Experiences, 10 March 2006', Colombo: Practical Action. Retrieved from http://www.janathakshan.org/gats_reforms/c/elecreglobal.html (accessed on 17 April 2013).

Prelis, M. 2005. 'CEB's Financial Crisis—Facts and Some Misconceptions'. *Financial Times,* 11 December 2005.

Ragavan, C. 2001. *GATS—Fact and Fiction: At Best a Partial Truth.* Penang: Third World Network.

Sauve, P. 2005. *Structure of the GATS.* A Presentation Made at ITC Capacity Building for Trade in Services in Sri Lanka, Colombo.

Shah, A. 2005. 'WTO Meeting in Hong Kong, 2005', Global Issues, 26 December 2005. Available at http://www.globalissues.org/article/570/wto-meeting-in-hong-kong-2005 (accessed on 17 April 2013).

Sinclair, S. and J. Grieshaber-Otto. 2002. 'Facing the Facts: A Guide to GATS Debate', Ottawa: Canadian Centre for Policy Alternatives. Available at http://www.policyalternatives.ca/sites/default/files/uploads/publications/National_Office_Pubs/facing_facts.pdf (accessed on 17 April 2013).

Singh, S. 2000. 'Uruguay Round: A Historical Perspective', Third World Network. Retrieved from www.twnside.org.sg/title/hist-cn.htm (accessed on 17 April 2013).

Thomas, S. and D. Hall. 2006. 'GATS and the Electricity and Water Sectors', Public Services International Research Unit, March 2006. Available at www.psiru.org (accessed on 17 April 2013).

Wallach, L. and P. Woodall. 2004. *Whose Trade Organization?: A Comprehensive Guide to the WTO.* New York, NY: The New Press.

Wesselius, E. 2002. 'Behind GATS 2000: Corporate Power at Work', The World Trade Organization Series No.4/TNI Briefing Series No. 2002/6. Amsterdam: Transnational Institute. Available at http://www.tni.org/sites/www.tni.org/files/download/wto4.pdf (accessed on 17 April 2013).

Witharana, D. 2007. 'Electricity Reforms and the Poor in Global Electricity Reform Experiences', Liberalisation of Services and Reforms. *Discussion Papers 2.* Colombo: Practical Action (ITDG) South Asia.

World Bank (WB). 1995. Sri Lanka: Private Sector Assessment. *Report No. 12514-CE.* Washington, D.C.: The World Bank.

———. 1996. Non-Plantation Crop Sector Policy Alternatives. *Report No. 14564 CE.* Washington, D.C.: The World Bank.

———. 1998a. Sri Lanka: Country Assistance Strategy: Progress Report. *Report No. 18711.* Washington, D.C.: The World Bank.

———. 1998b. Sri Lanka: Recent Economic Developments and Prospects. *Report No. 17761-CE.* Washington, D.C.: Poverty Reduction and Economic Management South Asia Region, the World Bank.

———. 2000. Sri Lanka: Recapturing Missed Opportunities. *Report No. 20430-CE.* Washington, D.C.: Poverty Reduction and Economic Management South Asia Region, the World Bank.

———. 2003a. Memorandum of the President of the International Development Association and the International Finance Corporation to the Executive Directors on a Country Assistant Strategy of the World Bank Group for the Democratic Socialist Republic of Sri Lanka. *Report No.* 25413-CE. Washington, D.C.: The World Bank.

———. 2003b. Sri Lanka: Promoting Agricultural and Rural Non-Farm Sector Growth. Vol. (1) Main Report. *Report No.* 25387-CE. Washington, D.C.: Rural Development Unit South Asia Region, the World Bank.

———. 2005a. Sri Lanka Development Forum: The Economy, the Tsunami and Poverty Reduction. *Report No.32221-LK.* Washington, D.C.: Poverty Reduction and Economic Management Sector Unit, South Asia Region, the World Bank.

———. 2005b. 'Sri Lanka: Improving the Rural and Urban Investment Climate', World Bank. Available at http://www.worldbank.lk/WBSITE/EXTERNAL/COUNTRIES/SOUTHASIAEXT/SRILANKAEXTN/0,,contentMDK:20569 317~menuPK:287057~pagePK:141137~piPK:217854~theSitePK:233047,00. html (accessed on 17 April 2013).

World Development Movement. 2001. *Summary Response to the WTO Document 'GATS: Facts and Fiction'.* London: World Development Movement.

Water Resources Secretariat. 2000. *National Water Resources Policy and Institutional Arrangements.* Colombo: Water Resources Secretariat.

———. 2001. *Proposed Revisions for the National Water Resources Policy and Institutional Arrangements.* Colombo: Water Resources Secretariat.

———. 2004. *National Water Resources Act (a Draft).* Colombo: Water Resources Secretariat.

World Trade Organization. 1995a. 'Annex 1B: General Agreement on Trade in Services', WTO. Available at http://www.wto.org/english/docs_e/legal_e/26-gats.pdf (accessed on 17 April 2013).

World Trade Organization. 1995b. 'Annex 2: Understanding on Rules and Procedures Governing the Settlement of Disputes', WTO. Available at http://www.wto.org/english/docs_e/legal_e/28-dsu.pdf (accessed on 17 April 2013).

————. 2003. 'Communication from Sri Lanka: Initial Conditional Offer on Services'. Council for Trade in Services, 8 September 2003. Available at http://www.esf.be/pdfs/gats_initial_offers/Sri%20Lanka%20intro.pdf (accessed on 17 April 2013).

————. 2005. 'Doha Work Programme: Ministerial Declaration Adopted on 18th December 2005 (WT/MIN(05)/Dec)', WTO. Available at http://www.wto.org/English/thewto_e/minist_e/min05_e/final_text_e.pdf (accessed on 17 April 2013).

————. 2006. 'General Agreement on Trade in Services: An Introduction', WTO. Available at www.wto.org/english/tratop_e/serv_e/gsintr_e.doc (accessed on 17 April 2013).

WTO-Watch. 2006. 'Analysis of the Hong Kong Ministerial Declaration on GATS. A Document by WTO-Watch (Sri Lanka)', WTO-Watch. Available at http://www.janathakshan.org/gats_reforms/a/hk-mindec.html (accessed on 17 April 2013).

Glossary

bandhs	strikes in which shops, schools and offices must close, and wheeled transport is banned
basti	slum
Brahmans/Bahuns	colloquial Nepali term for members of higher castes (traditionally educators, scholars and priests of Hinduism)
Cherumas and Pulayas	(one of the main) social groups in Kerala
Chetris	a caste in Nepal
Chipko	an ecology and livelihoods movement in the lower Himalayas
Dalit Sangathan	Dalit Non-Governmental Organization
Dalits	former 'untouchable' castes in India
Dharma	philosophical/religious concept of Indian origin
Didarganj Yakshi	a famous Indian/Mauryan sculpture
dolar kheti	'dollar farming' (characterizing many big NGOs in Nepal)
ganja	Cannabis
gram sabha	village assembly/committee
great exodus	the LTTE ordered the population to move to the areas further east and to the Vanni located to the south of Jaffna
harijan	scheduled castes
harijan basti	slum of *harijan* or scheduled castes
Jagrut Adivasi Dalit Sangathan	Dalit Non-Governmental Organization
Janadesh	Maoist newspaper

JRY	a poverty alleviation scheme designed to generate supplementary employment opportunities for the rural poor during agricultural slack periods by creating social assets such as public roads, ponds, and forest
kamaiyas	bonded labourers
kasippu	illicitly brewed liquor
KPAC	the cultural wing of the Communist Party in Kerala
loktantra	a new translation of 'democracy" without monarchical implications
Mahakali Treaty	signed in February 1996 between India and Nepal, pertains to sharing water of Mahakali river
mahar	a caste
MKSS	a rural-based NGO
Naadan Pattu	classical songs/music of Kerala
naib-sarpanch	female vice-head of the panchayat
Nair	a hindu caste
Operation Romeo	repression by the Nepali government on people in some districts who started to organize to enact their own land reform and to gain some power over their lives in the face of usurious landlords (1992)
padhnu	to read (reciting and studying)
pajero culture	a derogatory term to describe corruption of politicians in Nepal
pallisabha	village committee
panchayat	the most important adjudicating and licensing agency in the self-government of an Indian caste/a village council in India
panchayati raj	literally, rule by local councils

panchayat samiti	*panchayat* organization
PAR	an approach of engaging communities in the process of their own development, incorporating a more democratic outlook and attempting to break down the hierarchy between the villager and the expert
popular front movements	broad coalition of different political groupings
pradeshiya sabhas	councils at town and village levels
praja	a word for the subjects of a king or queen
prajatantra	a term with monarchical implications adopted for 'democracy' (etymologically something like 'rule by subjects')
raktasakshi	(the first) martyr
Rama	an Indian deity
Ravana	an Indian deity
Right to Information Act	an Act of the Parliament of India ('to provide for setting out the practical regime of right to information for citizens')
salwar kameez	traditional dress worn by both women and men in South Asia
*samitisabhya*s	members of the *panchayat*
sangathan	class organizations for ex-soldiers, women, peasants, (university) graduates, workers and youth
sarkar	government of the people
Shramik Mukti Sangathan	Workers' Liberation Organization
sarpanch	an elected head of the gram panchayat. The sarpanch, together with other elected panchas (members), constitute the gram panchayat. The sarpanch is the focal point of contact between government officers and the village community

Sita	an Indian deity
Swadhyaya	a movement for village renewal in Maharashtra
Tamangs	indigenous inhabitants of the Himalayan regions of Nepal
Tanakpur agreement	treaty on the sharing of waters between India and Nepal (1993)
thinking spatially	referring to (social) spaces in any society
vikas	(promoting) development (in school textbooks)
WUNC	the four essential claims of demonstrations according to C. Tilly
zamindar	a zamindar in the Indian subcontinent was an aristocrat, typically hereditary, who used to hold enormous tracts of land and control over his peasants, from whom the zamindars reserved the right to collect tax

About the Editors and Contributors

THE EDITORS

Siri Hettige is Senior Professor of Sociology at the University of Colombo. He is former Head of Sociology, former Dean of the Faculty of Arts at the same University and former President of the Sri Lanka Sociological Association. His other current positions include Chairman, Social Science National Committee of the NSF, Sri Lanka, Adjunct Professor at RMIT University, Australia, and Adjunct Research Associate at Monash University, Australia. He has many publications to his credit on such diverse topics as social inequality, social protection, youth unrest, education and health policy, ethnic conflict and migration. These include a number of books, edited volumes and more than a hundred papers published in edited volumes and refereed journals. He has also served on a number of government commissions and committees as a member as well as an advisor over a period of 20 years. He has been a consultant to a number of international organizations such as the ILO, the World Bank and IOM.

Eva Gerharz is a Junior Professor of Sociology of Development and Internationalization at the Faculty of Social Sciences, Ruhr-University Bochum, Germany. Formerly, she was a senior researcher at the Department of Social Anthropology at Bielefeld University, Germany. Her main research interests are empirically grounded perspectives on development sociology, activism and identity politics, diaspora and devel opment, and transnational and translocal dynamics. She has conducted empirical fieldwork in South Asia since 1999, especially in Bangladesh and Sri Lanka. Her book *The Politics of Reconstruction and Development in Sri Lanka* will be published with Routledge. She has edited *The Making of World Society: Perspectives from Transnational Research* together with Remus Anghel Gabriel, Gilberto Rescher and Monika Salzbrunn (2008).

THE CONTRIBUTORS

Laxman Acharya holds an MPhil in Education from Tribhuwan University and is currently a Ph.D. candidate at Kathmandu University, Nepal. He also teaches Statistics for Educational Research as a visiting faculty in School of Education, Kathmandu University. He has worked as a development economist with International Alert in Nepal and evaluated various development projects both in the governmental and non-governmental sector. As an independent freelance researcher he carried out a number of studies on the role and effectiveness of foreign aid and published several policy analysis papers with renowned international non-governmental organizations (INGOs).

David N. Gellner is Professor of Social Anthropology at the University of Oxford and a Fellow of All Souls. He has been working on Nepal and the Himalayas since 1982. His most recent edited volumes are *Varieties of Activist Experience: Civil Society in South Asia* (2010) and *Ethnic Activism and Civil Society in South Asia* (2009), both published by SAGE. *Borderlands of Northern South Asia: Non-State Perspectives* will appear with Duke University Press. He is also the co-author (with Sarah LeVine) of *Rebuilding Buddhism: The Theravada Movement in Twentieth-Century Nepal* (2005).

Natalie Hicks holds a B.A. in Politics and an M.A. in International Studies: Asia Pacific Region from Nottingham University, UK. She has completed a Ph.D. focusing on government reform in Vietnam from the Department of Political and Social Change at the Australia National University. Natalie was the Country Director of International Alert—a peace building INGO— during the conflict period in Nepal. She is the founder of the international development consultancy company Ratio International. She specializes in research and evaluations in fragile and conflict-affected states.

Vinod K. Jairath is currently Professor of Sociology at the School of Social Sciences, University of Hyderabad, India. He has previously taught at the Department of Humanities and Social Sciences, Indian Institute of Technology, Kanpur and the Department of Sociology at Delhi School of Economics, Delhi University. He has carried out and supervised

research in the areas of agrarian social structure, scientific communities, development and popular culture. His current research interests are social movements and sociology of Muslim societies. He has published papers in various journals and has recently edited the book *Frontiers of Embedded Muslim Communities in India* (2011). He has also directed and scripted more than three dozen documentary films on development-related themes.

Ravinder Kaur teaches sociology and social anthropology at the Department of Humanities and Social Sciences at the Indian Institute of Technology Delhi. She has previously taught at New York University and Delhi University. Her current research interests are in the areas of development, gender, new reproductive technologies, family, marriage and kinship. She has been engaged for over a decade in mapping causes and consequences of adverse female sex ratios in India and is the author of several scholarly articles on this topic. She is the co-editor of a forthcoming book on marriage in South Asia titled *Marrying in South Asia: Shifting Concepts, Changing Practices in a Globalising World*.

Dilip M. Menon holds the Mellon Chair in Indian Studies and is the Director of the Centre for Indian Studies in Africa, University of Witwatersrand, Johannesburg. He has worked on issues of caste and culture in modern India and is presently researching on histories of and from the global South. He currently finishes a monograph titled *The Uses of History: The Historical Imagination in South India, 1860–1960*. His publications include *Caste Nationalism and Communism in South India: Malabar, 1900–1948* (1994); *The Blindness of Insight: Essays on Caste in Modern India* (2006) and *Cultural History of Modern India* (2008).

B.B. Mohanty is presently a Professor in the Department of Sociology, Pondicherry University, Puducherry. He obtained his Ph.D. degree from Sambalpur University, Odisha, in 1993. He taught in undergraduate colleges of Odisha for five years (1992–1997). In 1997, he joined the Gokhale Institute of Politics and Economics, Pune, as a lecturer and subsequently promoted as a reader in 2002. Mohanty published numerous research articles in journals of international and national repute. He has visited the US, France, Canada, the UK, Sweden and Sri Lanka on academic assignments. His recent publications include the book

Agrarian Change and Mobilization (ed.) published with SAGE in 2012. Currently, he is working on agrarian transformation.

Dileepa Witharana is currently a Senior Lecturer at the Department of Mathematics and Philosophy of Engineering of the Open University of Sri Lanka. His research interests are in the areas of engineering and nationalism, energy policy, education policy and the changing aid context. From 1998 to 2008 he worked as a researcher and activist for various local and international organizations involved with community peace-building, electricity- and water-sector reforms, multilateral and bilateral free trade agreements and energy policy.

Index

accountable, 18, 87
  governance, 41
accumulation, 38, 47, 55
action(s), 41, 52, 88, 109, 120, 122, 142
  of business community, 88
  collective (see collective action)
  democratic, 120
  dialogical, 34
  of people, 57
  political, 28
actors, 2, 26, 28, 30–32, 34, 37, 45, 88,
  195, 208–9, 268
  international, 186–87
  non-state, 41
  political, 117
administrators, 26, 33
adverse incorporation, 38
Africa/African, 70
  South Africa, 121
agency(ies), 14–15, 35, 39, 87, 132–33,
  190, 218, 243, 254
  -based participation, 24
  budgetary, 222–23
  corporate, 155
  of local people, 28
agitprop, 45
Agricultural Development Bank, 140
agriculture, 26–27, 31, 151, 157, 159,
  162, 170, 176, 224–25, 228–29, 232,
  244, 257, 260
  peasant and plantation, 74
aid, 94, 107, 217–37
  foreign, 16, 206, 209, 217
  international projects, 140
alliances, 35, 38, 40, 86, 114, 138, 142
American Express, 244

American International Group, 244
animators, 32, 34
anthropologist, 27
anthropomorphized, 44
anti-democratic, 10, 75, 95
anti-fascist, 58
anti-globalization movements, 34
anti-state, 12, 76–77
approach
  bottom-up, 25
  neo-classical, 228
  top-down, 26
Araniko Highway, 221
art, 44, 49, 52, 60
  Buddhist, 53
  folk/tribal, 50
Asia/Asian, 7, 70, 132, 135, 142
Asian Development Bank (ADB), 220,
  222–24, 229, 231, 233–34, 236,
  263–67
atomic, 51
Australia, 70, 207, 219–20
Austria, 220
authoritarian, 3, 8, 15, 83, 95, 117, 121,
  199, 210, 242
authorities, 80, 87, 151, 173, 248, 255,
  257
autonomous, 17, 136, 142, 160
autonomy, 54, 74–75, 84, 86, 92, 111,
  115, 139, 142, 145, 154

backward areas, 30, 139
Backward Society Education (BASE),
  118–20
Bahuns, 103, 105
balance of power, 41

Bangladesh, 2, 4, 7-9, 277
Bangladesh Rural Advancement Committee, 27
basic needs, 70, 154, 226, 228, 230-31
Bharatiya Janata Party (BJP), 166
Bhils, 30
Bhutan/Bhutanese, 9, 114
Biju Janata Dal (BJD), 166
bilateral, 94, 206, 218-20, 222-23, 246, 251-52
aid, 224
donor agencies, 81, 228, 230
Botswana, 121
Brahmans, 103, 105
Brazil, 34
British, 3, 8, 51, 58, 63, 74, 159, 219, 221
aid agreement, 229
colonial rule, 72
education, 107
model of purely ceremonial monarchy, 107
notion of refinement, 45
Buddhist, 53
bureaucracy(ies), 12, 31, 40, 44, 49, 84, 86-87, 113, 146

Canada, 219-20, 229-30, 232, 245
caste(s), 6, 14-15, 36, 47, 58, 62, 102-5, 136, 157, 160-64, 182-84
-based bureaucratic arrangement, 159
distribution of beneficiaries of major schemes, 180-81
Dhoba, 170
hierarchy, 59
Khandayat, 177
lower, 100
Mahar, 64
scheduled, 158, 165-73, 175, 177-79
upper-caste Nairs, 63
ceasefire agreement, 188, 190-91, 193-194, 202, 205-7, 209
ceremonial, 102, 107, 117, 122
Ceylon, 74

Ceylon Electricity Board (CEB), 257-59, 264-66
chairmen, 137
challenge, 32, 39-41, 91-92, 96, 159, 182, 242, 247-49, 255, 258, 267
to governance after colonialism, 3-6
posed by GATS to government services, 245
for South Asian countries, 2-3, 11, 18
Sri Lanka in water, 257
of US to EU's policy, 256
change, agents, 32-34
chauvinistic, 192
Chetris, 104-5
China, 9-10, 70, 104, 134, 148, 217, 219-23, 227, 229, 232
Chipko movements, 32, 34
Citicorp, 244
citizen/citizenship, 6-7, 11, 13, 18, 24, 29, 36, 39-40, 45, 49, 52-54, 64, 70, 87, 108-9, 111, 181, 201, 240
civil
services, 104, 231
society, 6, 8-9, 12, 16-17, 30-31, 40, 72, 79, 81-82, 84-85, 113, 187-88, 240, 242, 245, 261
organizations, 8, 17, 30, 72, 79, 85, 240, 245, 261
civilizational, 50, 53, 55
class, 14, 17, 36, 44, 47, 56, 58-60, 62, 74, 95-96, 99-100, 102, 108, 159, 171, 181
-based discrimination, 178
bureaucratic-capitalist, 138
evil, 117
of rich peasants, 157
social, 74
urban middle, 82, 85, 90
collective action, 14, 32, 37, 120
Colombo Tamil, 191
colonial, anti-colonial, 6, 70-71
colonialism
agents, 47

ex-colonial, 70
rule, 6, 45, 47, 72
committee, 37, 59, 86, 112, 168–69, 193, 262
commonalities, 38
Communist Party of India (CPI), 58
communists, 64, 102, 107–10, 136, 142–43, 148, 154, 218, 220, 227
Communist Party of Nepal, 135
ministry, 59
politics in Kerala, 58
revolution in Vietnam, 132
community(ies), 11, 13, 16, 23, 25, 27–28, 30–32, 36–37, 47–48, 74, 77, 88–89, 91–92, 109, 111–12, 134, 141, 146, 149, 152–53, 155, 163
companies, 40–41, 244, 246, 254, 257, 259, 261, 266
complex(es)/complexity(ies), 1, 10–11, 13, 36–37, 40, 49, 71, 79, 147, 169, 175, 189–91, 193, 208, 241
concept, 11, 15–16, 23–41
conclusion, 40–41, 120–22, 153–55, 181–84, 190, 200, 206, 235–37, 266–68
conditions, 5, 17–18, 24–26, 39, 47, 69, 95–96, 119, 133, 150, 158, 166, 183, 190, 196–97, 203–4, 211, 220–22
conflict
mitigation, 217–37
resolution, 188, 203, 234, 250
post-conflict reconstruction, 16, 208
Congress, 45–46, 107, 117, 144, 160, 164, 166, 171, 177
conservative, 59, 72, 86, 188
Constitution, 29, 46, 53, 64, 74–75, 83–85, 108, 139, 159, 182
constitutional monarchy, 219, 234
constraints, 27, 39–41, 70, 256, 266
construct, 28, 191
contest, 163, 166, 177
contestation, 24, 41, 101, 131
control, 10, 15–16, 38–41, 86, 111, 131, 139, 146, 149, 152–53, 155, 157–58,

160, 162–63, 170, 187, 189, 192–93, 195–98, 201, 203, 206, 209–10, 247, 260
political, 73–74
restriction on market, 253–54
of upper castes on state policies, 159
co-optation, 40–41
corruption, 3–4, 12, 79, 82, 84, 87–88, 108, 140, 202–3, 243, 257, 259
Council
of Canadians, 245
for Trade in Services, 254
counter-insurgency, 195
critiques, 26, 48, 63, 99–100, 109, 201
of contemporary participation, 35–36, 40
of Maoists, 114–18
Cuba, 70
cultural variables, 28

Dalits (former untouchable caste in India), 33, 103, 105, 116, 132, 139, 141, 154
Darjeeling, 110n12
decentralization, 29, 110–11, 136, 139, 203, 230, 235–36
democratic, 30, 34
decolonized, 49
deconstruct/deconstruction, 30, 35, 38
debate(s), 11, 29, 35, 46, 59, 85, 89, 119, 138, 147, 168, 205, 241, 245
on development, 55
devolution in Sri Lanka, 203
public, 44, 258
on reconstitution of ethnographic field, 189n4
on tradition *vs* modernity, 54
Delhi/New Delhi, 45, 52–53
democracy, 99–122
democratic
governance, 29, 211, 236
undemocratic, 76, 199
Denmark, 219, 222–23
Department of Commerce, 244

depoliticized/depoliticization, 28, 32, 37
developing country(ies), 17, 26, 70–71, 88, 225–27, 228, 230, 242, 245–47, 249, 252–54
  GATS rule selected for discussion, 247
  welfare approach adopted by, 228
development
  agendas, 31, 33, 226, 233
  community, 11, 24, 47–48
  critiques of, 99
Development Assistance Committee (DAC), 220, 223
developmental NGOs, 30
diaspora, 7, 205, 207–9
dictatorship, 70, 107
difference, 33, 37–38, 48, 56, 59, 102, 108–9, 112, 115, 177, 183, 234, 260
discourse(s), 9, 11–12, 23, 41, 46, 52, 59, 118
  of egalitarianism, 121
  hegemonic, 241
  of modernization, 61
  post-colonial, 60
  public, 1, 195
disempowering, 113
Dispute Settlement Body (DSB), 248, 250–52, 256
District Development Chairperson (DDC), 146–47
District Development Committees (DDCs), 144, 146–47
diversity(ies), 2, 36, 45, 56
  cultural, 255, 267
  ethnic, 7
  religious, 7
doing
  fashion, 112
  goals, 11, 225
  post-development, 35
  sustainable, 12, 96, 202, 219
  theory, 35, 132, 261

domestic, 8, 71, 211, 228, 230, 236, 246–47, 251, 257
  governance, 94
  public debts, 92
  resource mobilization, 218
  services, limitations on favouring, 252–53
  violence, 141, 145, 154
domination, 9–10, 12, 39, 74, 105, 182–83
donors, 16, 30, 32, 34, 100, 110, 193, 202–3, 206, 217–37
Dravidian, 59
dynamics, 201
  of balance of power, 41
  of emerging political alliances, 40
  of ethnic struggle, 191
  of Maoist mobilization, 132
  of power, 39

economy, 7–8, 10, 12, 17, 72–74, 76, 78, 90, 170, 255
  global, 71, 96, 228
  household, 115
  Jaffna, 204
  liberal, 88
  market, 31
  national, 47
  open, 80
  political, 44, 70–71
  rural, 78
  urban-based service, 79, 81
education, 5–7, 9, 14, 24, 26, 31–32, 72, 79–80, 82, 86, 89–90, 93, 99–100, 103–7, 115, 118, 139–40, 143, 150–51
egalitarian, 6, 56, 74, 89, 121
elected, 44, 59, 76, 83, 102, 107, 137, 158–59, 161, 163, 165–66, 171, 177, 187, 200, 240
elections, 72–75, 81–83, 85–86, 91, 96, 101, 109, 117, 160, 163–65, 170–71, 173, 177–78, 182, 211, 241

Electricity Reform Act, 257, 262
elite(s), 29, 36, 49, 54, 103, 111, 114, 134,
   136, 141, 152, 159
   landed, 47
   political, 3–4, 13, 45, 70, 79
emancipator, 35
employee, 74, 82, 92, 171
employment, 55, 80, 87, 91–92, 109,
   162, 176, 181, 183, 234
   distribution in Sri Lanka, 74
   departures of foreign, 78, 93, 96
   non-agricultural, 93
   overseas, 81
   preference of, 77
empowerment, 11, 23–25, 33–35, 38,
   40, 110, 112–15, 121, 137, 141, 158,
   161, 182–83, 231, 242
   of disadvantaged, 100
   rules of, 111
   through participation, 28–32
enabling, 3, 38, 88, 154, 196
enclave, 75
engagement, 25, 39, 41, 49, 57, 64, 208,
   228, 237
English, 75n4, 76, 91, 107, 113, 118–19
Enhanced Structural Adjustment
   Facilities (ESAF), 228
entrepreneur, 204, 206
   political, 136, 143, 154
   subject to forced tax collections, 205
enterprise(s), 15, 39, 44, 53, 73, 82, 87,
   264–65
entities, 31, 253
environment, 38, 76, 78, 90, 94, 142,
   154, 231, 243, 254–57, 259–60, 267
epistemology, 36
ethnic, diversity, 7
ethnicity, 6, 77, 102, 136
ethnicization, 203
ethno-linguistic, 75
ethno-religious, 8
ethno-science approaches, 27
Eurocentrism, 28

European
   Commission, 220, 244
   Services Forum, 244
   Services Network, 244
evidence, 33n5, 35, 39, 49, 220
exclusion, 11, 17, 27, 39, 141, 169,
   233–34
   Dalit, 154
   of minorities and conflict, 2, 6–8
   participatory, 37, 41
experiment, 40, 54, 158
expert, 26–27, 45, 51, 86, 258

facilitator, 36, 88
feasibility studies, 227
female, 14–15, 78, 115, 141, 149, 161,
   163, 165–67, 169–70, 172, 178,
   182, 201
feudal/feudalism, 47, 50, 55–56, 58,
   62–63, 138, 158–59
field(s), 5–6, 13, 24, 26, 31, 47, 55, 62,
   82, 86, 90–91, 115, 134, 151, 190,
   199, 208
fieldwork, 15n4, 112, 140–41, 189, 195
finance, 90, 92, 96, 264
financial, 10, 16–17, 71, 87, 118, 142,
   150, 207, 225–26, 231, 236, 241–42,
   244, 257, 259, 261, 264
Finland, 219–20, 222–23, 234
focus, 9, 24, 29, 32, 40, 133–35, 148, 189,
   226, 228–30, 234
food, 26, 78, 82, 90, 147, 159, 167, 186,
   211, 255–56, 267
Food and Agriculture Organization
   (FAO), 228
forced participation, 30
foreign aid policy, Nepal, 217–19
Forest User Groups, 110–11, 121
France, 219–20, 226
freedom of choice, 17, 242–43
freedom of expression, 12
free trade zones, 76, 78
Friends for Peace (FFP), 134, 140–41,
   143, 147, 150, 152n11, 153

fundamental, 17, 46, 48, 59, 64, 120, 153, 236, 247, 261

gender, 14, 93, 99–100, 115, 136, 154, 176, 181–83, 201, 231
discrimination, 141
equality, 141
genealogy, 50
General Agreement on Tariff and Trade (GATT), 243–44, 250
General Agreement on Trade in Services (GATS), 240–68
Germany, 58, 219–20, 228
Ghising's Gorkhaland movement, 110n12
globalization, 71
Global Services Network, 244
Gorkha/Gorkhali, 110n12, 137
governance
democratic governance, 29, 211
good governance, 2–4, 6–7, 10–12, 16–18, 49, 69, 79, 87, 146, 226, 230–31, 233–35, 237, 240–68
participatory, 11, 24
government, 3, 10, 12–13, 15–16, 18, 29, 34, 36, 39, 46, 49, 52, 62, 74–76, 80–83, 85–88, 92, 104–5, 107–10, 113, 117, 119, 131–33, 135–37, 142–44
government agencies, 34
governmentality, 39
gram sabha, 168, 172–73, 179
grassroots
activists, 32
organizations, 29
Green Revolution, 27n1, 28, 29n2
grievances, 14, 74, 77, 135–36, 143, 154, 204–5
gross national product (GNP), 112, 226–27
growth, 17–18, 73, 75, 109, 160,
economic, 82, 219, 225–28, 231, 233–34

of lower middle class, 90
of Maoist movement, 64
Guerrilla, 136–37, 141, 187
Gurkha, 105–6, 219
Gurung, 106

Halcrow, 265
Headquarters, 131, 137, 146, 151, 208
health, 4, 9, 26, 31, 72, 79–80, 82, 86, 90, 100, 104, 109, 112, 192, 207, 229, 231, 246, 252
heraldic, 49
heritage, 53, 55
heterogeneity, 36
hierarchy(ies), 27, 36, 39, 48, 56, 59, 64, 105–6, 118, 149, 179, 182
Hindi, 55–56, 64, 103
Hindu, 13, 53, 63, 102–3, 107, 207
historical, 1–2, 9, 12, 23–24, 44, 46–47, 49–50, 117, 132, 135–36, 141, 158, 192, 220, 236, 260
homogenous, 36
Hong Kong Coalition of Service, 244–45

icons, 53
identity, 13, 15, 55, 57, 77, 103, 141, 191–92, 200
ideological, 8, 23, 35, 41, 70, 76, 85, 91, 95–96, 132, 138, 147–48, 221
ideology, 14, 30, 73, 104, 114, 132, 143, 147–48, 154, 220
illicitly brewed liquor, 193
imperialism, 138
inclusion, 15, 28–32, 38, 40–41, 100, 158, 161, 175, 181–82, 219, 233
of Dalits, 116
empowerment through participation, 28–32
formal, 14
institutional, 14
Maoist agenda, 142
participatory, 11

social, 16, 234–35, 237
of women into politics, 14
independence, 3, 5, 9, 18, 44–65
independent, post-independence, 14,
  69–96
India/Indian, 14, 29, 31, 44–65, 108–9,
  152–53, 157–84
indigenized, 47
indigenous knowledge, 27, 267
individual, 10, 24, 32, 37–40, 47, 54, 71,
  90, 92, 94, 110, 133, 146, 155, 207,
  232, 249, 265
Indo-Lanka Peace Accord, 203n15
industrial, 44, 47–48, 52, 76, 82, 94,
  224, 257
industrialization, 5, 48
industrialized countries, 70
industries, 8, 71, 73, 76, 90, 109, 140
inequality(ies), 14–15, 17, 27, 32, 35,
  38–39, 59, 62, 157, 159, 176, 181,
  183, 226–27, 233, 237
  economic, 71
  ethnic, 89
  horizontal, 12, 89
  social, 13, 71, 100, 235
  structural, 41
  vertical, 12, 89
inflation, 228
infrastructure, 6, 9, 72, 76, 81, 89–90,
  92, 99–100, 104, 110, 116, 146, 224,
  226–27, 229, 231, 236, 258, 265–66
initiatives, 10, 37, 52, 100–1, 141, 196,
  203, 206, 208, 228, 241, 267
injustice, 17, 37, 75, 87
insidious modes of inclusionary
  control, 38
institutionalization, 2, 110, 234
institutions, 2–5, 7–10, 14, 17–18, 37,
  41, 44, 47–48, 51–54, 71, 74, 80,
  82–84, 86–89, 91–92, 102, 107,
  111, 119–21, 155, 157, 161, 187–88,
  193–94, 196, 200
instrumental, 24, 40, 244
insurgency, 195

Maoist, 13, 16, 109, 120, 144, 147,
  232–33, 236
military, 114
Tamil, 7
intellectual property, 243–44
interaction, 13, 15, 26, 39, 112–13, 134,
  181, 190
interdependence, 225
International Finance Corporation
  (IFC), 266
International Fund for Agriculture
  Development (IFAD), 220
International Labour Organization
  (ILO), 228
International Red Cross, 194
interventions, 3, 17, 26–28, 31–34, 39,
  60, 73, 92, 236, 243
interview, 134, 147, 197, 201n13, 207
investment(s), 94, 205, 228–29, 244, 258
  Nepal's, 226
  private, 8, 72
  productive, 73
  public, 8, 90
  social, curtailment of, 8
invited spaces, 37, 39, 41
irrigation, 26, 27n1, 157, 176, 225–26,
  229, 257, 260, 264–65

Jaffna, 15, 186–211
jan andolan I and *II*, 131n1, 135, 143
jan sarkar, 131, 144–45
Janata Dal, 166
Japan Services Network, 244
jobs, 64, 76, 92, 106, 115, 134, 197, 259
judicial processes, 88
judiciary, 12, 17, 84, 88, 104, 242

Kashmir, 109
Kasippu, 193
Kaski, 106
Kathmandu, 13–14, 100, 103, 105–9,
  112, 114, 118–19, 131–32, 134,
  136–37, 141, 153–54, 219, 221, 227
Kerala, 34, 40, 48, 57–59, 160

Kilinochchi, 193–94, 198–99, 206, 208–9
King
  Birendra, 104, 107–8, 135, 218
  Gyanendra, 109, 114, 141, 144
  Mahendra, 101–2, 104, 107, 110, 218
  knowledge, 26–28, 38, 167, 267
Korea, 90, 219, 249n2
  South, 9n3, 10

Lamnasa, 106
land reform(s), 45, 72–73, 90, 104, 142, 144–45
language, 6, 59, 75n4, 76, 91, 103, 107, 110, 113, 139, 197
Latin American, 70
Least Developed Countries (LDC), 249–50
legitimacy, 7, 40, 74, 108, 117, 195, 198–202, 209
level, 69–96, 99–122
liberal, 3–4, 10, 40, 70, 72–73, 77–78, 81–83, 88–89, 91, 109, 228–31
Liberalisation of Trade in Services (LOTIS) Committee, 244
liberalism, 74, 94, 96, 228
liberalization, 251–52, 254
  economic, 4, 9, 76, 77n5, 78, 80, 109n11
  market, 12
  progressive, 249
  Sri Lanka, post-, 81–95
  pre-, 74
Liberation Tigers of Tamil Eelam (LTTE), 13, 15–16, 91–92, 96, 186–202, 204–11
Lichhavi, 102
Limbus, 105
linking, 38, 221
literature, 1, 35, 40, 70, 101, 132–33, 157, 193, 253
lobby, 150, 244–45, 259–60
local
  democracy, 40, 111n14, 121, 157–84

knowledge, 26–28, 38
localism, 40
localist approach, 37
locality, concept of, 15, 37–38, 171, 189–93, 195–98, 200, 209–10

Macroeconomic, 229, 231, 264
Mahendra, King, 101–2, 104, 107, 110, 218
mainland, 191, 193
majority, 31–32, 61, 77, 80, 82–83, 99, 133, 139, 141, 154, 161, 166, 171–72, 175, 177, 181, 199, 211, 240
Malayalam, 48, 59–60, 62
Malaysia, 9n3, 10
male, 14, 78, 93, 161, 165, 167, 170, 172, 177–78, 182–83, 196
management, 16, 30–31, 37, 40, 65, 74, 96, 112, 202, 231–32, 236, 260–62
Maoism/Maoist, 13–14, 16, 64, 109, 114–18, 120, 131–33, 138, 140–55, 232–34, 236–37
marginal, 27n1, 28, 39, 41
marginalized, 2–3, 12, 28, 32, 35, 96, 143, 182, 200, 237
markets, 4, 9–10, 12, 40, 71, 78–79, 246, 253–54
Marrakesh Agreement, 243
Marshall Plan, 226
martyr, 63, 116–17, 121
martyrdom, 62, 117n19
Marxism, 48
Marxist, 59–60, 72, 114
masculinity, 46
media, 1, 12, 17, 74–75, 79, 84, 88–89, 161, 186–87, 261
Medical Institute of Tamils (MIT), 207
methods, 25, 27, 29, 34, 38, 114, 151, 228
micro-level, 38, 268
migration, 5–7, 78, 86, 88, 93, 115
military, 7, 9, 13–15, 70, 79, 91–92, 114, 117, 137–38, 141, 147, 149, 153, 187–89, 194, 196–200, 205–6, 209–11, 220, 222

Ministry of Defence, 210
minority, 74–75, 77, 89, 103, 110, 118–19, 136, 142, 189n5, 192, 202, 211
missionary organizations, 218, 222
mobilization, 3, 40, 47, 53, 63, 85, 101, 132, 218, 230, 232
modern, 5, 8, 11, 44–45, 48–51
modernism, 49, 52, 120
modernity, 11–13, 34, 44–50, 52–56, 62, 64, 106, 112–13, 116, 120–22
modernization/modernization theory, 26, 44, 49–50, 54, 57, 61, 157
monarchical system, 221
monarchy, 58, 102, 107, 135, 141, 219, 234
Moors, 77
Morocco, 243
Most Favoured Nation (MFN), 251, 254
movement, 17, 30–32, 34, 40, 47, 58–60, 64, 76, 92, 106, 115, 117–18, 135–36, 138, 141–43, 145, 147–48, 151, 160, 199, 201, 210, 217, 226, 245–46
multilateral, 17, 31, 81, 88, 94, 100, 206, 218–20, 222–24, 228, 241, 243–44, 249–50
Multilateral Investment Guarantee Agency (MIGA), 266
multiplication, 37, 41
Muslim, 36n7

nation, 11, 46–47, 49–50, 52, 63–64, 108, 115, 140, 217, 221
democratic, 45
panchayat attempt to mobilize, 101–7
post-colonial, 53
national, 2–4, 6–8, 12–13, 17–18, 26, 31, 33, 45, 47, 49–54, 60, 63, 82, 87, 90, 92, 100, 103–4, 106, 109, 119, 140
nationalist, 6, 31, 46–47, 49, 52–53, 71, 90–92, 94, 96, 140, 190n6
National Water Resources Authority, 264, 266

nationhood, 49
natural resource, 37, 231, 260
nature, 1–2, 24, 26–28, 41, 55, 83–85, 95, 114, 122, 134, 161, 174–76, 179, 202, 231, 251–52, 257
Nehru, 45–48, 51–52, 219
neo-liberal, 25, 69, 71, 88–91, 96, 109–14
Nepal/Nepalese/Nepali, 13, 16, 99–122, 131–55, 219, 221, 232, 235
Netherlands, 219–20, 222–23
networks, 80n6, 85, 111, 120, 136, 193, 202, 207, 210
Newari, 103, 107
newness, 49
new orthodoxy, 34, 38, 112
non-conforming, 39
non-governmental organizations (NGOs), 25, 29–34, 110, 111n14, 112–13, 115–16, 118–19, 139–40, 205, 207–8, 223
non-state, 7, 30, 37, 41
norms, 38, 61, 133, 149, 182
North American Free Trade Agreement, 250
Norway, 219, 222–23

official participation, 35
capability based participation, 40
efficiency based participation, 24, 32, 40
oil crisis, 228
oppression, 24–25, 35, 119, 192
Organisation for Economic Co-operation and Development (OECD), 1, 222, 245
Organization of Petroleum Exporting Countries (OPEC), 220
organizations, 8, 17, 25, 29–31, 34, 72, 79, 82, 85, 102, 110, 112, 114, 118–19, 121, 141, 160, 186–87, 193–94, 205–8, 218, 220, 222, 240
outcomes, 2, 30, 32–33, 37, 71–72, 119, 133, 138, 150, 243

pro-poor and pro-democracy, 39
social, 75

Pakistan, 8–9, 46, 107
Panchayat
    local government unit, 104, 135
    regime (Nepal), 100, 103–4, 107–10
Parbatiya, 13, 103, 105
parliament, 46, 76, 82–83, 86, 119, 144,
    200, 240, 262–65
participation, citizenship, 11, 24
participatory development, 26, 35–36,
    38
participatory exclusion, 37, 41
partition, 8, 44, 46
party, 14, 59, 76, 82–83, 85, 87, 107–8,
    110, 114, 118, 142, 154, 158
passport, 110, 146–47, 149
patronage, 52, 63, 90, 144, 146, 158
peace, 3, 11, 18, 116, 134, 188, 193, 197,
    201–4, 219, 234–35
per capita income, 9n3, 17, 70
performance, 1, 13, 18, 58, 96, 101,
    120–22, 200, 203–4, 206, 264
performative, 101, 122
Pokhara, 106
policy(ies)
political, 2–10, 12–14, 16–18, 23, 25,
    28, 32–33, 38, 40, 46–48, 50, 53, 56,
    60–62, 64, 69–79, 81–89, 92, 94, 96
politicians, 3, 45, 61, 79, 82, 86–87, 109,
    111, 113, 145, 158, 188, 200, 259
politics, 9, 13–14, 37, 45, 50, 58, 62–64,
    75, 77, 101, 104, 120, 133, 234, 237
    democratization of, 3, 6
    everyday, 148–50
    mass-regarding, 148
    national, 8
    Odisha, 158–62
    parliamentary, 114
    South Asian, 5
polity, 89
popular front movements, 142n5

popular spaces, 37, 39
population, 2, 5, 10, 12, 15–18, 70, 73,
    75, 80–82, 91, 93, 103, 111, 147,
    162, 170, 173, 176–77, 188–89, 191,
    193–95, 197, 200, 204
populist participation, 24, 35
power
    equations, 36
    relations, 38, 241
    structures of power and control, 40
poverty alleviation, 26, 30, 80–81, 181,
    227, 236
Poverty Reduction Growth Facilities
    (PRGF), 228
practice, 2–3, 9, 11, 17, 23–24, 27–28,
    33–38, 40–41, 46, 50, 57, 59–61, 63,
    72, 80, 87, 92, 100, 103–4, 111–13,
    118, 121, 162, 178, 198, 204–5
price de-regulation, 228
PricewaterhouseCoopers, 265
primordial, 6
privatization, 17, 41, 82, 110, 231, 259,
    262–63, 265
privileging, 37
problem, 12, 15, 31, 38, 47, 53, 62,
    64, 71, 73, 76, 81, 84, 87, 119, 146,
    150–52, 168, 175, 196, 200
process(es), 3–4, 6–7, 9–11, 14, 16, 23,
    25–32, 34, 36–40, 45–47, 49–50, 52,
    58–59, 64, 84–86, 88, 101, 105, 109,
    121–22, 135, 138, 144–45
professionalization of change agents,
    32–34
projects, 12, 26–27, 30–32, 36, 40–41,
    72, 80–81, 92, 99, 104, 110–12, 116,
    140, 218, 224, 226, 229, 232, 243,
    257, 263, 265–66
property, 48, 139, 150, 190, 207, 211,
    243–44
public, 1–8, 12, 14, 17, 31–32, 44, 72–74,
    76, 79–93, 104, 108, 118, 121–22,
    138–41, 146, 153, 155, 169, 181–82,
    193–95, 197, 200

Public Utility Commission Act, 257, 262

Punjabi, 112

radical, 4, 12, 23–24, 29, 32–36, 39, 45, 47, 49–50, 61, 63–64, 72–75, 104, 108, 142
  theatre, 57–60
Rajasthan, 33n5, 34
Rana, 105, 117, 217
rebellion, 76, 131
reconciliation, 18, 90, 92, 203
reforms, 202–7, 240–68
regime, 7, 73, 75, 82, 88, 91 92, 94, 96, 100, 102–4, 107–10, 117, 144, 150, 187, 217, 221
relations, 10, 15, 36, 38–40, 94, 96, 121, 137, 139, 145, 157, 161, 176, 178, 183–84, 190–91, 201, 217–20, 241
religious, 7–8, 36, 53, 103, 105, 116, 120–21
remittances, 4, 94, 96, 204, 207
representatives, 3, 14, 16–17, 31–32, 44, 47, 52, 114, 139, 158–59, 162, 182, 188, 193, 200, 205, 207, 211, 240, 244, 246
research, 13, 28, 90, 94, 107, 113, 132–34, 140, 142–43, 146–50, 153–55, 194–95, 210
resistance, 4, 12, 39–41, 75, 81–82, 87, 133, 163, 191–92, 258, 261–63
resources, 3, 5, 16, 27, 29, 32, 71, 73, 89–90, 121, 146, 157, 220–21, 228, 230–31, 236, 242, 253, 257
responsibilities, 31, 40
responsive, 41, 154, 203
revolution, passive, 45–48, 50, 56
rights, human, 2, 94, 119, 153, 187, 193, 199, 205, 210–11, 226, 230–31, 234–35, 260–61
ritualization, 122
rituals, 28, 38, 101, 106, 116, 119–20, 122, 157
Rolpa, 116, 136–37

romanticization, 49, 54–57
roots, 5, 33–34, 243
Royal Nepal Army, 138, 147, 152
rupee, 64, 119, 176, 208
rural, 157–84
Russia, 227

sanitation, 26
Sanskritization, 50
Santiniketan, 46
Satyagraha, 45
Scheme for Reorganization of the Electricity Industry, 262
schools, 32, 75n4, 79–80, 90, 99, 103 6, 117, 120, 139, 142–43, 147, 150, 164, 166–67, 171–72, 187, 207, 248
Science, 5, 8, 11, 51–54, 90
scientific, 27, 44–45, 51, 138, 140
sector
  agricultural, 14, 151
  corporate, 72, 76, 85, 90, 94, 133, 155
  defence, 90
  educational, 4, 90
  industrial, 94, 224
  informal, 78
  private, 6, 12, 16, 72, 77, 80–81, 88, 90–91, 229–31, 240, 257, 259–62
  public, 76–77, 80, 82, 93
separatist group, 191
service, 240–68
settlement, 243, 247, 250–51
Seven Party Alliance (SPA), 138
shifts, 6, 12, 16, 32, 40, 74–76, 95, 225, 232, 236–37, 259, 262
Singapore, 10, 82
Sinhala, 75n4, 77, 91, 192, 198, 204
Sinhalese, 77, 89–92, 96, 188, 197–98, 211
social
  action, 39
  capital, 23–24, 30, 34, 38, 154, 219
  movements, 34–35, 40–41, 118–20, 160
  reforms, 3, 6
  upheaval, 50

Socialism, 48, 50
socialist, 6, 8, 10, 26, 36, 51, 69–70, 72–75, 89
sociality, 37, 190
society, civil, 6, 8–9, 12, 16–17, 30–31, 40, 72, 79, 81–82, 84–85, 113, 187–88, 240, 242, 245, 261, 267
socio-cultural, 2, 33
socio-economic, 4, 16, 81, 136, 158, 171, 219, 227, 229, 235–37, 257
socio-political, 1–2, 4–5, 18, 161
soldier, 105, 108, 197–98, 219, 221
South Asia/Southasian, 1–18, 39, 71
Southeast Asia, 90, 110, 134
Soviet-Union, 8, 58, 70
space, 240–68
Sri Lanka/Sri Lankan Tamil, 69–96
Sri Lankan Monitoring Mission (SLMM), 194
standards of living, 26
state, 2–4, 6–12, 14–17, 25, 29–33, 40, 45, 47–50, 52–55, 57–59, 61, 64–65, 72–77, 82–92, 94–96, 99, 105, 109
strategies, 217–37
structural, 27, 32, 37–38, 41, 70, 92, 114, 228, 230–31, 264
Structural Adjustment Programme (SAP) WB's, 228–29
subversion, 39, 41, 198
suppression, 10, 81, 210
sustainability, 34, 232
Swadhyaya movement, 32
Switzerland, 220, 249n2

Taiwan, 90
Tamangs, 105, 113
Tamil
    Batticaloa, 191
    Eelam, 190, 192–93, 198–99, 210
    police force, 187, 193, 197–99
Tamil Rehabilitation Organization (TRO), 208
Tamils Health Organization (THO), 207

Tarai, 103, 112, 114, 118
tax(es), 14, 76, 105, 140n4, 145, 153, 193, 204–5
technical assistance, 220, 222–23, 243, 263, 265
techniques, 25, 27–28, 36, 38–39, 153, 225
technology, 5–6, 8, 11, 27n1, 51, 71, 208, 226
teleguided, 33
terms of trade, 4, 73, 105
Thabang, 116
Tharu, 118–20, 146
Third World, 25–27, 133, 225
Third World Network, 245
Tibet, 219
Trade
    Related Intellectual Property, 244
    rights, 244
    investment measures, 244
transformation, 4, 10, 23–24, 35, 38–41, 50, 56–57, 60–63, 76–77, 219
    in rural China and Vietnam, 133–34
    social, 133, 136, 183
transformative, 36, 144
    development, 35
    participation, 24, 39
    social action, 39
transition, 44–45, 47, 53, 79–80, 137, 143
tribals, 27, 33, 50, 118, 160n3
Tribhuvan University, 113
trusteeship, 47
tyrannical, 35
tyranny, 35

UK, 220–21, 223, 226, 228–29, 231, 234–35
underdevelopment, 5, 8–10, 26, 100
underprivileged, 3, 36, 73, 161
unemployment, 71, 73, 75–76
United Nations Development Programme (UNDP), 220, 227, 230, 232

university, 75n4, 85, 102, 107, 205, 248
graduates, 90–91, 99, 171
untouchables, 33, 59, 61–62, 139, 163
urban, trade unions, 85
Uruguay, 242n1, 243–44
US, 25, 220, 222–23, 226, 228–29, 235, 244
US Coalition of Services Industries (USCSI), 244
USSR, 219–20

Vanni, 191n7, 192–93, 195–96, 198–99, 206, 208, 210
vernacular, 33–34, 75
Vietnam, 70, 132, 134, 148
violation(s), 4, 17, 94, 252, 255
violence, 5, 76–77, 118, 137, 148, 153, 197
culture of armed, 136
domestic, 141, 145, 154
election-related, 96
of partition, 44
political, 8, 133
voice(s), 17, 24, 29, 36n7, 38–39, 102, 132, 183, 187–88, 192
vote banks, 47, 85

war(s)
civil, 7, 186
Cold War, 26, 219, 230
ethnic war, 18, 89, 93
People's War, 58, 114, 116, 135–37, 142, 147–48
Second World War, 8, 25–26, 70, 225–26
Western countries, 70–71, 195, 207, 218–19
women, 14, 28–29, 33, 46, 62, 102, 112, 115, 141, 158, 161–62, 165–67, 169, 171, 173, 175–79, 181–84, 195–201
work, 30, 32, 48, 51, 61 63, 80, 85, 99, 108, 112–14, 133, 142, 146–47, 149, 153, 169–71, 174–77, 183, 194
workers, 4, 28, 61, 76, 80, 87, 102, 140, 246
construction, 56
local, 29
migrant, 5
NGO, 112–13
political, 117
urban, 82
World Bank (WB), 30, 71, 202, 220, 263
World Trade Organization (WTO), 242–54, 256, 268